POLICE CRIMINOLOGY AND CRIMES

POLICE CRIMINOLOGY AND CRIMES

James Vadackumchery

KALPAZ PUBLICATIONS
Delhi-110052

Police Criminology and Crimes
(*Police Criminology*)
Rs. 790
ISBN: 81-7835-094-7

Published in 2002 in India by
Kalpaz Publications
C-30 Satyawati Nagar
Delhi-110052
E-mail: kalpaz@hotmail.com

Lessertype setting: A.A. Computer
Printed at Chawla Offset Printers, Delhi 110 052

To

Mary,
Neethu and Neethie

Contents

Preface

Police Criminology is a new branch of scientific study in the area of enforcement criminology. My researches in criminology have helped me a lot to open new concepts in understanding crimes and criminal behaviour. Nexus crimes, enforcement crimes, consensus crimes, noquisitorial system of justice, equal justice, policization of criminals, politicization of police, criminalization of police and politicians, etc., are new fields in criminology. This book on Police Criminology exposes the causative aspects of police crimes and introduces Push-Pull-Ego Factors theory to understand crimes and criminal behaviour.

Police criminology represents an analysis of the crime problems in law enforcement by police. The discussion is placed on the problems principally seen in Indian police. Much of the discussions, nevertheless, may be applicable to the police service throughout the world. The tendency for committing enforcement crimes is seen to be to the upward direction, perhaps, all over the world.

I am indebted to my wife, Mary and daughters, Neethu and Neethie for their assistance and encouragement to do research and to write this title. I am grateful to Kalpaz Publications, Delhi for bringing out this title in print.

I wish to state that the views and opinions expressed in this book do not reflect the views and opinions of the Government of India, State governments, Home offices and police departments. They are the personal views derived through observations, study and research. Dr. James Vadackumchery affirms that he has the moral rights to be identified as the author of this title.

Thiruvananthapuram,
February, 2002.

Dr. James Vadackumchery

Introduction

What is police criminology? In the interest of realism, criminology may be defined as the scientific study of crime and criminal behaviour. If so, crimes committed by police and other enforcement officers will also come under the scope of criminology. If a person with a high paranoid factor is given authority to enforce law, he is likely to misuse his power and abuse his authority—this is what a criminologist may say when he speaks about crimes committed by police during the course of law enforcement or in the pretext of enforcing law. A policeman must have a sense of integrity. Today, I read in the news paper about a liquor tragedy. More than 35 people died and several became blind. If the news paper report could be believed, the enforcement officers received regular payoff from the bootleggers. Allegations are always heard that some policemen/officers keep a group of political office-holders reasonably satisfied and happy. How? They do so by obeying their commands and not by enforcing law in a fair and just way. Police service needs members who possess enviable mental and physical qualifications to perform many intricate tasks in the field of human relations. There is no room for the use of filthy expressions and epithets in professional police-human relations. Policemen expect phenomenal results from their works through short cut methods and they employ third degree methods during interrogation of suspects. To be more blunt about the police work, they violate human rights of people—many people think so. No doubt, there is a breakdown of respect for police authority and a distrust on police honesty and integrity. The strength of any policeman/officer depends upon his internal control, self-control and self-discipline. Do they have the expected or required self-mastery? Respect for law is essential in the life of a man—and particularly so in the life of a policeman. Do we notice it among those who are corrupt or vulnerable for corrupt practices? Some of them interpret illegal acts as legal just because they are done by the law enforcement functionaries.

This, doubtlessly, reflects the tolerance of police behaviour which will eventually destroy the service itself. Registration of false cases, concoction of evidence, production of touts, if they happen in the service, are of bad taste.

Criminology studies law violations and violators. If the laws are violated by those who are bound to enforce them, then it comes under the scope of criminology. Why do they commit crimes? The criminologist must envisage the gamut of enforcement criminality—misdemeanor cases such as informal arrests, illegal detentions, drunkenness, callous indifference to protect civic rights and citizen's safety, disorderly conduct by policemen, traffic violations by those who must enforce traffic laws etc. The problem of recidivism is a subject matter coming under the scope of criminology and the corrupt police officer repeats his crime even when he is deeply involved in detecting, controlling and preventing crimes and correcting criminals. Is he not a habitual offender?—not a hard-core criminal?

Custodial rape, custodial suicide, custody-murders, assaulting people in lockup, plundering articles from a scene of search, misappropriating valuables when mahazars are prepared, theft by policemen are reported in the press and media. The offenders have uniform and it does not mean that they have immunity for what they do. Thievery is thievery, no matter who commits it; pilfering is pilfering, no matter it is committed by a constable or the director general of police. A behaviour becomes criminal not only when it is reported to the police to set the law into motion, but also when it is committed by the police and not acted upon by them. What are the crimes committed by the law enforcement agencies and why do they commit them? This forms a part of police criminology. Criminologists today identify enforcement crimes, nexus crimes, simulated encounters and human rights violations that take place within law enforcement and make attempts to estimate the frequency of occurrences. Even today, many of the enforcement crimes are not recognized or identified as crimes and the penal statutes do not give any special identity for such lawless law enforcement. Police criminology is a developing branch which makes attempts to give a distinct identity to crimes committed by law enforcement functionaries. A superintendent of police got angry at his subordinates who attended a conference and he became so because he found that petty cases were not registered in their jurisdiction. The young subordinates who were blamed wildly by the superintendent of police went back to their respective jurisdictions and registered as many cases as possible on that day, next day and subsequent days. 'Was it law enforcement-or-misuse of authority/abuse of power? There is the story of an young man who attacked some women who resided in his neighbourhood just because he was jilted by his sweetheart. He had the physical strength to do so and he was caught at last. He transferred his aggression to his sweetheart who jilted him to some women who were helpless before his superior strength and power. Likewise, the 'petty offenders' caught by the activated subordinates of the angry superintendent of police were helpless and defenseless before the police uniform which decided to register as many petty cases as possible against people who were in their jurisdiction. Criminologists study behaviours as well. When the law enforcement officers do so—creating offences just to multiply the number of petty cases to satisfy a superior and domineering authority—do they have guilt feelings? Are they having a 'psychopathic personality? Do they suffer from character disorders? Or, do they have only personality traits disturbances? These areas were not subjected to deep analysis and study by criminologists, psychologists and sociologists. Now, a situation has come into being that the crimes committed by law enforcement officers must be scientifically studied, for, they are more conspicuously seen now than what they have been in the past. Crimes and criminal tendencies committed and expressed by the law enforcement functionaries make it impossible for the people to steer them in the expected ways as they fail to follow the norms of the society. Why? They are treated as inadequate people in law enforcement and justice administration. These inadequates are poor performers in society, because they have no respect for the laws they enforce and administer. There is the erosion of values in them. How can they torture a person who is suspected to have committed an offence? Yet they do so and the United Nations in their Convention Against Torture emphatically say that torture of any kind is a human right violation. Why do the police resort to third degree methods and other degrading strategies during crime investigation and law enforcement? I do not think that any serious studies were conducted to learn the etiology of torture, third degree and degrading treatment in police custody. Some police officers, when they wear the uniform, forget the conventionalized norms of society which they had once internalized and the norm was that 'torture of any kind is a sin against man, humanity and God". One sees an alienation from the norms and the people who reinforce them—a withdrawal from the established norms of the society which supports such principles for human coexistence, harmony and peace.

A corrupt policeman—a policeman who tortures the suspects—who manipulates records to see that the accused is punished—who pads up evidence to convict a person— who establishes *nexus* relations with underworld criminals—all of them go away from the approved norms. This is a subject matter which comes under criminology. When a policemen does so, a criminologist understands that the approved norms erode within his uniform and/or he becomes estranged and normless. He becomes a criminal, but he neutralizes his criminality by convenient rationalization and gives a colouring that he does everything for the larger interests of the society—fair administration of justice and proper enforcement of law.

In popular view, criminology is what criminologists study. For the last 10 years, my wife has been engaged in keeping news paper cutting of police violations of law and the file is indeed very thick. Looking into the file, one may be shocked to see the extent, magnitude and intensity of police violations of law and naturally, it becomes an area for the criminologists to study. Sometimes, it may be seen that the police violate laws under pressure. A superior authority in the hierarchy may force a subordinate to violate the law and he may employ intimidation and threats to pressure the subordinate to do an illegal act. Subsequently, he may yield to such strategies. The victimized or exploited individual suffers the police as he does not have the power and strength to resist the police force. In the company of two or more policemen, spontaneous behaviour is often generated. Death in police custody is reported from many parts of the Country and a close scrutiny of the entire situation which results in the murder of a person in police custody may reveal that the death takes place as a result of the spontaneous behaviour generated from the policemen who exhibit the dynamics of mob behaviour. This is otherwise called *the interactional explosion*. When third degree is employed on a suspect by a group of policemen, suggestion works as a mental force. Suggestion is found to be a behavioural trigger in human interaction. Spontaneously generated suggestion operates even in animals. Under the influence of the interactional explosion, a policeman may employ excessive force on the suspect. Criminologists ought to study such behavioural dynamics.

Imitation is another behavioural trigger and the law enforcement officers may be tempted to imitate a role model in the work environment—a role model presented by the associates, superiors, subordinates and so on. Concoction of evidence may ensure success in criminal trials and certainly, a person who does not possess ego strength, upright conscience, self esteem, self resistance or internalized norms may be tempted or pressured to imitate the perverted role models. A senior deputy superintendent of police said that he used to plant evidence whenever he was convinced morally of the involvement of a person in the commission of crimes. He further stated that he got the idea to do so from his superior officer who did the same in previous occasions and his strategy resulted success in his work. He found his superior enjoying prestige in the police service and that was the sole reason for his imitation of the prestige model. Police criminology smells an expression of criminal tendencies in such officers who pad up evidence during criminal investigation. Imitation, criminologists consider, is a conscious learning process. Some criminologists call such behaviour as model takeover rather than an imitation which according to them may imply a lot of conscious development of skills.

Violation of professional ethics in police may be seen. Why do they do so? Every legal action has a moral dimension. A policeman's weakened resistance to temptations or a neutralization of the unethical aspects of his behaviour may be responsible for his moral violations. Police criminology takes note of this aspect of police behaviour. Some policemen/officers have earned notorious names and they are called *lions*, *tigers*, *leopards*, *vultures* and *thunders* by the people. They have such names because their behaviour is such that it shows an animal like pattern. How does such pattern of behaviour come in them? Police criminology makes analysis of such behaviours.

Criminal behaviour must never become a way of life. But it is a way of life for some. Corruption, corruption-money splitting, corruption-money fixing and corrupt practices must not become a way of life. If it becomes so, a subculture of corruption comes into being. A person involved in corruption and corrupt practices may be close to a way of life. A criminologist tries to find out explanations for such behavioural patterns in law enforcement.

Locating Crimes and Criminal Behaviour in Law Enforcement

Criminologists today try to locate crime and criminal behaviour in law enforcement. When crimes are reported to police, they are investigated. The criminals are located and in a quite few cases, crimes are proved. So far so good! And the system works well. Nevertheless, criminologists ask: "How?" In other words, how are the criminals located?—How are the crimes proved?—How are the criminals punished? Are there any law violations when the crime is investigated and the criminal is detected? Does the police behaviour turn out to be a criminal behaviour? Behaviour is observable and there come criticisms against police behaviour during law enforcement. Sometimes, cases are registered against the police and their behaviour is punished. Sometimes, the Human Rights Commission awards compensation to the victims of police misuse of power/abuse of authority. Criminal laws in many countries are codified and India has a penal code enacted in 1860. It is an antique piece of legislation and certainly it does not contain a chapter on enforcement crimes committed by the enforcement agencies during the course of their job although the Code has some scattered legal provisions on such crimes. Criminology studies the making of laws and police criminology researches in to such areas of police criminality.

What is behind police criminology? The press and the media point out crimes committed by policemen and their allegations are not altogether baseless. Police are to enforce the law and the question is: "Who will enforce the law against the police?" *Nexus Crimes*—i.e., the crimes committed by the bureaucrats (police included), leaders (political or otherwise), go-betweens, and dadas (*goondas*) after entering into a *nexus* understanding with the criminal *nexus operator*—are discussed every where today. Criminologists today admit that nexus crimes are more harmful and more serious than any other types of crimes. I have authored a book titled *Indian Police and Nexus Crime* and I have brought out the fact that the nexus crimes have the ingredients of organized crimes, white collar crimes and enforcement crimes. Nexus crimes are to be handled differently by professional investigators. Police crimes and nexus crimes, like the Mafia crimes and white collar crimes, are terribly reprehensible and ought to be thus dealt with. But how? Police criminology must study these aspects as well. When police behaviour is seriously considered a threat to human life, safety, morals, decency, dignity, etc., criminologists may agitate for law enforcement against the enforcers of law. Custody rape/murder and calling of epithets and other human rights violations come under criminologists' concern. Social and criminological values decide the nature of police behaviour. Criminologists are and ought to be special '*interest groups*' to see that crimes are treated as crimes, no matter who commit them. Their studies must put pressure on the Legislature, Parliament and people to pass new laws or amend the old ones. The criminologists have concerns based upon their observations, studies and system of values and they have started to think that it is high time that a special branch in criminology which studies exclusively the crimes committed by law enforcement agencies is developed. Police criminology belongs to such a branch. The laws against enforcement crimes are and ought to be based on the perceived need to maintain conformity to people's aspirations and expectations.

Police and Enforcement Crimes as Social Problems

The society today becomes increasingly concerned with police and enforcement crimes. When they become threat to society and its security, then they become social problems. For example, corruption and corrupt practices during law enforcement have become threats to society. They generate grave concern. Cries are heard from the people and media. Agitation for a solution is set in motion. There are recurring episodes of informal arrests, indecent searches, illegal detentions, gender injustices, custodial deaths etc. and certainly, they generate grave public concern. Quite recently, a group of political activists went to a police station and demanded the release of people taken into custody by police for their alleged involvement in the commission of crimes. The activists said that they were innocent people. The police acts in such situations frighten people with threatening images or perceived threats. During the internal emergency in India (1976), there were many such incidents and necessarily, they caused great consternation.

When India became independent in 1947, the planning commission put control of crime and delinquency at or near the bottom in the list of priorities. Corruption and fight against corruption did not receive any concern then. No one thought about enforcement crimes, nexus crimes, police crimes etc. to be serious social problems. Not even a penal code was drafted and still India has, as said earlier, an old penal code which has outlived its utility. Even today, there is no national campaign organized to ensure public support to fight against crime and delinquency. The campaigns are organised for polio eradication, malaria prevention, family planning and birth control. Terrorism, naxalism, insurgency, corruption, nexus crimes, political crimes, white collar criminality, food adulteration, Mafia operations are in full swing in many parts of the Country. There is no praiseworthy programmes for crime prevention. The power elites are not having any serious concern over the emerging and emerged crimes in the Country. They do not demand actions and formulate solutions. On the other hand, the politicians, bureaucrats, *dadas*, underworld criminals establish nexuses to promote crimes and Mafia operations to serve and protect their self interests. Recently, the President of India in his address to the Nation on the eve of the Independence (2000) day spoke loudly against and about nexus crimes. His push against crime, I doubt, could not evoke serious anti-crime and delinquency campaigns and fund raising for them. I also do not think that there is any serious researches in criminology encouraged and promoted. The realistic situation in the country is that there is no one to fight against crime and delinquency. No member of the power elite, no government, no politician, no man of God, no teacher, no university, no scientist, I feel, will come forward in the near future as a champion of a purposive movement to control crime and delinquency. If that is the truth, there may not be any one who will be interested to conduct researches in police criminology and other enforcement crimes. In this deplorable situation, this book 'Police Criminology and Crimes' receives great importance.

Reporting Police and Enforcement Crimes

Any crime committed by an enforcement agency must be reported. But, where? The crimes committed by police are recorded by the National Crime Records Bureau, but the criminologists feel that the statistics provided by the Bureau shows only the tip of the iceberg. As such many crimes committed by enforcement agencies exist as unreported violations and no one besides the crime-doers, crime-observers and victims of crime know of their occurrences. As the mortality rate of enforcement crime is exceedingly high and incredible, only a drop of the crimes comes to the notice of the press, people and authority. As the enforcement crimes are not reported, there comes no solution to the problem. The crime-doers keep out of trouble and they continue to involve in committing more crimes. Recidivism is seen. They do not consider their illegal or unlawful behaviour to be crimes—not even abnormal acts. Since the statistical or epidemiological fact of enforcement/police crimes is accepted by the people, criminologists make attempts to learn the reasons for their non-reporting to official sources. One of the main reasons, I consider is the fear of the people towards police. They are afraid of the foul police strategies if and when the police crimes are reported. Once sees the unwillingness of the victims of crime or observers of enforcement crimes to report to official sources. Though the police may misuse their power/abuse their authority, it so happens, sometimes, that the victims do not come to take note of the fact at the appropriate time. The degree of invisibility of the police abuse/ misuse of their power/authority is an accepted fact. A policeman/officer who concocts an evidence in a criminal case may be the only person who knows about the act. The act is invisible from the standpoint of reporting at the appropriate time. Hence, fear, unwillingness and invisibility of the enforcement/police crimes may be a very powerful cause of non-reporting of police crimes. An authority who can use the law for the investigation and prevention of crimes can also misuse/ abuse his authority, if he so desires and chooses. My studies on the non-reporting of enforcement/ police crimes reveals—

1. The offence is done in a clandestine way so much so that the offenders only know the commission of crimes.
2. If at all the colleagues/associates know about the crimes, they are unwilling to report them. There exists a sort of fraternity even in the commission of crimes and in the maintaining of their secrecy.
3. The victims of abuse of power/misuse of authority have fear of the police and it prevents them from reporting enforcement crimes.
4. People are generally ignorant of the laws, procedures, rights, privileges etc. and there exists no service to educate them. They do not know where to report and how to go about it.
5. Some people are indifferent about many things and they are just not bothered about anything.
6. There are vested interests which do not allow people to report enforcement/police crimes. It is better to suffer than to react against. The victims are individuals and the crimes-doers represent a mammoth agency which has muscle and money power.
7. Fighting against a mammoth agency is expensive, time-consuming and laborious.
8. In some instances, the offence committed may not be of a serious nature—may not be directly against some individuals—may be distributed in the society. Hence, the victims may be indirect.
9. The victims may not be interested to see that the enforcement crimes are detected/discovered. There may be *nexus* understanding for mutual benefits.
10. The botheration, harassment and inconvenience in reporting and aiding detection, proving crime and testifying in courts are unthinkable for some people. They may show a blind eye to the continuance of nexus crimes.
11. There exists public tolerance to police crimes. The people are not prepared to resist police abuses, nay, they allow them. They think that such police abuses are necessary for maintaining law and order, harmony and human welfare in society. There are many such areas which police criminology must study. It must concentrate on the reporting of law violations during law enforcement, arrest procedures, detention, identification and thus a variety of legal action

against the crime-doers. Since, there exist no laws specifically enacted for punishing enforcement offenders, police criminology may have to devote its resources to such areas. New laws have be framed and old ones to be amended. The study of recidivism and habitual criminals, and the identification of first offenders, hard-core criminals among the policemen/officers including offenders with perverted value system or character disorder must be extended to the study of enforcement criminality. Police criminology may devote its time to (1) the study of enforcement crimes, (2) prevention and control of all types of crimes including police/enforcement crimes etc. (3) investigation and detection of enforcement/police crimes and (4) implementation of laws for the effective administration of equal justice to all.

Police Criminology For the third Millennium

India is in a transition stage from colonial rule to a mature democracy. During the transitional stage, enforcement criminality/police crimes may be seen—or may be a necessary evil to reach a mature democracy (?). No doubt, the police system may have difficulties to fight against their own people. There can be the inability or unwillingness either to suppress the criminality or to correct the crime-doers. From 1860, the police in India have travelled a long way and after India's independence in 1947, the police have travelled further and now are in the third millennium. Ours is, in the language of the United Nations, a developing democracy and in such a democracy, the police can commit many crimes or can withdraw themselves from committing crimes. A fluid state is seen in any young democracy during its transition. Two professors from Netherlands came to me and while discussing on the social and cultural trends in India in the millennium, they said that "corruption and corrupt practices put down the progress of this developing nation". And they continued: "Police can control the corruption and corrupt practices, but the forces which operate in the society operate on police more powerfully so much so that corruption and corrupt practices are more encouraged than curbed down". And it was a time a liquor tragedy took away almost three dozen lives. Among the dead, there were policemen too. Policemen who are bound to book bootleggers and sellers of poisonous liquors encourage the crime by consuming them. What is more frustrating is that the names of policemen/officers appear in the press and media in connection with the commission of several other crimes including sex crimes and prostitution. Crimes which the police commit can never be tolerated. The authority and power which must control and prevent crimes/criminal activities can not abuse them. If they do so, there will be conscientious objection from many walks of life. A senior deputy superintendent of police once said : "I have investigated many cases and chargesheeted many. But, I do not claim that I have chargesheeted only true cases". I have seen him repenting over his past doings and he told me that police criminology must be a topic that must be taught to police officers during their induction training courses.

Of course, the Central Committee on Police Training instituted by Government of India has recommended the inclusion of criminology in the syllabus. Nevertheless, the syllabus does not contain subjects under Police Criminology. The criticism against the syllabus is that the young recruits are taught to study criminology and criminogenic factors among the people outside the police—and not the same of those working inside the police service. I think that the Indian public have made it extremely difficult for the policemen/officers to work in a favourable atmosphere and the reasons for the emergence of such a situation must be analysed and identified. Behind the situation, one may notice police involvement in activities which the people do not approve of. Police criminology then comes into being. People isolate the police and many are afraid of the police. Some think that they may be victimized if they go closer to the police. I find a state of *dynamic tension* between the people and the police in India. Most people want to isolate the police and the police want to integrate their work with people by coming closer to them. The concept of isolation-integration can be used to understand the public-police relations in India. Police isolation also refers to the lack of public trust on proper functionings—that the people have suspicion over police integrity—that they sense criminality in police exercise of their power and authority—that they find abuse of power/misuse of authority. Amidst the isolation strategies and attitudes, I take note of the fact that the police can not be totally isolated like that by the people. No doubt, the general public dislike those policemen/officers who represent arbitrary authority or who commit nexus crimes or who promote enforcement criminality.

Criminology has its causative, detective, legal and correctional aspects. Police criminology too has the same aspects. The sociology of police crimes, psychology of police criminality etc. become a part of police criminology. They are dealt with in this book in separate chapters. I have authored a book "*Wounded Justice and the Story of Indian Police*" and I have treated historically and elaborately the crimes committed by police from the colonial past to the democratic present. When life is challenged by terrorism, naxalism, insurgency, poisoning of food, environmental pollution, nexus crimes, harships, maladjustment, bureaucratic indecisions, political vandalism, corruption and corrupt practices, enforcement crimes, misuse of authority, abuse of power, Mafia crimes, white-collar criminality—a police service with an upright conscience is an eloquent expression of what the law enforcement is able to devise in order to give everyone new reasons for hope and harmonious coexistence. When a crime-free existence draws to a close, it is the conscientious law enforcement which finds the most appropriate means for enabling the people—especially the abused, victimized, the handicapped and those who can no longer look after themselves to receive an adequate response to their needs, in particular their anxiety. In these cases, the role of police authority is indispensable and they can take advantage of the police services provided the service is crimefree ensuring fair justice. Can this be done? Police criminology discusses it. Police functionaries need to be directed by people and principles with this perspective in mind. The police profession calls for all functionaries from constables to the director general of police to be guardians of law and protectors of the people. In today's social and cultural contexts, the allegation is that police functionaries lose sight of their inherent ethical and legal dimensions. Police criminality is resulted and they become, as the allegations are again seen, criminals in uniform, What to do?

CHAPTER—1

Police Crimes Down the Millennia

Police crimes are not of recent origin. In *Valmiki Ramayana*, there is the mention of police patrols. *Apastamba Dharmasutra* (600-300 B.C.) tells the King to appoint only pure and truthful officers for protecting the subjects from thieves. It means that the officers entrusted with the duty to maintain the safety and security then were not people who had integrity and character. If precautions were not taken, then impure people could creep into the then existed police service or whatever the service it was then called. Kautilya spoke about government officials who were evil minded. He wanted the spies to have a watch on government officials who exhibited criminal tendencies. He specifically refered to corruption by public servants. There is evidence to show that use of judicial torture was in vogue at that time and the torture was employed to elicit a confession from the suspects. During his time, the officials who performed police functions were paid fat salaries and the objective was to prevent corruption and corrupt practices. It was believed then that a handsome pay would make them to have no recourse to foul and fraudulent means to multiply their regular income. There were arrangements made to see that the officials did not become corrupt, oppressive and partial in their duties. Certainly, some did show criminal tendencies and the precautions became thus necessary. If they were caught, then they were punished. Corporal punushments, dismissal and banishment from service were inflicted on corrupt personnel.

Westerners claim that victimology is their baby. According to the principles in victimology, the victims of crime must get compensation or restitution as the case may be. Arthasastra says: "Whatever of the property of citizens robbed by thieves the king can not recover, shall be made good from his pocket". The *Vishnu Samhita* repeats: "Having recovered the goods stolen by the thieves, let the King restore them entirely to their owners to whatever caste they may belong. If he has been unable to recover them, he must pay their value out of his own treasury". The Yagnavalkyasmriti (100-300 A.D.) the Naradasmriti (100-400 A.D.) and the Katyayanasmriti (400-600 A.D.) put heavy responsibilities on the officials who had the duty to detect the stolen property. They said that the restitution to the victims was to be paid by the officers. They said further that the losses on the roads were to be made good by the officers entrusted with the authority to apprehend thieves. As it may be seen today in some cases, the officers could not plunder the property recovered then. The law then existed made them directly and personally liable to make good the losses incurred by the victims. However, there is no evidence to show that the officers in ancient India involved themselves in thieving properties seized or recoyered. Nevertheless, the officers employed torture, inhuman and degrading treatment on the suspects to extort confessions in criminal cases. It has been seen that they tortured people when they had strong suspicion (not certainty) about the involvement of a person in the commission of crimes. The authority was often misused/abused by unscrupulous policemen/officers. Offenders received harsh treatment and mutilation was resorted to.

Coming to Akbar's administration, the Subedars (Suba means a province and the Subedar was to administer criminal justice and maintain law and order) were required to employ only "honest, unavaricious and truthful men" to collect intelligence about crime, law and order. The instructions indicated that there were corrupt and avaricious people who came forward to maintain law and order in the Subas (Provinces). The Subas were subdivided into *Sarkars*. A *Faujdar* was appointed in each Sarkar. He was the commander of force in the Sarkar. He was to police the Sarkar under him. Every Sarkar was divided into Thanas or Chowkis and Thanadar was appoonted by the *Faujdar*. The Moghals were essentially an urban people. There were Kotwals in big cities and they were the chiefs in the city police. The police were made responsible for restoring the articles stolen. If the police failed in their duty, then they became responsible for making good the loss incurred by the victim. In all police transactions, integrity and probity were very much insisted. Nevertheless, there were violations and the violators were severely punished. Accepting bribes was considered by the Moghals to be a most reprehensible act—or—practice. History gives ample evidence to show that the police functionaries were notoriously corrupt. They did not perform their duties impartially, justly and lawfully. The timidity of the people to make complaints against their police and the weakness of the government were found to be two important causes for the prevelence of corruption among the law enforcement functionaries.

In the Deccan, Shivaji appointed *Paripatyagars* (Havaldars) and *Mukhya Deshadhikaris* (Subedars). They were to look after administration including the police. They too were found to be corrupt and Shivaji punished them mercilessly. After Shivaji's death, Mamlatdars were appointed to maintain law and order. They too were found susceptible to corruption. There was abuse of power/misuse of authority. The Mughal police system broke down by the middle of the eighteenth century.

Police Crimes Up to 1861

During the period of Clive, the Zemindars were authorized to maintain peace, law and order at their expense. They were to appoint adequate number of Paiks and Thanadars. They could not do the job. They neglected their police duties and did many things in league with dacoits. The officers oppressed and plundered the people at will. Police crimes thus became a social problem, whatever might be the reasons for the same. During the period of Hastings, orders were issued stating that the Thanadars and Paiks ought to be dismissed or fined if they neglected their duties. Whatever might be the compelling reasons for the police to neglect their duties, one might see that they were not serious of their functions as police officers. Dacoity was found everywhere and the dacoits were protected by the police functionaries. Hastings further wanted all persons (including police officers) convicted of abetment, connivance or collusion with dacoits should be adjudged equally guilty as the dacoits and accordingly punished with death.

On 29th June 1782, Hastings issued a proclamation and the said proclamation contained references to the misconducts of Thanadars (police officers) and their disobedience to the orders issued to them. The orders and proclamation issued then spoke about the non-discharging of police responsibilities and abuse of power by the law enforcement officers. In this context, Anandswarup Gupta writes: "Thanadars and Paiks etc. were appointed and dismissed by the Zemindars. . . . . .They had to purchase their appointment at most exorbitant rates at public sales and were subjected to annual exactions for their continuance in their office. To indemnify themselves, they, in their turn, realised large considerations from dacoits for granting them protection or screening them from justice. They also made the inhabitants within their jurisdiction pay heavily and punished them with excessive fines on pretences of murder, robbery or adultery". Even today we notice the same pattern of behaviour. As the allegation goes, policemen/officers offer corruption money to politicians or other influential people to get a lucrative posting. Afterwards, they establish nexus partnership with criminal businessmen or underworld criminals to make money. They also accept corruption money and other favours. The evils seen today therefore have a history of three centuries. As the police were corrupt then, scholars saw lawlessness in the country during the period of East India Company.

Cornwallis became the Governor General in India and soon after his arrival in India in September 1786, he found that the police could not protect the life and property of the people. Frauds, peculation and corruption were seen everywhere. In 1787, it was decided that the collector's or magistrate's authority ought to be exercised to prevent any abuses by police by inflicting severe punishments on those who neglected their duty or who showed gross breach of duty. Cornwallis found that the collectors were deeply engaged in commerce rather than punishing police officers who neglected their duties or showed gross breach of duty. He also found that the police functionaries were notoriously corrupt. The bottom level policemen were ill-educated, underqualified, poorly paid and unscrupuloulsy dishonest. The policemen had unholy relations with criminals and naturally the criminals often escaped punishments. The crimes continued to show an upward trend.

What was happening then? There is evidence to show that the Thanadars were keeping dacoits with them. They were receiving consideration from them for protecting them. They never caught hold of the dacoits even when they were ordered by the magistrates to do so. The same behavioural pattern may be seen even today. If they were dacoits at that time, today they are 'nexus partners' who involve in the commission of many kinds of nexus crimes such as bootlegging, corruption-money fixing, corruption-money splitting etc.

Cornwallis decided to take over the police directly into the Government's own hands. He passed Regulations for the purpose on December 7, 1792. In the preamble of the Resolutions, mention was made about the collusion which subsisted between the robbers and the police functionaries then for the purpose of multiplying robberies and other disorders for plundering property. Thus the police came under the exclusive charge of the Government. The landholders and farmers were asked to discharge their police establishments. The magistrates were required to divide their districts into police jurisdictions of an area of 400 square miles each. The guarding of each jurisdiction was entrusted to a Darogah who was selected and appointed by the magistrates. A Darogah had an establishment of officers. Paiks and Village watchmen of all types and descriptions were put under the Darogahs. They could be dismissed or inflicted with other types of punishments if they were found to be harbouring criminals or having connivance in their malpractices. Evidence is there to show that the Darogahs involved in corruption, extortion and oppression. Hence, provisions were made to initiate civil and criminal actions against such people who exhibited corruption, extortion and oppression. Although the concepts of human rights which are now recognized in India were not known to the people at that time, nevertheless, one sees that the police during Cornwallis's period committed many types of human rights violations.

A Regulation was again passed imposing a police tax on merchants, traders and shopkeepers and so on. The Regulation stated that a police jurisdiction should have a Darogah, a Jamadar, ten Burkundauzes and a Mohurrir. If necessary, there could be additional Burkundauzes. Later, the same Regulation was reenacted with some alterations and amendments. The Darogahs were made removable on proof of incapacity. They could be placed under suspension for misconducts. It has been found out that the Darogahs used to furnish incorrect reports to magistrates. If they were detected to do so, then the matter would be intimated to the Governor General who might dismiss them if found necessary. Manipulation of records, concoction of evidence, filing of incorrect statements, production of tutored witnesses, preparation of false documents are seen today and history shows that the malady has a long history in Indian administration. The Regulation made it clear that the officers under the Darogah's authority found guilty of corruption, extortion or oppression or of committing any act repugnant to the Regulation could be prosecuted by the party injured either criminally (before the Court of Circuit) or for damages (before the Dewani Adalut). The same provisions exist even today. Until the Human Rights Commissions were appointed, (i.e., after 1993 when the Protection of Human Rights Acts was enacted), people used to go to courts for getting damages for human rights violations. Private complaints are filled by people if the police resort to oppression, extortion or third degree methods. However, it is an expensive affair and therefore some people are reluctant to go to criminal courts for prosecuting police functionaries. One thing is certain and that is to say that the lawless law enforcement was in vogue in India during the period of Cornwallis or even before.

Marquis Wellesley became the Governor General in 1798. He wanted to improve the police in India. Mr. H. Strachey, a Judge and Magistrate stated that the police were 'inefficient' and 'bad'. In a report giving a graphic description of the Darogahs of the time, one could read: "In the duties of his office, a darogah is hardly occupied half an hour a day; and he often becomes negligent, indolent, and in the end, corrupt. His dishonesty consists in taking bribes from poor people who have petty foujdarry suits, in conniving at the absconding of persons summoned through him, in harassing ryots with threats or pretended complaints, creating vexatious delays in settling disputes, or preventing their being settled by razaeenamah; and chiefly, in deceiving the poor and ignorant, with whom he has to deal[2]". Receiving of 'razeenamahs' was found to be a source of making improper emoluments by police functionaries. Confessions were extorted and witnesses suborned. The same procedure is a human right violation now and is condemned by many as crimes during crime investigation.

In his letter dated January 25, 1805, H. Strachey stated that the police officers in certain areas were ignorant and inattentive to their duties. As a result, the people were not coming forward to give information to the police. He further stated that the delay and expenditure to prosecute the culprits were intolerable to the poor people. Even today, the same situation prevails. Regulation III of 1805 provided for severe punishments to police officers of any rank who aided, abetted or connived with a gang which committed crimes. A number of instances in which police functionaries aided, abetted and connived with gangs came to the notice of the authorities during that time.

E. Strachey, a Judge in Calcutta Court in 1808 drew the attention to the fact that the police were not giving protection to person or property. He said that the existing "wretched, mechanical, inefficient system of police was a mere mockery". He continued: "no civilized country ever had so bad a police". E. Strachey noted that the dacoits taken to police stations (Thanas) got them released by paying huge amount of money. The police did help the dacoits in many ways even by altering dacoity into triffling cases. The police compromised with the dacoits and sometimes their cases were suppressed. In criminology, these sort of crimes are now called enforcement criminality or nexus criminality. Police can alter or amend the sections of law to make a grave crime to a simple one or vice versa and they do so on the basis of considerations they get from sources interested in miscarriage of justice. In another report, E. Strachey spoke about the way the police managed to get acquittals from the courts. They converted simple cases to severe ones and did not produce strong and convincing proofs to win the cases. Resultingly the cases were acquitted. For doing so, they accepted corruption money. J. Stuart, a Judge in Benares Court on February 5, 1808 attacked the police by telling that they were not men of character or qualifications having any estimation in the eyes of the people. They were treated with rigour and disgrace. According to him, the police neglected their duties, oppressed the people and even colluded with criminals. Today, the people speak of police—politician—underworld criminal nexuses and the collusion with criminals seen during the early part of the 19th century was nothing but a forerunner of what is alleged to be seen now. G. Dowdeswell, Judicial Secretary to Government filed a report on September 22, 1809 in which he stated that the defects in Darogahs were due to their lack of education, habit of concealing crimes and approach of extortion of every species.

Police, Crimes and Madras Presidency

How was the picture of police crimes in the erstwhile Madras Presidency?

In Madras, there were no regular police establishments. The revenue officers and the military of the Zemindars performed police duties. Hence, in 1775, the Court desired Madras Government to find out whether or not the Regulations similar to those established in Bengal could be introduced? Whatever that be, in the instructions issued to the collectors under the Government of Fort St. George in June 1791, one could read that the Zemindars were suspected to have connived at or concerned in robberies and murder. It was also seen that such Zemindars (who abetted, practised, or connived at robberies and murders etc.) were to be proceeded against. The Court actually wanted to reduce the military force of the Zemindars. Lord Wellesley in 1798 wanted Madras Government to enforce the desires of the Court. The Supreme Government wanted Madras Government on December 31, 1799 to establish the same form of internal administration seen in Bengal in the Presidency. The Government was fully aware that the Zemindars abused their police power and authority. The Government wanted to forfeit their property if they were found to have connived at robberies or promoted robbers or other disturbers of public peace. Actually, they involved themselves in open plunder by violence and oppression. Wherever one had the power, strength and authority, he misused them or abused them for his advantage. The same is seen even today. In due course, the Company abolished the Zemindari police administration and police duties were transferred to officers appointed and paid by the Company. Darogahs were provided and 'Tanedars' appointed for each station.

Lord Bentinck, on December 22, 1804, formed a Police Committee to enquire into the state of police in Madras Presidency. Colonel Munro stated in his report to the Police Committee that the "existing police system was not as efficient as it ought to be, not because of any defect inherent in it, but because it had been perverted from its original purposes during times of disorder". He said that a large number of the police personnel were themselves thieves—some were either themselves robbers or did employ robbers and many of them were murderers. He pointed out that no traveller could pass through the territory without being robbed and everything took place as desired, directed and encouraged by the then existed police functionaries. Most unfortunately, same or similar allegations are heard against the police even today. The police are sometimes accused of encouraging, conniving at, keeping silent at, accepting corruption money, involving in nexus activities etc. of Mafia criminals, crime syndicates, political whims and fancies etc. and such news often appears in the media. Colonel Munro emphatically said that the encouragement of banditti by police functionaries ought to be put down by iron hands and the root of the evil ought to be identified. The same voice is heard loudly even today against the police that their protection and encouragement of banditti ought to be discouraged and eradicated with a strong will. The Government fails to do so because there exists some unholy nexuses among the police, politicians and criminals of various descriptions including the criminals of the underworld.

On June 10, 1806, there had been a mutiny of the Indian troops at Vellore. A number of people died and Lord Bentinck was greatly agitated over the incident.

Thanadari System in Bengal and Police Criminality

The rules were consolidated and Regulation XX was passed on the 7th October 1817. Accordingly, the rules prohibited the irregular practices by police officers. It was necessary because the police involved in the commission of many irregular practices and they indicated their tendency towards law violations. The irregular practices prohibited were:—

(1) Not to trade or keep any warehouse or shop, for wholesale or retail, within the limits of the Thana to which they were appointed.

(2) Darogahas not to employ Burkundauzes on their own private affairs and to be liable in default, to fine and imprisonment from office.

(3) No diet money or other allowance or gratuity to be demanded

or received by a Burkundauze from the complainant or the accused or witnesses or other persons while serving processes. Any such demand or receipt was made punishable as a criminal offence and also with dismissal.

(4) No established *Vakeel* or *Mukhtar* to be allowed by the Darogahs to be permanently employed at their Thana by any landholders etc.

(5) No Vakeel or Mukhtar to be employed by the *Darogahs* at the Magistrate's stations to receive and transmit the salaries of the Thana establishment, or for any other purpose connected with their public functions.

(6) No unauthorized Moharrirs or writers or gōyendas or spies to be employed at Thanas without the permission of the Magistrate, but individuals to be encouraged to give information with a view to the apprehension of heinous offenders.

How did such rules come into being? It presupposes that such irregularities were in vogue during the period. It also means that the police then exhibited criminal tendencies which were to be punished by criminal sanctions.

Crimes by Police during Interrogation

In the introduction to the Convention against Torture and Other Cruel, Inhuman or Degrading Treatment or Punishment, the Secretary General of the United Nations, Javier Perez de Cuellar noted on December 10, 1984: "Surely one of the most insidious evils in this supposedly modern age is the continued practice of inflicting torture upon individual human beings. This Convention marks, therefore, an extremely important milestone in the continuing efforts of the United Nations to promote and ensure greater respect for human rights. The world community has thus outlawed once and for all the abominable practice of torture". The observations of the Secretary General was true in every letter of his statement in India for centuries. Regulation XX which was called by Harington in 1817, 'The Police Officer's Manual' contained provisions relating to torture by police. The rule stated that the prisoners questioned by police officers deserved to be treated with human dignity. The rule insisted that the free and voluntary confessions by the interrogated ought to be recorded in the presence of three or more credible witnesses who were not police officers or connected with Thana establishment. The police interrogators were not allowed to induce confessions by hopes or fears or prospects of pardon or threats or other persuations or intimidations. The rule continued to say that any maltreatment inflicted on any person or witnesses by a police interrogator, landholder or other person to extort confession or to procure information was not allowed. Police officers who resorted to torture or violence were punished by the pain of immediate dismissal from service. In spite of such hard and merciless rules against the employment of torture, the fact remains that there exist allegations of using inhuman and cruel methods of torture even today. Why? Why do the police exhibit criminal tendencies even at a time when the psychology of interrogation has developed as a science now?

Madras System and Crimes by Police

The native officers of police were found to be involving themselves in extortion, oppression and other abuses of authority. Hence, Regulation III of 1819 made native police officers guilty of such offences to be liable to civil suits as well as criminal prosecution. If convicted for the offence, they could be fined or awarded an imprisonment not exceeding one month. However, it was later learnt that the said Regulation III of 1819 could not check abuse of authority or afford relief to a sufferer from the immediate exercise of undue authority. The police handled a large number of people and the exceedingly huge number of people could not be protected by law against the abuse of police authority. The police misused their authority without much risk of punishment or exposure. The people had no means to file complaints against police abuse of power. Of course, they refrained from making complaints against the police to magistrates as they were afraid of the aftereffects or consequences of resorting to such courageous steps against the police.

What was happening in Bombay? Bribery, extortion including receipt of presents, abuse of authority and misconduct by native police officers were made punishable as criminal offences with fine and imprisonment upto 7 years and "public disgrace". They were also made liable for civil actions. What did they indicate? They revealed that the police in Bombay indulged themselves in the commission of many sorts of crimes and their involvement necessitated for the enactment of criminal laws with deterrent punishments. The law in Bombay empowered the district police officers to look into the cases of oppression, or extortion committed by subordinate police officers.

A Select Committee of Parliament enquired into the affairs of the Company again in 1832. The Committee examined police administration as well. Evidence was given before the Committee that the frequent instances of the use of torture for extracting confessions or gathering evidence caused serious anguish and anxiety among the European gudges to be more cautious about even well-authenticated confessions unless they were supported by other reliable and trustworthy evidence. The Committee found out that the native officers were lavishly resorting to extortion, coercion, torture and violence for eliciting confessions. India had laws against torture, but not effectively used. The laws are defective now, nay, are a sort of encouragement for the culprits to commit crimes. Whatever that be, one observes the fact that the police have been committing various types of crimes down the millenia.

The Torture Commission

In 1837, Faujdari Adalut directed the Board of Revenue to issue a circular order for the trial of all persons who employed torture, violence and cruelty on people while they exercised police and revenue duties. Employment of torture on people in their helplessness and defenselessness was certainly a lawless law enforcement and no civilized police would be pardoned for their cruelty, violence and torture. Cruelty, violence and torture would mean deterioration in police service and expression of criminal tendencies among law enforcement functionaries. In Madras Presidency, "torture was frequently employed by native officers" and the House of Commons had a debate on the issue in 1854. Earlier in 1852, the Faujdari Adalut issued a second circular and the circular dated 12-6-1852 was provoked by a case which occured at Talook Treasury at Ellore. On 23-3-1838, the Talook Treasury was attacked by armed men who killed 2 sepoys on guard. The Zemindar of Ellore and 20 of his dependents were taken into custody. Four of them confessed that they did it under the orders of the Zemindar. Two of the accused were convicted to transportation for life. It was done on the basis of the statements given by those who confessed that they committed the armed robbery as per the orders of the Zemindar. They were made approvers in the case. The Zemindar pleaded that he was innocent. On inquiry, the approvers of the case confessed that they had no knowledge of the armed robbery and their confessions were recorded under coercion and torture. They also alleged that their former confessions were extorted by the police.

In 1847, several members of a gang of Kunjar docoits were taken into custody. Some of them confessed that they committed the armed robbery at Ellore. Further investigation proved that their confessions were true. As a result, the two innocent people convicted earlier were ordered to be released. By the time, one of them was dead. What an injustice? Even today, allegations are raised against torture by police and commissions are appointed. The reports of many commissions hitherto appointed reveal that torture continues to be an evil in police custody. National Human Rights Commission award huge compensation to the next of kin of the deceased. Custodial rape, custodial violence, gender indecency and human rights violations come on the front pages of the news papers and some papers write editorials about such police atrocities on human beings. They call the police officials "criminals in uniform".

On September 9, 1854, the Madras Government appointed the Torture Commission to conduct an inquiry to the employment of torture by police. The Commission observed that the then existed police organization lacked adequate supervision—was extremely defective—suffered from a want of an efficient, preventive and detective policing. Police could not get public trust and their proceedings were ineffective. The police extorted confessions and concocted evidence to save themselves from the stigma and consequences of failure in the detection of crimes. The Code of Criminal Procedure, The Indian Penal Code and the Indian Evidence Act do not approve of any confessions by coercion and torture. Police investigators in many parts of the Country plead for accepting confessions before police officers as evidence in criminal trials. At a time when the Torture Commission was appointed, none of the above Acts were enacted in India. All of them were enacted during and after 1860. But, one notices the fact that torture was employed by the police even when the above said Acts were not in operation. Hence, the counter argument is that the admissibility of confessions before police officers will not and can not take away the evil of torture unless the police officers themselves decide not to employ it. Police officers who have aggressiveness and criminal tendencies are found to use torture on people when they elicit confessions from the suspects during criminal investigation.

The Torture Commission submitted their report on April 16, 1855. The Commission found that torture in police custody in India had a long history. They quoted at length the findings of Col. Munro during 1802. The also quoted the Court's letter to Madras (March 11, 1826). Moreover Faujdari Adalut had time and again—repeatedly—issued several circulars against the practice of torture by police. The fact was that the Faujdari Adalut had a mass of information collected from various sources about the use of brutal torture by police. For what did they use it? Did they employ torture for administration of justice? If they did so; what type of administration of justice was ensured by such cruel methods? Was it not criminal to employ torture on people who were helpless? If the practice has been in existence for centuries in India and is still in existence, then the evil is a curse in administration of justice and the people are condemned to suffer the evil and evil doers. Police criminology has no option but to study the causative and preventive aspects of torture-crimes by police in India.

The Torture Commission stated categorically that personal violence was practised by the police functionaries and the despicable evil was seen all over the Presidency. Exortion of bribe was universal. Torture was very aggravated and cruel in police stations and the victims of torture had no option but to suffer. They confronted great difficulty in obtaining any redress whatsoever.

During the time the Torture Commission spoke about torture in police stations, the medical science was not developed much. Hence the victims of torture could not prove any visible marks of torture to anyone. The torture employed by police did not leave any tell-tale marks on the injured person's body. People were afraid of the police. If some victims of torture made a complaint, then their future lives, mental peace and safety would be jeopardised and the police invariably saw to it that such people were harassed and persecuted. False cases might be registered against them and every means of annoyance and oppression would be lavishly brought to play against them. The Commission observed that the torture, oppression, annoyance, harassment continued till such time the victims of torture who made complaints and their family had their ruin or consummation. What type of justice was that?—If they were there? Criminology was not a developed subject then and therefore the criminologists could not devote any time to study police crimes at that primitive stage.

The Commission analysed the causes of police crimes and asserted that the then existed laws were inadequate. They were of no use to prevent and punish the police personnel who employed torture and violence during the enforcement of laws. The laws could be twisted to satisfy their aggressive tendencies. Lack of conscientious police personnel in the service was identified as the prominent cause for police crimes. To quote the Commission: "the collection of land revenue was entrusted to the very class who had from time immemorial been accustomed to practise the most cruel and violent tortures upon the persons of the unfortunate prisoners in their custody, accused or suspected of crime". The nexus crimes now seen in police service—i.e., the nexus among the policemen/officers to make exorbitant profits by way of corruption-money fixing, corruption-money splitting and other corrupt practices—were in existence even during the time of Torture Commission. For, the Commission noted that the police and revenue officers from the collector down to the peon jointly committed nexus crimes to make corruption money. It further shows that the nexus crimes which are seen today have their roots deeply gone to the nexus practised and perpetuated for centuries in this great country. The Commission said that the entire police was notoriously corrupt and they committed various types of crimes without any moral restraint, self-esteem and an upright human conscience. To quote the Commission once again: "there was but too good reason to suspect the existence of a league in which the native officials, with some bright exceptions, are branded together from the highest to the lowest, for the common purpose of extorting illicit gains, and for mutual protection from discovery". The same observation is valid in full measure even today. Sir. H.C. Montgomery, the Member of the council once observed that the deterrence caused by infliction of punishment to police personnel who used torture, violence, ill-usage and coercion failed to ensure the desired results. Mr. Walter Elliot, the Member of Council, noted further that tampering with evidence in criminal cases could not be prevented because the people who tampered the evidence were men of influence. The same deplorable situation continues even today and allegations are plenty in the media showing that there take place concoction of evidence, padding up and production of tutored witnesses and touts in criminal cases. Such crimes committed can help only to administer wounded justice, injustice or miscarriage of justice. The Governor, in the meantime, observed that the agents of the police were not faithful people. They resorted to many strategies which were not justifiable in law.

The Second Law Commission and Police Crimes

A second law commission was appointed on November 29, 1853. The Commission submitted their first and second reports in 1855 and the third and forth in 1856. The Commission observed that the police were armed with "very extensive powers in the investigation of more serious offences and that the evidence taken by the Parliamentary Committees on Indian Affairs in 1852 and 1853 and other papers abundantly showed that these powers were often abused for purposes of extortion and oppression". The Commission observed further: "confessions are frequently extorted or fabricated". The fact was that the police, if they could not get the true culprits used to catch hold of some people whose circumstances or characters were such that they could justify their action under some pretext or other and the Commission noted that the police resorted to such obnoxious practices quite frequently. They extorted or fabricated false confessions from such unfortunate men. The police actions thus offered impunity for real offenders and greatly encourged people to commit crimes further. For, the real criminals were never brought to book. Truth was never brought out, rather the real culprits were safe under the maladministration and miscarriage of justice. How do the police perform their duties now? This is a question and the answer to the question will give a picture (partly) of the extent and intensity of police crimes in the present conditions.

Torture Commission and After

The Torture Enquiry brought out many unfortunate truths about police. In 1856, an important directive was issued. It contained: "Our attention has been directed, on various occasions of late, to the character and proceedings of the police in different parts of India, and the reports which from time to time have been laid before us have combined with many incidental notices of failure or abuse to deepen the conviction that an immediate and thorough reform of the police in all the old provinces of British India is loudly called for". It continued further: "That the police in India has lamentably failed in accomplishing the ends for which it was established is a notorious fact; that it is all but useless for the prevention, and sadly inefficient for the detection of crime, is generally admitted. Unable to check crime, it is, with rare exceptions, unscrupulous as to its mode of wielding the authority with which it is armed for the functions which it fails to fulfill, and has a very general character for corruption and oppression". It wanted to effect necessary changes in the constitution and organization of the police. It emphacized the need to convince the people that the Government was earnest and serious in its endeavours to administer fair justice and proper law enforcement. It emphatically stated: "the existing force is so condemned by the authorities, and so hated by the people, that a mere attempt at reform, without such changes, would be a serious error, and would bring about its own failure, from the public and general conviction of its inadequacy to the great object in view. We observe with deep regret the long continuance to this evil under our administration". What a disappointing situation indeed!

The conditions in the Country changed a lot and the revolt which was earlier called the Sepoy Mutiny and now known as the First War of Independence broke out at Meerut on May 10, 1857 and was spreading all over the country. On November 1, 1858, the Proclamation which Queen Victoria issued announced that the Crown had taken over the Government of all the Company's territories in India and the Government of India Act, 1858 was passed by the British Parliament at the same time.

The First Police Commission and the Indian Police Act—1861 on Police Crimes

Lord Canning decided to set up a Police Commission in India and it was done by a notification dated August 17, 1860. It was done with many objectives and one such objective was to improve the reputation of the police service. A perfect and economical police was what Lord Canning wanted—a police service, which was devoid of corruption, extortion, coercion etc. He wanted a civil police and not a military police. The duty of the civil police was to protect the people and community against all local classes. Although it was seen in the general objects of the Commission, one might think that the people at that time wanted protection from the police as well. Even today, people want to get protection from the police and their abuse of power/misuse of authority. The Supreme Court of India in D.K. Basu Vs. State of West Bengal issued certain directions to police and they were intended to protect the people and their interests when they were arrested by the police. The Commission was told that the police should have a uniform and the communication was: "It need not vary more from the usual dress of their class than is sufficient to make them as public officials on duty, without anything peculiar to catch the eye, or to feed the vanity of the wearer. In most parts of India uniform colours in the various parts of the usual national costume, will be quite sufficient as a distinction". Whatever that be, the police in many parts of the Country when they were in uniform felt that they could afford to do many things to people which they might not do if they did not have the vanity of having the uniform.

Crime by police against the people was not a concern of the Commission. The presemption was that a service which was created and maintained for preventing crimes could never become an agency to commit crimes. But history shows that the presumption has been far away from being real. Hence, criminologists become interested in studying more about crimes committed by police and thus a new area called *Police Criminology* comes into being.

On 29th September 1860, a Bill was introduced in the Legislative Council by the Hon'ble Sir. H.B.F. Frere and while doing so, he said that complaints of the inefficiency and corruption of police became universal. He said further that the police was everywhere oppressive and corrupt, indisciplined and ill-supervised. The Bill was passed on the 16th day of

March 1861 and became the law of the Country—i.e., the Indian Police Act (V of 1861) on the 22, March 1861. The Act, however, did not deal with crimes committed by policemen or misconducts by them in the discharge of their duty like threats and extortion etc. Of course, the provisions were in the Indian Penal Code—1861 and in the Code of Criminal Procedure Code which was in the process of enactment then. All said and done, subsequent history from 1861 shows that the police continued to commit crimes in spite of adverse criticisms against them by the people, press, courts and research scholars. The story of police crimes from 1861 to 1947 when India became independent is treated in the chapter that follows.

References

1. Anandswarup Gupta, *Crime and Police in India* (upto 1861), Sahitya Bhawan, Agra, 1974.
2. Fifth Report, 1812 (1917) Vol. II.

CHAPTER—2

Police Crimes in British India

The British were fully aware that the crimes committed by police were a problem to be tackled with. In 1860, the India Penal Code came into existence, and sections 330 and 331 of the Penal Code were enacted with a purpose to book the crime-doers in police uniform. Voluntarily causing hurt or grievous hurt to extort confession or to compel restoration of property were treated as serious offences. According to section 331, I.P.C, whoever voluntarily caused grievous hurt for the purpose of extorting any confession or any information which might lead to the detection of an offence, or for the purpose of compelling or causing the restoration of any property was punished with imprisonment for a term which might extend to 10 years and was liable to fine. Though the law was very specific on the matter, history proved that third degree methods were lavishly employed by the police investigators. They were caused within the four walls of a police station so much so that the visibility of law violations was minimum. No one subjected to torture dared to speak out anything that happened in police custody. This gave a confidence among the police that they could torture anybody with immunity. The practice thus became an unwritten law in due course of time. Victims of police torture died either in police custody or within a short period after their torture. The Code of Criminal Procedure which was enacted in 1861 made clear provisions under section 176 of the Code empowering a Magistrate to conduct an inquiry into deaths in police custody. This section required an inquiry to be conducted into the cause of death by a Magistrate either instead of or in addition to the investigation held by a police officer. The law permitted the Magistrate to inform the relatives of the deceased to allow them to remain present when he held the inquiry. However, there was no provision to make victimological compensation to the victims of torture or to the next of kin of the deceased.

Earlier the police could retain an arrested person for 48 hours in their custody without producing him before a Magistrate. The long stay of the arrestees in police custody was detrimental to the interest of the arrestees and paved the way for employing more torture on them. The 1861 Code of Criminal Procedure by virtue of section 57 made it mandatory for the police to produce the arrestees before the Magistrate within a period of 24 hours of the arrest excluding the time necessary for the journey from the place of arrest to the court of the Magistrate. Nevertheless, allegations were plenty against the police functionaries that they resorted to inhuman, degrading and oppressive methods within that short stay of 24 hours. When the arrestees were produced before the Magistrates they were asked to state whether or not they were mistreated by the police. To the question thus asked, the arrestees invariably used to say that they were not ill-treated by the police. Researchers attested to the fact that the arrestees had no option but to say so before the Magistrates. They had no courage or were helpless to speak against the police. The arrestees who were roughed up by the police prior to their production before the Magistrates could not but shiver before the policemen/officers who too were present in the court when the Magistrates asked them to speak about the treatment in police stations. In due course, the question and answer session in the court by the Magistrate and the arrestees became a ritual in criminal justice administration.

The Code of Criminal Procedure 1861 made a distinction between cognizable and non-cognizable offences and empowered (section 41, new Code of 1973) a police officer to arrest a person without warrant only when he was concerned in a cognizable case. Critics to police attitude to the arrests were of the view that the police did not give much weight to such a provision of law. They arrested anyone if they wanted so and they manipulated the cases as they desired. A simple hurt could be made an attempt to murder and wrongful confinement/restraint etc. could be put in the F.I.R. at the sweet discretion of the police authorities. In short they could make a non-cognizable offence to a cognizable one or vice versa and researches conducted in the recent past too showed that the present day police too resorted to such objectionable practice in the pretext of justice administration. Who could question the police authorities if they have determined to violate the laws?—if they are adamant in committing crimes?

The police in the British India thought that the Indian Penal Code and the Code of Criminal Procedure were enacted to initiate actions against offenders other than policemen/officers. The superior ranks too were not keen in enforcing the law in their department against their subordinates. All of them were, therefore, blamed that the laws were licences issued to them to take action against the people other than against the police functionaries. The most misused/abused section in the Code of Criminal Procedure—1861 might be section 151 which empowered a police officer to arrest a person without warrant to prevent the commission of cognizable offence which could not be otherwise prevented. Under this provision of law, a police officer could take any person into custody provided he was prepared to manage and manipulate evidence against the arrestee. Some policemen/officers used subjective scales to asses the behaviour of others and they arrested people, sometimes, to satisfy their ego and grandeur feelings. No doubt, a police officer could arrest a person if he had a mere suspicion that he would commit a cognizable offence and the provision was misused by some unscrupulous police officers. The arrestee was not even charged with the commission of any cognizable offence and the power was given indiscriminately to all police officers.

Offences were classified into cognizable and non-cognizable. In 1861, the classification was made and it was made so because the police caused serious harassments to people who were alleged to have committed petty offences. The law made distinction between cognizable and non-cognizable offences for preventing police officers from misusing their power of arrest. In spite of the distinctions so made in the Code of Criminal Procedure—1861 (Act XXV of 1861), the police continued to effect the arrest under some pretext or other.

The Code of Criminal Procedure (Section 46 of new Code—1973) authorized police officers to touch or confine the body of the person to be arrested only if the person did not submit himself to the custody. Researchers found that some police officers literally lifted the arrestees and threw them to the police vehicles even when they were meak and mild. It was seen even in the recent past and of course, police vehicles were not available when the Code of Criminal Procedure was enacted, on 1st January, 1862. But they were treated brutally at the time of arrest. The law was very clear and specific that it was only when the person forcibly resisted the endeavour to apprenend him or attempted to evade arrest that a police officer could use "all means necessary to effect the arrest". But, the criminal in the policemen did not give due respect to the provision of law and the defenseless arrestee had no option but to yield and suffer. No one thought seriously about the expression of criminal and aggressive tendencies among the then law enforcement functionaries, for, illiterate people took it for granted that the police were empowered to employ torture on the arrestees. The law was very categoric that the police officer could use only that much force which was necessary to overcome the resistance of the person arrested. Who could weigh the force and resistance? In certain instances, the arrested persons met with tragic death while they were in police custody. The law insisted that a police officer ought not cause the death of the person sought to be arrested, even if he was resisting or evading arrest, unless the person concerned was accused of an offence punishable with death or imprisonment for life. Researches would show that people who died in police custody were not accused even in involving any serious or heinous crimes.

Even before human rights were recognized in India as they are today, the Code of Criminal Procedure—1861 made it certain that the person arrested ought not be subjected to more restraint than was necessary to prevent his arrest. Somehow or other, handcuffs played an important role when arrests were made not only in films and other cultural programmes, but also in real life. The Supreme Court of India issued special instructions regarding the use of handcuffs. When the Code of Criminal Procedure was enacted, very poorly paid and overwhelmingly illiterate policemen/officers were enforcing law. They were vested with vast powers which they did not know how to exercise. As the historians put it: 'the vast powers given to police by the Code of Criminal Procedure—1861 had unbounded scope for the abuse of their power and authority'. Historians say that the inspector general of police of the north west provinces had his own views about the provisions of the Code of Criminal Procedure—1861, but his voice was very feeble. The then Government thought that the superintendents of police would be able to check the malpractices of the policemen/officers. History proved that the superior ranks could not prevent the malpractices. Anandswarup Gupta writes in this context: "if the provisions of the Police Act, the I.P.C and the Cr. P.C. to which attention has been drawn are viewed together, the conclusion is irrestible that the criminal administration was sought to be run with brute force and by instilling in the people a fear complex with regard to the police[1]".

The Code of Criminal Procedure—1861 (Section 50 of the new Code—1973) said that the person arrested had to be informed of the grounds of his arrest and of his right to bail in non-bailable offences. In bailable offences, bail was a matter of right while in non-bailable offences, it was left to the discretion of the court whether or not the arrestee was to be released on bail. Old people say that they had no courage to ask a police officer the grounds of the arrest or if they dared to ask such a question, it would, in all probability irritated him and nobody could predict what would happen afterwards. According to them, torturing the arrestee then and afterwards would be the natural outcome of such a question to a police officer in uniform. If this is what old people speak about police behaviour and if that is what people see today in police work, certainly, it would have been worse in the past when the Code of Criminal Procedure—1861 was enacted. For, every police behaviour seen today has a history, sometimes extending to several decades or centuries. The Supreme Court of India in D.K. Basu Vs. State of West Bengal reiterated the rights of the arrestee to know the grounds of his arrest at the time of the arrest.

How did the police grant bail in nonbailable offences? Sometimes, the arrestee had to humour the police to obtain bail. Section 98 of the Code of Criminal Procedure insisted that no police officer should offer to an arrestee any inducement by threat or promise or otherwise, to make any disclosure relating to the commission of crimes. Voluntary confessions or disclosures out of the free will of the interrogated alone were accepted as evidences. Police officers could search the person and places and seize property. There were allegations that the searching officers plundered property during their search. The Indian Evidence Act 1872 too made several provisions to protect the interest of the suspects/arrestees in criminal cases. Section 24 of the Evidence Act stated that the confessions ought to be voluntary and if it was made under any inducement, threat or promise, then it was irrelevant in criminal proceedings. Moreover, sections 25 & 26 of the Indian Evidence Act made any confessions made to a police officer or in his presence inadmissible in evidence. Why did the British law makers make so many provisions in law for creating difficulties for the police? The simple answer to the question would be to check and prevent the criminal tendencies of the police personnel. Describing the police in Bengal, Trevelyan who travelled from Calcutta to Bihar wrote in 1864—that is, immediately after the Indian Penal Code, the Code of Criminal Procedure and Police Act were enacted—that the detective capacity of the police functionaries was very weak. Hence, they used force on people to make confessions. They were corrupt to the core. The policemen involved in many corrupt practices. A policeman was considered as an unskilled worker and he was paid very poor salary when the inspector general of police received the pay scale of Rs. 2500-100-3000. The Chaukidars received their pay and it was Rs. 3 to 6 per month. They therefore went after alternate means and methods to make money. In 1864, the lowest grade constables got Rs. 5 as their salary. The higher grades received Rs. 6 and 7 as the case might be. Mr. Temple, the Chief Commissioner then observed that the police were fairly successful in identifying, detecting and repressing ordinary crimes, but were quite unsuccessful in dealing with organized crimes or with cases of an intricate nature. He said further that the police did not have good detective skills and ability to find out organized crimes. They were not up to the mark or deficient in the scientific and intellectual parts of their profession. No one asked why the police were inefficient in the detection of organized crimes. Was it because the police had any understanding with the organized criminals? Today allegations are heard about police nexuses with crime syndicates/Mafia criminals and my book on *Indian Police and Nexus Crime* deals entirely with the unholy nexuses of policemen with criminal politicians, underworld criminals, criminal businessmen and organized criminals. If the police in India purposefully failed or refused to identify organized crimes even during the British rule in India, the presumption would be in favour of police having *nexus* dealings with organized criminals. If that was the case, one might say that the police nexuses with criminals could be traced back to the British regime in our Country.

The administration reports of the police during 1864 would show that the mail robberies continued to show an increasing trend and the police then were suspected to have involved in the commission of mail robberies. Whatever that be, it has come to notice that only 52 per cent of the cases of burglary and theft reported to police were investigated during 1866. Why? Even in the cases investigated by the police, it might be stated that the police were very deficient in their detective ability. In order to cover their deficiency, some police officers resorted to abuse the power and authority. They were found to have recourse to the use of torture to obtain confessions from the suspects. An Inspector General of Police in 1865 complained that the police recorded false confessions which the accused retracted before the magistrate. Indian Evidence Act (I of 1872) came into force from 15th March, 1872.. The Code of Criminal Procedure—1861 had sections 148—150 relating to confessions before the police. These sections were reproducted in sections 25—27 of the Indian Evidence Act and they were found necessary to control the police. Torture by police was an aching problem and precisely therefore section 24, Indian Evidence Act—1872 laid down that a confession made by an accused person was irrelevant in a criminal proceedings, if the making of the confession appeared to the court to have been caused by any inducement, threat, or promise having reference to the charge against the accused person proceeding from a person in authority and sufficient, in the opinion of the Court, to give the accused person grounds which could appear to him reasonable for supposing that by making it he would gain any advantage or avoid any evil of a temporal nature in reference to the proceedings against him. What might have necessitated the British to enact such a law in the Indian Evidence Act—1872? The reason was simple and it was to discourage the police functionaries who misused their muscle power for the disadvantage of the people. Mr. Inglis stated in the Council that the police were placed in a position of maximum possible moral degradation by virtue of such provisions of law in the Indian Evidence Act. All ranks in police were treated alike by the Evidence Act. He admitted that the police in India suffered from a bad reputation. The law of evidence thus did not trust its law enforcement officers and the history of police thenceforth showed that the police resorted to many more improper and evil strategies to convince the court about the involvement of the accused in the commission of crimes.

The more the police employed improper and objectionable methods, the more they earned the distrust of the people. In an overenthusiasm to prove the cases before the Courts of law, the police resorted to several brutal and short cut methods exhibiting and expressing their criminal tendencies and aggressive behaviour. The police also were found to use torture not only when they interrogated the suspects (with their ingnorance of the psychology of interrogation) but also when they arrested them—when they handled law and order situations—when they searched places and seized articles—when they interacted with people. The people considered the police to be a brutal force expressing animal instincts and aggressive behaviours. Even after several years of independence, the police could not earn the reputation of being people friendly. Even in 1873, it was found that the morale and discipline of the police in India were far away from being satisfactory. The people evaluated the morale and discipline of the police on the basis of the same seen in the dominent culture and society. The people did not and could not assess the morale and discipline of the police from what they showed in the parade ground when they did drill. The use of filthy language, epithets and third degree methods kept the people away from the police even in 1873. The Lieutenant Governor in 1874-75 found that the lower grades of the viative officers enjoyed only a low status in society and they behaved as "low status men" as they did not want to impress upon any one with their sober behaviour and decent conversation. To quote Anandswarup Gupta again" "There were complaints of the tendency of the police to make hasty arrests and to be harsh and rough in bearing. This was inevitable because their calibre was as poor as it could be. Only 897 men could read and write and nearly half the force was wholly uneducated. There were also several well founded charges of extortion or bribery[2]". He continues: "crime increased in 1876. Police failures were reported to be 'most lamentable' in burglary cases and 'not creditable' in thefts. The conduct of the police continued to be unsatisfactory. Judicial convictions and dismissals were numerous and there were several instances of torture, maltreatment and extortion [3]".

Looking into the history of Indian police, a criminologist may ask: "Why did the police resort to torture, inhuman and degrading treatment for several centuries?" The answer can also be given by a criminologist. In any case, the criminality in Indian police is as old as the police system itself, but it has not attracted much research attention. One reason for the neglect is that the police has been treated as a force fighting against crime and criminals and as such the criminologists did not look at the police and their behaviour from a criminological angle. Criminologists in India and abroad, until recently, went to the Central Jails and Sub-Jails to study the personality, personality traits, attitude to crimes and family backgrounds etc. of criminals. For, they thought that the convicted criminals were the real criminals. Criminologists did not devote much of their attention to the crimes committed by the law enforcement agencies to increase convictions from the courts of law. In a way, that was a major drawback in the development of criminological thoughts. Today, the crimes committed by the law enforcement officers attract a lot of media attention so much so that the criminologists can not close their eyes shut to the hard and aching realities.

Police Crimes: 1877—1889

Police wanted to prove their worth, efficiency and capacity to detect crimes and apprehend criminals. In Gaya, some policemen were found to commit dacoities, mail robberies and many other offences. Later, they caught hold of innocent people and charged them with the commission of the above said offences. The purpose of doing such illegal and unethical acts by policemen was not merely to earn a reputation as good detectors, but also to amass money by way of dacoities and robberies. As the culprits caught by the police ultimately got acquittals from the courts, the dishonest police activities could bring ill-fame and bad image. A Police Gazette in English, Bengali and Hindi was sanctioned in 1879 and the pay of the constables was raised. A new post—subinspector of police—was created to attract educated candidates. No doubt, the police service was unattractive for many as they had low pay, status and emoluments. Necessarily, they had to do hard work and to face many risks while they performed their duty. In 1880, some policemen were suspected to have connived with dacoits among the *Bheels*. They were identified and some of them were convicted.

The British introduced "Punitive Police" and the purpose was to cause deterrence among the people. The punitive police were not people friendly and they could put down crimes in Poona district and other places during 1880-81. In another sense, the licence given to the police to handle situations in an atrocious way made them to employ lavishly torture on people indiscriminately. Almost a police raj or police *goondaism* could be seen then. Certainly, it had its short and long term effects on police crimes in India.

In 1884, The Calcutta Review published an article[4] which said: "there was not much complaint against the spread of violent crimes as against the existing protective organization". Police was described as "an engine of oppression of the most exquisite and pernicious kind". The article continued:

"The disrepute and unpopularity of the police force is undoubtedly a very frequent cause of its demoralization. It is curious that a service which exists ostensibly for the benefit of the public should stand so low in public estimation . . . . . In India, there are special reasons for the bad 'odour' which attaches itself to the very word 'police'. Police stood for fair justice and the people could not sense it. It was of bad taste and precisely therefore ought to be corrected". For, the article said further that: "The force is invested with enormous powers, and paid at inadequate rates of salary, and at the same time very little care is exercised in the selection of candidates for the various posts". Even today, one doubts very much whether or not we have devised fool-proof methods for the selection of upright candidates having the required aptitude, good will and sincerity in the job! The ailments, critics say, continue to damage the image of the police in public estimation. What was seen in 1884 in the British India has been in existence throughout the history of police. "The police officer, when once appointed, has ordinarily little to fear in the way of really efficient supervision, and, as a natural consequence, he too often systematically preys on the people from the date of his appointment to that of retirement"—noted by the author of the article. Today, human rights are accepted and the police functionaries take extra-caution when they involve themselves in preying on the people—say the researchers. Nexus criminality is an evil of Indian democracy and the unholy nexuses established by police with criminal businessmen/underworld criminals provide facilities to prey on the people. Necessarily, the *nexus* transactions make the police unpopular in the eyes of the people.

The observations of the Calcutta Review could reveal the nature, extent and intensity of police crimes during 1884. The Review said: "The best appointments constantly fall to low-caste men, who have, as such, far greater powers for evil than an aristocratic incumbent would possess because of the injury they can inflict on any high-caste person who should happen to offend them; and, besides, from the accident of their birth they are restrained by no sanctions and no considerations of any kind from making their appointment as lucrative as possible........ and dishonesty is found to enjoy a practical immunity from punishment-.......... the result is that the police are usually useless....... or else, they are a positive evil".

Muslim fanaticism in Malabar (erstwhile Madras) resulted in periodical riots and a new unit called Malabar Special Police was instituted. In 1885, again a *punitive police* force was created to deal with the Mapilla outrages in Malabar. Punitive police force—the concept itself was of a questionable nature. The police ought to be people friendly and the punitive police force could never become so. Muscle power ruled the punitive police. Whatever a punitive police would do even with the best intentions, the people would not take it for its face value.

Police Crimes: 1890—1904

Mr. J. Beames, Commissioner of Bhagalpur was appointed as the Chairman of a Committee instituted to look into the causes of imperfection in police in Bengal. He submitted his report in 1891. He accused the police for:

1. Careless recording of the first information report;
2. Undue delay in taking up investigation;
3. Refusal, omission, failure to send up material evidence in criminal cases;
4. Placing undue reliance on confessions and he found that they resulted in large scale acquittals of criminal cases.

Why did the police do so? Were they ill-motivated? Necessarily, they resulted in miscarriage of justice or administering injustice to people involved in criminal cases. During the trial of cases, it was brought out that sometimes the police registered false cases and presented false charges. Sometimes, the evidence was tampered and tutored witnesses were produced. If that was what the police did, certainly it was indicative of the existence of a criminal mind in those officers who did such acts unscrupulously. The Committee made several recommendations to check the malpractices by the policemen/officers during investigation.

A similar committee was appointed in the N.W.P. and Oudh in 1890 under M.W. Kaye, the Member, Board of Revenue. The Committee inquired into the defects in the police system. The Committee found that the accusations of tyranny, oppression, torture, corruption, manipulation, concoction of evidence, fabrication, abuse of power, misuse of authority of police were due to the defective material with which the police force was composed. Of course, the legal system and the laws under which the system worked were also responsible for the commission of crimes by the police personnel. A radical change was recommended. In other words, a radical change in the material (police personnel) could only guarantee eradication of crimes by police.

Section 161, Code of Criminal Procedure contained the word "truly" and the section related to the recording of statements made by witnesses to the police interrogator. The police were found to coerce the witnesses and to threaten them saying that they would prosecute them incase they did not tell the same thing before the Court when their statements were recorded during the trial. The statements recorded by police under coercion thus became sources of harassment and mental aches for the witnesses who had no option but to surrender to police threats. The misuse/abuse was so much that ultimately, the section 161 Code of Criminal Procedure was amended and the word "truly" was omitted. The fear of prosecution for perjury did hamper investigations.

In 1898, policemen/officers were deployed for plague duty in Calcutta. It was found that the police lacked discipline. 13 cases of torture and 85 cases of extortion were reported against the policemen. Some of them ended in conviction. There were 3278 departmental punishments in 1897 and 3856 in 1898. What did they show? It meant that the police consisted of people who had violent tendencies. They suffered from lack of character.

Lord Curzon on February 3, 1902 said: "a Government that gives good laws or good eduction or the wherewithal to live, but the places the preservation of internal order and the detection, prevention and punishment of crime in soiled or incompetent hands can not escape reproach[5]". He found that the number of departmental punishments inflicted on policemen was unimaginably large and quite demoralizing. The higher levels in police exhibited criminal tendencies in their own way and inflicting punishment was one way they were expressing the vengeance, retribution and aggression. Even today, the same nature in seen among some of the higher-ups in the hierarchy so much so that the lower ranks feel quite desperate at the way they are punished by the disciplinary authority. As a result, some commit suicide while others take to drinks/drugs. During 1902—1904, the administration reports of the police showed that the discipline of the police force was not satisfactory. The punishment remained heavy in many provinces. Resignations from police went up in Central Provinces, NWFP, Assam and N.W.P. The lower ranks in police suffered a lot and the higher ranks enjoyed a lot.

The police during the period of the East India Company and during the British India were involving themselves in lawless law enforcement, nexus crimes, corruption, malpractices, oppression, abuse of power, misuse of authority and what not? The period that ended by 1900 from the moment Robert Clive landed in this Country was a period during which the police in India, by whatever way they were called, committed many crimes and atrocities. No one took serious notice about the law enforcement agencies committing law violations. As a result, anything by name 'police criminology' did not come into being. It took another 100 years for us to study the police behaviour from a criminological perspective down the millennia and the police in India need to look to themselves to see how they commit crimes and how do they perpetuate crimes in society.

Indian Police Commission: 1902-03 evaluated police and made many recommendations for the police for the 20th century. The report of the Indian Police Commission contained vivid descriptions of police criminality and now 100 years are over since the Commission made their views on police crimes and criminal tendencies. No serious studies were undertaken to study police behaviour from a criminological perspective although some research articles or journalistic reports are seen here and there on police crimes and criminality. The next chapter is on police crimes during the pre-independent period in India—that is up to 1947.

It is a fact which must be accepted that the police in India, down the centuries, committed many crimes and they themselves did not study seriously the causative and preventive aspects of police crimes and criminality. The police committed crimes under the colour of their uniform and muscle power—under a consensus that they have reached and with the fund the people have entrusted. 'Criminals in Uniform'—under such a large banner headline, a national daily gave great prominence to a crime committed by 'some policemen in a south Indian State. The courts of law, time and again, wrote judgements on police criminality and policemen's involvement in the commission of crimes. Films and video projected them and the policemen and hierarchy did not probe into why crimes took place in police service! Police department collected the statistics of police crimes and it was intended for publication by the National Crime Records Bureau, Government of India. The statistics did not serve any useful purpose till date. No significance was attached to the crime committed by the people in uniform and no one studied the problem of police crimes as a criminologist might do it. Policing the police or guarding the guardians were words or phrases which meant very little to the policemen, for they were guarding other people, policing the society, investigating crimes which others had committed, preventing crimes seen in society while some of them were actively committing, conniving, cooperating, participating and propagating crimes and criminal behaviours. Police crimes are now well recognized and thus police criminology or criminology of law enforcement becomes a reality. Law enforcement, crime detection, commission of crimes by policemen, nexus crimes, crime prevention, crimes by hierarchy, maintaining law and order, keeping peace, criminogenesis of police crimes, victimology and victimgenesis of police crimes, victims of abuse of police power/ misuse of authority, third degree methods, enforcement crimes etc. are words and phrases which people discuss in these days and they try to give some operational definitions to crimes which police commit while they enforce law or do things in the pretext of enforcing law. Even a sphere where people might have supposed the police role (expected and effected) to be clear-cut and specific, they would not see the police doing anything. Why? Nexus, nexuses and what not make the police to be lethargic, indifferent, negative etc. in their work? Police criminology studies such issues in law enforcement. At the moment, there is the reason to think that public trust or confidence in the police, as an institution, may not be great or enviable in India and the policemen do sense it. To the extent that the people see the police as authoritarian thief catchers and to the extent that the police involve themselves in the commission of various crimes from simple theft of seized articles from the scene of crime to nexus criminality in union with criminal politicians and underworld criminals, there is a strong basis for studying scientifically the criminology of policing the society. A good number of crimes which the policemen commit may come under petty corruption and corrupt practices. Unfortunately, the petty corruption rises into well organized gang activities and some of the crimes committed by certain people in uniform really become prominent in the media and the crime-doers figure as men challenging the whole basis of criminal justice administration. Increasingly, it is being recognized today that in sharp distinction to the traditional criminals, a demonstrably successful criminal class has emerged and they are caught only infrequently and as such they continue to commit crimes with impunity. 'Crime police' and 'Criminal policeman'—both mean a lot in these days. To understand police crimes means to understand the law enforcement in a fuller way.

Indian Police Commission: 1902-03 wanted to better the police system in India. They have observed police behaviour and misbehaviour, nevertheless, as shown elsewhere they did not approach the issue from a criminological perspective. The next chapter is about police crimes during the pre-independent India.

References

1. Anandswarup Gupta, *The Police in British India*: 1861—1947, Concept Publishing Company, New Delhi, 1979.
2. Anandswarup Gupta, *ibid.*
3. Anandswarup Gupta, *ibid.*
4. The Calcutta Review, No. 157, 1884.
5. H.D., Police—A Progs., March, 1902.

CHAPTER—3

Police Crimes during the Pre-Independence Period

"Police force is far from efficient; it is defective in training and organization; it is inadequately supervised; it is generally regarded as corrupt and oppressive; and it has utterly failed to secure the confidence and cordial cooperation of the people"—emphatically said by the Indian Police Commission appointed by Lord Curzon in July 1902. The Commission was speaking how the police was in British India and was suggesting how the police ought to be in the 20th century India. The terms of reference to the Commission did not contain anything relating to police crimes or criminology of law enforcement although they had put to examine whether the general supervision exercised by the Magistracy over the police, and the control of the superior officers (including inspectors) over the investigation of crime were adequate to prevent oppression on the part of the subordinate police, and, if not, how they could be made so.

The British administration was fully aware of police corruption and police involvement in various types of crimes. But, the terms of reference did not specifically contain anything about police crimes. Mr. J. Beames Committee and many other committees appointed subsequently made specific comments on police crimes and Lord Curzon was fully aware of them. To quote once again Anandswarup Gupta: "The detailed investigations which were undertaken in Bengal and the N.W. Provinces following the enquiries of 1888 showed that the state of the police was thoroughly discreditable to the administration, but they revealed also that there was no intention to examine the system in depth. Even so, these enquiries and investigations highlighted at least one major defect in the system, i.e., that the status and emoluments of the subordinate police were grossly inadequate and unsatisfactory, but that the action that resulted was superficial in the extreme and failed inevitably to bring about any improvement to the performance of the traditional functions of the police and the criminal courts or the reputation and polularity of the force".

Looking into the attitude the British administration had towards the police system here, one may come to a conclusion that the British wanted a brutal force to retain their rule in the country. They were just not bothered about police crimes although they spoke against them here and there just to show others that they were really concerned about the prevention of police crimes and correcting them. They wanted a *punitive police force* and they wanted the police to perform their duties under European control. Even the Indian Police Commission: 1902-03 suggested that the European control ought not be diluted. If the police in India committed crimes and involved in corruption or corrupt activities, the Europeans under whose control the police worked here could not run away from the responsibility and liability. The Commission was concerned more with the criminality of the people and the offences they committed. The Commission did not study the crimes committed by the policemen. The Commission stated or repeated what many other authorities were telling time and again that the police force was far away from being efficient. They did not say much about the 'why' of the problem. The British administration could do a lot to make the police efficient, but they did not. Why? The Europeans had the control over the police and the inefficiency of the police meant the inefficiency of the European masters. According to the Commission, the police were inadequately supervised and what was the responsibility of the European masters for it? The Commission further noted that the police was generally regarded as corrupt and oppressive. Then, what was the role of the European masters to carve out such an image? The Commission loudly stated that the police utterly failed to secure the confidence and cordial cooperation of the people. Why? The British knew the reasons for the deplorable state of affairs even without a high powered commission making such observations. Beames Committee analysed the causes for the sad state of affairs. There were illiterate constables and officers. They treated the constables as labourers and head constables as skilled workers. They entrusted investigation of work to head constables. They were not given any training worth its name. The Kaye Committee too made the same observations. When ignorant people were given wide powers to investigate, naturally and necessarily, oppression came into being as a substitute or compensatory mechanism for their ignorance. Though many suggested to institute a special wing for conducting the investigation work, nobody took any serious notice of such a recommendation. The authority at the decision making end felt that it had superior wisdom than those who made recommendations and they ignored the suggestions under some count or another. Police crimes, tyranny, oppression, corruption, fabrication, concoction, abuse of power, misuse of authority thus became the inevitable outcome of such culpable refusal and negligence of the authorities who were supposed to take decisions and implement them. It further shows that the police crimes that one sees presently had a history and background which were older than a century. The cliches like unpracticability, unnecessary expenditure and unwise strategy etc. were as old as police crimes in the Country. The decision making authorities rejected the ideas on silly and simple grounds.

Indian Police Commission: 1902-03 and Police Crimes

The Indian Police Commission: 1902-03 observed that important and responsible duties were entrusted to untrained and ill-educated officers recruited in the lowest ranks. The Commission observed further that the superior officers too were insufficiently trained. What could be done if the blind were asked or necessitated to lead the blind? The blind superiors and the blind subordinates together committed atrocities on crime investigation. As ignorant people, they had no option but to do things in the way they wanted and many a time they resorted to illegal and immoral strategies during crime investigation. The commission accused both European and native officers of corruption—officers of all ranks including magistrates and so to say, the criminology of law enforcement had its origin in the remote past and its development down the centuries. The Commission took note of the fact that corruption prevailed at every stage of crime investigation and law enforcement. To quote the Commission:

"The police officer may levy a fee or receive a present for every duty he performs."[3]

"The complainant has often to pay a fee for having his complaint recorded."

"He has to give the investigating officer a present to secure his prompt and earnest attention to the case."

"More money is extorted as the investigation proceeds."

"People are harassed....... sometimes by having to accompany him from place to place, sometimes by attendance at the police station. . . . .

sometimes by threats of evil consequences to themselves or their friends (especially to the women of the family) if they do not fall in with his view of the case, sometimes by invasions of their houses by low-caste people on the plea of searching for property........ From all this deliverance is often to be brought only by payment of fees or presents in cash".

One century is now over since the Indian Police Commission made observations on the criminality which prevailed in police. Has the situation changed to the better?-to the worse? Police criminology may better answer the question; but no such criminology developed over the years. For, the criminologists and researchers, it may be reiterated, thought that crimes were committed only by those who were convicted by the courts. All of them rushed to jails to study more about crimes and criminals. They never went to a police station to study on police crimes and criminals in police uniform. Justice Mulla of the Allahabad High Court in a landmark judgement observed that there was no organized criminals in the Country whose record of crime would come any way near to that organized group called the Indian police.

Indian Police Commission 1902-03 observed criminality in police work, but did not study the issue as a criminologist would do it. The Commission enumerated some causes for the criminality and the etiological analysis was not deep enough to learn the real causes of police crimes.

Police Crimes Develop to a Social Problem!

The history of Indian police may show that the crimes in police and by police got developed and thus a culture of police criminality emerged—note some criminologists. As early as 1902, the Police Commission said: "The station house officer will sometimes hush up a case on payment of his terms; he will receive presents from parties and their witnesses; he will levy illicit fees from shopkeepers and others for services rendered; or to obviate vexatious espionage. He has a specially rich vein in cases concerning disputes about land, water or crops......" Was the Commission talking about the various types of nexus crimes which the police commit in these days—or are accused of committing presently? If they were done on a small scale then, the situation has worsened in an alarming proportion in these days! On November 4, 2000 when I write this chapter I read in the morning news paper that many police officers are just suspended from service for their nexus transactions with Abkari Mafia who engineered a Hooch tragedy in a south Indian State. The entire State is contaminated with news and views relating to nexus crimes—i.e., the unholy relations among the police (excise), politician and Hooch Mafia in the State. The media is full of news about nexus crimes and the nexus partners play "*deaf-dumb games*" to fool the people who become victims of enforcement crimes.

Police criminality may be, like any other social problem, centuries old. While criminologists have devoted a lot of time for studying various criminal problems, they have not taken up police crimes as a serious problem till date. The reasons for this neglect and indifference may have helped only to multiply the seriousness and intensity of the problem. Corruption and corrupt practices, nexus crimes and enforcement criminality, simulated encounters and human rights violations, custodial torture and custody rapes etc. attract research attentions from some research quarters. When the Indian Police Commission: 1902-03 spoke: "He has a specially rich vein in cases concerning disputes about land, water or crops", the Commission was talking about police nexus criminality. To quote the Commission once again: "A body of police comes down to the village and is quartered on it for several days. The principal residents have to dance attendance on the police all day long and for days together. Sometimes all the villagers are compelled to be in attendance, and inquiries degrading in their character are conducted *coram populo*. Suspects and innocent persons are bullied and threatened into giving information they are supposed to possess. The police officer, owing to want of detective ability or to indolence, directs his efforts to procure confessions by improper inducement, by threats and by moral pressure . . . . Sometimes suspects, whom the police officer does not desire to report as under arrest, are kept for days together under "so-called surveillance" which is nothing else than unauthorized confinement or restraint, a system which affords serious opportunity for malpractices. All this is done to secure evidence in support of the view which the police officer from time to time holds regarding the case. If in his opinion, enough of evidence is not thus obtained to secure a conviction, he will not hesitate to bloster up his case with false evidence. Sometimes this leads to an innocent person being prosecuted through police mistakes. More often perhaps it leads to guilty persons escaping through the suspicion thrown on the police evidence. Many a good case has been ruined in this way; but the police officer is unduly impelled by the statistical test to try to make his investigation end in conviction. When an investigation fails, the complainant is sometimes finally bullied or threatened into acknowledging that a mistake has been made, and the case is 'false'. When it is successful, the accused is often subjected to unnecessary annoyance; the law about bail is overlooked; the rules limiting the use of handcuffs are forgotten; and no serious effort is made to treat the accused with that consideration as to his food and comfort to which . . . . . he is entitled until he is convicted . . . ."

The Indian Penal Code 1860 and the provisions made thereunder were in full operation when the Indian Police Commission: 1902-03 made the above mentioned observation. The Code of Criminal Procedure—1861 and the laws of procedure enacted thereunder were effective when the police did the above mentioned illegalities. The Indian Evidence Act—1872 and the evidence laws were fully applicable then. Nevertheless, the police did not care them and they violated the provisions of law which they were bound to respect. Their acts and crimes were not counted when statistics on crimes was prepared. Why? Was it not a crime to tolerate crimes committed by police?

As one reads in the Commission's report prepared during 1902-03, I could see the police doing the same things during 1973—76 exactly in the ways the Commission has narrated. In a north Indian village, I noticed that the police officers going to the village demanding the villagers to feed them with "murgi" (Chicken) and liquor and I could not understand what they could do after a liquor party and how could they investigate the cases in a fair way! Was it the sort of investigation as contemplated by the Code of Criminal Procedure—1861? Were the hierarchy not aware of the crimes committed by the subordinate ranks? Perhaps, in a culture of police crimes, everyone from the bottom to the top became a part of that criminal culture! The Indian Penal Code—1860 makes confessions by improper inducement, threats and coercion to be crimes under law. What is happening today? How many cases of custodial violence, custodial deaths and degrading treatment are reported? The Penal Code says that killing of a human being by another human being is homicide and if it happens in police custody, then it is called custodial murder. Why do the police who ought to give protection to the life and property of people commit custodial murders? A criminologist must answer this question. A murder is a murder, no matter who commits it; a rape is a rape no matter whether it is committed in a police station or outside. If deaths, violence and rape etc. are reported from police stations—may be occasionally, then they certainly indicate a cultural milieu of criminality which must be studied in depth. A culture develops not in one day, too soon. The police culture of criminality has a history of many centuries so much so that a criminological analysis of the existing milieu may throw lights on many invisible areas of police crimes and their development.

The Commission: 1902-03 spoke about incommunicado detention in police custody. Even today, the same strategy is seen and in Joginder

Singh's case, the Supreme Court has issued special directives. The commissions of inquiry instituted in many States to probe into custodial deaths or rapes or violence often brought out incommunicado detentions which had a history of origin and development. The nineteenth century malady continues to be seen even in the 21st century. Abduct or kidnap a person and keep him in secret custody in a police station is an offence under law. When the police officers come to know about such detentions, some of them do not initiate any legal action against those who commit the offence. Criminologists now call it to be "lawless law enforcement or an enforcement crime", but one doubts whether or not a police officer may subscribe to the view of the criminologist in that regard. Such police officers may interpret such police crimes as a '*holy act*' done for the larger interests of the society. The Police Commission: 1902-03 made the observations, but illegal detentions continued to dominate the police culture which made attempts to justify the illegal detentions (wrongful confinement) in several ways. Improper inducements, coercion and use of third degree methods were seen in police lockups and the police culture interpretted it to be a necessary evil during the investigation of crime. Has the situation improved to the better?—or—has it deteriorated to the worse? A criminologist may have to answer the question. As it is today, no criminologist is seen to be assoicating himself when reports to reform the police in the Country are prepared or if at all he is associated, his views are not taken serious note of by the decision making authorities. Moreover, the police is always studied as law enforcing agency and not as a law violating agency although plenty of law violations are seen by police commissions, courts, researchers and police functionaries themselves.

The Police Commission: 1902-03 took note of concoction of evidence and padding up. The Evidence Act—1872 is categoric about the inadmissibility of such concocted evidence. Nevertheless, many judgements in criminal cases even today award acquittals on the basis of concocted evidence. It is nothing but miscarriage of justice and in every letter of the law, is a patent violation, a crime in its true sense. Where is the remedy for this oft-resorted criminal practice? What are the etiologically motivated factors to produce tutored witnesses and touts in criminal cases? A criminologist must study the criminal tendencies in police functionaries.

The crimes which the police commit during investigation of cases are issues which the people probably suffer and tolerate in these days. Police crimes still cause stress and anguish among the people. People are able to predict the type of crimes to which people in police custody are likely to be subjected. The press and the people today study the police in terms of crimes they commit, lawless law enforcement, illegal arrests, unauthorized detention, unlawful procedures, manipulation of records etc. and they do it under the light of human rights laws by exploring what is implied in the valued concern for fair and just administration of justice. People and the press, media and researchers make enquiries into the nature of police jobs in the millennium and they call police brutality and violence by their proper names which they did not do a century ago when the Indian Police Commission: 1902-03 prepared their report. The Commission said, it may be reiterated, that the police during the period under inquiry committed atrocities on innocent people just for securing evidence in support of the view which the police investigator from time to time held regarding the case. The Commission further pointed out: "If in his opinion enough evidence is not thus obtained to secure a conviction, he will not hesitate to bolster up his case with false evidence. Sometimes, this leads to an innocent person being prosecuted through police mistakes". This was nothing but crude administration of injustice on people who were helpless and defenceless before the police authorities. Do such obnoxious practices take place now? Researchers subscribe to the view that they do take place even today in a wider way. Those and similar acts in police culture must be considered before any improvement on police administration of justice is thought of. Police organization needs to be sensitive to these aspects and must acknowledge that it can achieve a name and fame only if it ensures a crime-free atmosphere in police stations. At every point, the policeman's judgement has to be in play with frequently complex sets of facts and the nature of his judgement will determine the nature of the action he takes. This discretion is a valued aspect of a policeman's work and if he takes a decision, as the Indian Police Commission noted in 1902-03, to bully the complainants, to threaten the witnesses, to torture the suspect, to create false evidences, to annoy the accused, to refuse the bail, to misuse the handcuffs, to deny food to the detinues in police lockups, then the policemen deciding so must be suffering from mental disorders. The psychopathy of police behaviour and the sociopathy of police culture are areas of great interest for criminologists today.

Causes of Police Crimes

Why do the police commit crimes during investigation of crime and enforcement of law? The Indian Police Commission: 1902-03 studied this issue and said that there were many reasons. According to them: "one is that the investigation of cases has been to far too great an extent entrusted to low paid and unqualified officers.......... In the police department, where the work is perhaps the most difficult and important in India, Government has been content to have the higher and more responsible offices filled by men deficient in education, intelligence and social status.......... Everywhere the demand of enlightened opinion is for the reform, of the station-house officer". Obviously, it becomes clear that the Commission did not study police crimes from the criminological perspectives. They could not be blamed for that because there were no criminologist in the Commission. Moreover, criminology in India during 1902-03 when the Commission analysed the causes of police abuses of their power and authority was not a developed science. The Commission, it seems, did not therefore look at and evaluate the abuses from a criminological angle. No doubt, low salary and lack of qualification could not be a direct cause of police crimes. People who got less salary or had no qualification would not commit crimes. Criminal motivations and facilitating environment might have been a better explanation for the police to commit crimes.

I cannot subscribe to the Commission's view that men who were deficient in education, intelligence and social status committed abuses of power. Criminologists have proved that people who possessed higher I.Q. committed crimes and low intelligence could never be a cause of crimes. The etiological analysis of police crimes by the Commission was superficial and they never brought out the real cause of police criminality. For example, lower level police functionaries enjoyed only a low social status then. It did not mean that people who had low social status would torture people, concoct evidence or treat people in a degrading way. I do not think that lack of education was a cause of police criminality. Today, a lot of highly qualified candidates are recruited to the police, but they too are found involving themselves in the commission of police crimes. The police ought to have values and the needed philosophy must rest on a set of human values conveying the idea that the police are to administer justice in a fair, lawful and moral way. The British did not inculcate such values to the police, instead the Commission blamed the supervisors. The Commission observed: "Supervision has been doubly defective. It was inefficient as regards....... inspectors, and it has been weak and inadequate as regards the superintendents. As to the inspectors...... the public do not regard them as honest....... there is incontrovertible evidence to show that success rather than honesty has been the qualification for promotion". Here too the Commission was not analysing the real causes of police crimes and criminality. They were beating at the bush and their approach did not tell the policemen/officers that they were committing offences and were liable to be punished. This approach could not succeed in making the police to introspect to themselves. How could the superintendents become weak and inadequate? How could the inspectors become inefficient? There was enough evidence to show that the Commission has been responsible for making sweeping judgements on higher officials in police hierarchy. Inefficiency of inspectors and inadequacy of superintendents could never become the cause of police crimes. They must have provided some opportunities for a policeman/ officer who possessed criminal minds. Indian criminology gives a lot of emphasis to the criminal mind of the offender. The chapters that follow will discuss more elaborately the causes of police crimes. The Commission made a lot of charges against the superintendents. They observed: "they are often-not well educated or intelligent men, that their training is defective, that their knowledge of the vernacular is not such as to enable them to have free intercourse with the people and to become acquainted with their feelings and circumstances, that they are too much in the hands of their subordinates, that they are not accessible or even courteous to natives, but their views are too narrow and their sense of responsibility too weak to allow them to pay due regard to complaints against their subordinates or strictures on their work or to take due notice of misconduct, that they are too burdened with clerical work and too little helped by qualified assistants to be able to exercise effective supervision and control over the police..... The Commission are of opinion that there is a great deal of truth in these complaints".

The Commission, it seems to me, was infectuated by the idea that crime, criminal tendencies, abuse of power, misuse of authority etc. were the aftereffects of lack of education, intelligence and training. They were not. We have plenty of evidence to show that well educated, highly intelligent and professionally trained people had involved in the commission of crimes—various types or crimes with intelligence and professional skills and competence. The education, intelligence and training would not decide whether or not someone would become a criminal, rather would decide how one would commit a crime if he became so. Education, intelligence and training could decide the manner in which the criminals committed the crimes. The Commission's observations were not helpful to understand the why of police crimes. Since the Commission's findings did not speak anything about the basic and fundamental factors of causative importance, the police crimes continued to be in existence in police subculture. For example, suppose the Government, in furtherance of the Commission's recommendations appointed educated, intelligent and trained superintendents to police the society, certainly they would have committed crimes in a better way with the help of their superior education, intelligence and training. Today, the police department has many educated and intelligent officers and men. If the allegations heard and seen are true, then the causes of police crimes are very much different from the education, intelligence and training of police personnel. My studies in the recent past and for the last 25 years have testified to me that a good number of police abuses take place as a result of a lack of an upright conscience correctly formed among the policemen/officers. More about it is discussed in the chapters that follow. Some of the crimes take place within the four walls of a police station—away from the public visibility—in isolation and there, no one except the human conscience will control the behaviour. Knowledge of the vernacular might have helped the superior ranks in police to have free social intercourse, but would never prevent them from committing crimes. Recent observations on police nexus with criminals prove that their knowledge of the vernacular was a helping factor to come closer and closer in their nexus crimes and transactions.

The Commission observed that the Superintendents of police were too much in the hands of their subordinates. What did the Commission mean by such an observation? Did they mean that all the subordinates were criminals so much so that the superintendents who were in the hands of the subordinates too became criminals? Some researchers say that a system becomes criminal if the administration is criminal and some others say that the system becomes criminal if the subordinates are criminal. There is a point in both arguments and therefore I may attest to the view that the superiors and subordinates have to share the responsibility of making a system criminal and one can not blame the other ignoring his share in the issue. One enthusiastic low caste police officer used to torture any suspect from a high caste birth when he interrogated him and he did so in spite of strong resistance from his subordinates. In many such instances, he was dissuaded by his associates and subordinates, but in vain. In some instances, he was cautioned, but the crimes continued to dominate his behaviour. It was found out that his perceptions about high caste structure was defective and perverted. The Commission, instead of evaluating the criminality in police culture in an objective way, found fault with the subordinates and observed that the superintendents were too often inclined to support their subordinates in an unreasonable manner and to receive complaints or strictures on police work in a hostile spirit. Why? It showed that the superintendents too had criminal tendencies which they expressed and exhibited along with their subordinates. The culture was defective and was perhaps pregnant with criminality.

Nevertheless, the Indian Police Commission: 1902-03 observed: "There are honest and efficient police officers of all grades, though they are represented as being very exceptional in the lower grades. . . . . . Neither do the Commission forget that much may be said in excuse for the misconduct of the police in the generally indifferent attitude of the people in respect of crime, in the encouragement of corruption by the readiness with which the people offer illegal gratifications and in the low pay and poor prospects of the police service. But honourable exceptions and mitigating circumstances can not efface the general impression created by the evidence recorded. There can be no doubt that the police force throughout the country is in a most unsatisfactory condition, that abuses are common everywhere, that this involves great injury to the people and discredit to the Government, and that radical reforms are urgently necessary. These reforms will cost much; because the department has hitherto been starved; but they must be effected".

The Commission found honest and efficient police officers amidst those who showed criminal tendencies. It showed that honesty and efficiency could exist in any culture which promoted criminality. How could the Government promote such honest and efficient police officers? Most frustratingly, the Commission did not deal with such issues. Instead the Commission found fault with the people who offered corruption money to police functionaries. Even today people do so, because they have no option but to yield to the greed of the police functionaries who administered justice to the people. The people tolerate the greedy police officers, for, they have learnt from their experience with police functionaries to adopt a policy which accepted the practice: "it is wiser to offer illegal gratification rather than fighting against a system which has institutionalized corruption and crime". In such a situation, indifference shown to police crimes may yield better dividends rather than showing reaction to police misconducts and crimes. The Commission's observation that the entire police force in the Country was in a most unsatisfactory condition was worth considering, nevertheless the administration was not keen in eradicating the unsatisfactory conditions. "Abuses are common everywhere, that this involves great injury to the people and discredit to the Government"—the Commission painfully noted. Even after a century, critics on police speaks the same thing more frequently and loudly than what it was during 1902-03. But the disease continues and the people suffer the consequences. Governments come and go in a democracy, but the people and the police remain as sufferers and abusers of power/authority respectively. Is there a salvation?—a cure from the ailment?

Whenever police crimes are detected or reported, disciplinary proceedings may be initiated or the crime-doer may be transfered. This is an oft-resorted strategy. Does it solve the issue?—cure the disease? A suspension or a transfer can not cure an old disease in police culture. The police is granted the only legitimate use of force in civil society. Regarding the use of legitimate force John R. Lambert says: "The legal recognition that there is a legitimate use of force by the police goes hand in hand with a recognition that in the use of force there lies a major risk and danger for police management and personnel because of the difficulty in practice in distinguishing illegitimate and legitimate use of force [1]". Abuse of power or misuse of authority certainly does not come under legitimate use of force by police. It is lawlessness and crime. Third degree methods to extract confessions, refusal to feed the detinues under custody, custody rapes and calling of epithets seem to have been commonplace events in the centuries gone by. These obvious abuses are seen, as the accusations and allegations of police brutality reveal—even today in the democratic India. Police brutality, as the allegations show, refers to aggressive patrol tactics, harassment to the kith and kin of the suspects in crimes, arrest on suspicion, verbal insults to the public on roads or other demeaning behaviour. Use of force to control and assert police authority in a violent or potentially violent situation is one thing and the use of force against a suspect in helplessness in police custody is quite another thing. After an arrest and in the four walls of a police station, use of force is clearly unjustified, but the police are accused of employing force on detinues.

Constant interference by the police in the private lives of people, constant espionage on the privacies of people, constant visits of the policemen in the houses of the suspects constituted an intolerable burden and vexation to the people of early 19th century India. The same situation continues without much change even in the 21st century. The 1902-03 Police Commission found men of even criminal classes appointed in the police service. The Commission recommended that the constables recruited to the police ought to belong to the "respectable" classes of the society and ought to be people of good character and antecedents. It was a good proposal if the Government could implement it and today many people subscribe to the view that the recommendations ought to be enforced to the higher grades including the director general of police. For, the history proves that some directors general who were appointed to hold the highest office were accused of corruption and nexus transactions.

The commission observed that the most important duty of the police was prevention of crime and the police ought to know all who were addicted to crime. But the observation was not applied to police culture of crime and no effort was made to identify the police functionaries who were addicted to crime during law enforcement and investigation of crime. The culture continued to prevail even after India became independent. Recidivists in police uniform, as a result, multiplied so much so that the courts passed several judgements punishing police offices and men of all ranks.

Regarding the culture of crime in police, the Commission observed: "serious offences were generally very fairly reported, though the corruption, oppression and inefficiency of the police already described and the delays, expenses and vexations too often involved in the prosecution of cases have led to the suppression of crime to a greater or less degree everywhere". The same situation continues even today and a director general of police who retired recently from the service said that he would not go to a police station to register a case, if that was possible, for he could not think about the expenses, heart-aches and uncertainities connected with the ordeals of registering criminal cases before the police. The people have fear, anxiety and anguish when they think of going to police stations to register criminal cases. The Commission wanted to check misbehaviour of police at the time they registered criminal cases. They wanted an immediate despatch of the F.I.R. to the magistrate having jurisdiction. The Commission recommended that no suspect should be detained if he could properly be released on bail. In many instances, the police simply refused to grant bail to the arrestees in bailable offences. This was nothing but miscarriage of justice and expression of criminal tendencies. The Commission condemned the practice of informal arrest which was very prevalent in many parts of the country. Even the books published in 1998 in India have brought out the existence of informal arrests in police culture. It is nothing but abduction by policemen of people who are incapable of resisting this illegal practice. The 1902-03 Commission observed that the informal arrests were found to be a source of abuse of police authority and many malpractices. But, their recommendation to put an end to such illegal practice had no effect even today when people take note of the fact that the practice is followed even today and some of them thus taken informally into custody have committed suicide or met with death in police custody. In D.K. Basu Vs. West Bengal, the Supreme Court of India had given a directive to the police to issue custody/arrest memo at the time they effected arrest of the people. Even after the Supreme Court's directives, allegations are levelled against some policemen/officers that they do resort to informal arrests and are accused of disobeying the orders of the Apex Court in the Country.

When the Indian Police Commission Report: 1902-03 came out, the Secretary of State wrote that the report contained "a very grave condemnation" and it was a condemnation of the police culture, tactics, crimes and behavioural patterns. Necessarily, the condemnation called for criminological researches particularly in the area of police crimes. That did not take place and as a result, though many innovations were brought by the British Government, the culture of crime in police continued to prevail. It dominated police activities in many areas including law and order and crime investigation. As the police committed several crimes and abuse of authority/power, they were not treated as a law abiding men belonging to a law abiding community. Whenever people hear that a policeman has committed a crime, they are not surprised at it, For, they think that the policeman can do so—can afford to do so—has been doing so—will do so and they thus tolerate police crimes to an extent possible. Experts on police—community relations affirm that the police in India can never come closer to the people so long as they live in a culture of crime—whatever may be the objective in remaining in that long established culture which could only damage their reputation.

Reference

1. John R. Lambert, *Crime, Police and Race Relations*, Oxford University Press, London, 1970.

CHAPTER—4

Police Crimes after the Police Commission: 1902-03

Enforcement crime may be a concept or recent origin in criminology. Whenever enforcement officers commit a crime as defined in law, they are not transacting Government works; rather do their private business or transactions which please them most. Whatever that be; people tolerate enforcement crimes and do not treat enforcement criminals as criminals in the traditional meaning and concepts. In British India, the police were found to commit a lot of crimes, but the people and administration said that they were misconducts and not crimes. Why? This attitude of leniency and consideration shown to law enforcement functionaries for several decades made them to feel that the crimes they committed were necessary strategies for performing their duties—until 1993 when the Protection of Human Rights Act was passed. Immediately after the passing of the Protection of Human Rights Act—1993, some law enforcement functionaries started to think that some of the enforcement crimes might be necessary evils and would not be necessary strategies. Today, many think that any human rights violation during law enforcement is a positive evil and a crime in every letter of the words. Such a feeling was not there in the British India particularly when the Indian Police Commission: 1902-03. prepared their report.

During 1906, communal riots broke out in Orissa and the Government once again quartered "punitive" police in the area. In Punjab too, the "punitive" police posts continued to function. The crimes were found to be on the increase and in 1906, the inspector general of police in Bengal said: "A good ratio of detection is indisputably the best incentive to full reporting. It is not altruism or high principle that furnishes the motive for the ordinary action of the average man but self-interest. What the ordinary man wants when crimes deprive him of property is first and foremost the recovery of that property; he does not care particularly about the punishment of the offender; that affects the State and not the individual; he wants to get back what he has lost, and his natural inclination to go to the police will vary directly with their capacity for achieving this object[1]". His observations related to the detection of lost property and in every sense, he spoke of victim justice. An organization meant for administration of criminal justice was bound to see that victim justice too was ensured. By whatever cause if the victim justice was denied, it could help only to the loss of public trust on police sense of justice. If it was due to any criminal tendencies among the police functionaries, or owing to their culpable negligence or corruption, the people would not pardon the policemen/officers. The Inspector general of police, Madras was candid enough to admit: "always unpopular, the department has become more than ever an easy and as it were an unauthorized target for aspersion both in the press and in the courts. Many weaknesses and malpractices...... have been exposed and discussed....... One of the most apparent of these is that the courts have undoubtedly become more suspicious of police work and of police cases, and the convictions are harder to obtain, while another is that, with diminished credit and prestige, the influence of the police has declined throughout the country and the respect, in which it was held, has decreased, with the inevitable further result of diminished efficiency[2]". The Indian Police Commission: 1902-03 condemned some of the methods police resorted to get confessions and to obtain convictions. Some of the methods and tactics the police employed were crimes under the Penal Code—1860, but were not treated to be so by the police themselves. These methods used by the police really created suspicion in courts and subsequent judgements pronounced by them. A crimefree police culture and police strategies were not contemplated and enforced. Even the recommendations of the Commission to eradicate corruption, torture, concoction of evidence by the police were either not implemented in full enthusiasm or were watered down and diluted. The same situation prevailed in India after her independence. After the Central Committee Report on Police Training had come into existence in 1973, many of the recommendations to improve police training were rejected, modified or diluted so much so that the implementation of the recommendation of the Committee was found to be frustratingly slow. Even today, the police are blamed for their strategies as they were accused of for their misbehaviour as early as during the early part of the last century.

During the early years of the last century, many policemen and officers were dismissed from service for misconducts; many were awarded various types of departmental punishments; some were convicted by magistrates for various offences. The percentage of punishments to the total strength of the police was roughly estimated to be 10 by researchers and almost the same percentage is seen even in independent India. Criminologists feel that the trend is frustrating enough and precisely therefore a criminological study must be seriously done to learn the etiological factors of police criminality and subsequent punishments.

During 1907-08, anarchist movement in India got developed alarmingly and the movement was suppressed with 'ferocity'. Lord Morley, Secretary of State wrote a private letter to the Viceroy in 1908 and he said: "We must keep order, but excess of severity is not the path to order. On the contrary, it is the path to the bomb[3]". Once the police force of any country was allowed to become ferocious to the people, then taming it would be very difficult. Although Lord Morley cautioned the Viceroy about the excess of severity, nothing was initiated to rectify the situation. A conspiracy of silence and inaction took the situation from bad to worse. It has been recorded that during 1909, a total of 16 'revolutionary' crimes were reported. Bombs appeared in Madras too. The maintenance of internal peace became indeed difficult. There was widespread disorder. The political unrest worsened the situation further. The British lost confidence in the Native police officers. The loyalty of the Native policemen/ officers was suspected and a proposal to create a Special Police Reserve composed mainly of Europeans and Eurasians was discussed. Crimes were on increase in many parts of the country and convictions were on the decrease. Police crimes too were on the increase.

Sir Edmund Cox once stated that the recommendations of the Indian Police Commission: 1902-03 did not have any perceptible changes in the working of the police. The conspiracy of indifference was, perhaps, a roadblock on the way. He said: "the police are not at all exemplary. Neither are the villagers. If the accused are well-to-do people, they are always ready to offer bribes to the police to hush the charge up. The charges of bribe-taking, usually made in anonymous or pseudonymous letters, are incessant. Sometimes they are true, in others they are certainly false".

Government of India was fully aware of the malpractices in police department. It was then decided to put down the malpractices and at the same time to protect the reputation of the department. "The importance of securing public confidence in the genuineness of inquiries into charges of ill treatment must be allowed to prevail over purely departmental considerations and be welcomed by all alike"—it was felt. More over, it was further noted: "The principles which....... should be borne in mind ....are first, that in all cases of a certain class and affecting a certain class of officers, both to be defined, a magisterial and not a departmental enquiry should be held and, secondly, that in no case should any charge of ill-treatment be dealt with by an officer in any way connected with the investigation of the original case[4]". The courts of law used to pass strictures in some cases. Such cases were taken serious note of.

Royal Commission on the Public Services in India

The Royal Commission on the Public Services in India was appointed by the British Government on August 31, 1912. The Commission received many memoranda from police organizations and they contained the cries and complaints of the police functionaries. Many in police were frustrated. The police was the worst paid department in the British Empire—the complainants said. "Police Reform"—a pamphlet was published by Dinsha Edulji Watcha. In the above pamphlet, he said: "The harsh and repressive laws have been largely contributing to crime and perjury, they have sown the seeds of wide discontentment and stimulated corruption in police". According to him the police is "the rotten organization which purported to protect life and property and detect life crime". He analysed the causes of the malady in police and found out the illiteracy, low pay structure, labour class background etc. as the etiological factors He lamented at the deterioration in police efficiency or of the police morale. He noted with anguish the large number of resignations, disertions, dismissals and discharges in the police department. He called the service to be "most disagreeable". He made several suggestions for the improvement of police efficiency and the most important among them was a hike in the salary of the constabulary. But, it seemed that his wishful thinking remained as a mirage in the police history of the country. On one side, the repressive laws and police atrocities continued and on the other, the terrorist activities got developed and magnified. Police were given arms and training in the use of fire arms to suppress terrorist activities. However, the administration doubted the loyalty of the police in dealing with the situations.

The Indian Police Act—1861 was found to be useless to make a police service with desirable personality traits. As early as in 1914, demands were made from several quarters to pass a new Police Act, but invain.

It was argued that "an up-to-date Police Act instead of the antiquated measure of half a century ago" could not serve any purpose. It is frustrating to note that the museum peace Police Act—1861 is in existence even today—an Act which the British India wanted to throw away. What a tragedy indeed! India is an independent country for more than half a century now and the old Police Act—1861 is still in operation. Police Act—1861 made the police unpopular in British India and how could it make the police in democratic India popular in the new millennium? Many States in India have passed Police Acts, but all of them were in tune with the Police Act—1861.

The police in the British India felt unhappy as the Government did not show any responsible care and concern for their problems. Necessarily, their dissatisfaction had adverse effect on their behaviour to the public. Mr. Alan Sykes, as early as in 1914 could sense the deep dissatisfaction among the police functionaries who felt 'that they were not getting their fair share. Even today, the deplorable conditions exist as they were about a century ago. The constables pay is said to be poor and their promotion prospects are poorer. They enjoy only a low status and they are authorized to enforce law with a lot of authority. Police crimes as a result of dissatisfaction could be seen in India even in the early part of the last century. Candidates from respectable classes of the society were not found coming forward to enlist as constables. This also affected the behavioural patterns of the constables. Even candidates from the labour class too were reluctant to join the constabulary and the reason was the low pay they received for the hard work they did for the people. As and when the Government realized the inadequately low pay to the constables, an allowance in the form of pea-nuts or fish-feed was allowed. Discipline in the police department was adversely affected by such measures and recruitment of candidates with good personality traits suffered a lot owing to the poor pay structure to the constabulary. In the Police Administration report, it was pointed out that: "It has become increasingly difficult to secure men of the required standard, and it is idle to expect that men entrusted with the powers of the police will refrain from abusing their position if they are not paid a fair living wage". To add insult to injury, the state of police buildings and housing conditions of the members of the police service were deplorably pathetic. The working environment too affected their behavioural patterns. If at all they wanted to be nice to people, they could not but project out their hostility to their working conditions. The same situation continues even today and the National Police Commission: 1977—81 had emphatically pointed out the deplorably deplorable conditions of furniture in police stations, lockups, police buildings and what not? The culture of crime may have its roots in such pitiable conditions and working environments and a study of police crimes means and includes these areas as well.

The British administration realized the gravity of the situation and the Statement of the Moral and Material Progress of India for 1917-18 stated: "It would be idle to deny that there is room for improvement in the present police system of India. Like every other service, it is cheaply run on account of the poverty of people. The total cost of the Civil Police in 1916 was £ 4.4 million, which worked out only 4 d. per head of population. The total average cost per man of the whole Civil Police of British India, officers included, is about £ 21 per annum. It is difficult to see how, when the cost of the force is so moderate, its standards can be expected to rise higher". The Statements continued: "It would not be too much to say that most of the defects of which the police can fairly be accused arise from the fact that in the subordinate ranks the pay is not sufficient to attract men of right stamp to perform the difficult and responsible task of safeguarding public peace". How is the situation now in India? Has the situation changed to the better? I think that the police service does not attract men of the right stamp even today and the question is: "Why so?" An answer to the question may solve many of the problems the department faces today. As it does not fall in the scope of this title, the area is not dealt with. After the Islington Commission's report which came out on August 14, 1915, the Government took immediate measures to improve the pay and prospects of the subordinate ranks. They were done to boost their morale. The Islington Commission's report was considered with some delay. After India became independent, several State Governments had appointed State Police Commissions and they have made several recommendations. But, as the allegation goes, many of the reports are still kept in the police archieves for research scholars to study and to prepare reports for obtaining university diplomas/degrees. What a deplorable situation indeed!

The disruptive impact of the life in police service and in the working environment ought to be studied if any Government want to initiate remedial measures. But that is not done even today. It may be remembered that crime, misconduct, abuse of power, misuse of authority etc. may result from the disorganization seen in the working environment. Criminologists take such behavioural patterns as indicators of disorganization within the police department. The British felt that the disorganization seen in Indian police had to be eradicated. Sir William Vincent, the Home Member said that the Indian police wanted character, power of decision and other qualities to offer enviable service to the people.

In England, the Desborough Committee was appointed in 1919 to review the conditions of police service there. About the policeman, the Committee observed: "His character should be unblemished; he should be humane and courteous and, generally, he should possess a combination of moral, mental and physical qualities not ordinarily required in other employments". It means that the Englishmen give top priority for the morality of police service followed by psychological and physical qualities. The Committee observed further: "When he becomes a constable, he is entrusted with powers which may gravely affect the liberty of the subject, and he must at all times be ready to act with tact, and discretion and on his own initiative and responsibility, in all sorts of contingencies. The burden of individual discretion and responsibility placed upon a constable is much greater than that of any other public servant of subordinate rank".

Though the Desborough Committee felt so for the policeman in England, one doubts very much whether or not the British had the same ideas about the policeman and his role in India. Of course, they wanted character, uprightness and power to take fair decisions for the Indian policeman. Nevertheless, in reality they did not do anything much towards those ends. The British believed that the policemen held a position of trust. But, what did they do for achieving that end? They created punitive police in India! In India, the British took a different policy, because they wanted Indian money for prospering and they were making only lip-services for improving the police. They wanted a brutal police and the police committed atrocities on Indians just to serve their English masters.

A Cop Personality and Crimes

The cop personality in England was different from what it was in India. The subculture of police that existed in India was such that the policeman was a creature deserving public contempt. The character of the work which the police did in India did not or could not deserve public acceptance, even remotedly. But, in England the police got public appreciation, good will and community cooperation. There, the people did not see criminality in police much whereas in India, people took note of criminal policemen of all descriptions. The people in India could see and experience only a hostile or apathetic policeman. Hence they kept a long distance from him. How could the people come closer to the police if the police commit crimes on them? Police agents were used to set fire to houses in different areas of Cuttack town. Later, the police found fault with the Congress volunteers for doing the same. Even today, the police are blamed by the press and people that they instigate people to commit crimes or they themselves commit crimes to achieve some political gains for the ruling party in Government. Allegations are heard that the mufty police do many things for the politicians in power—the police commit enforcement crimes—they participate in nexus criminality etc. The Cuttack police, after setting fire, resigned *en masse* in protest against them being misused by the authorities themselves.

The British repeatedly imposed punitive police in India and they did not do so in England. Punitive police meant police atrocities and it encouraged criminality among the policemen. On February 1, 1922, Mahatma Gandhi himself wrote to the then Viceroy about the virulent type of repression. He wrote about the brutal treatment of prisoners in jails, flogging, assault on the innocent and called them "official lawlessness" and "lawless repression". The British who wrote in law that the policemen were bound to obey only the lawful orders of the commanding ranks pressued the illiterate and ignorant police to have recourse to official lawlessness and crimes. "Listen to my order; Don't question me" approach of the British masters made many to become criminals in uniform.

The Police (Incitement to Disaffection) Act was passed and penalty was prescribed for spreading disaffection among the police. A situation was thus emerged that the police committed many types of offences. L. F. Rushbrook Williams prepared the Statement of the Moral and Material Progress of India 1922-23 and he wrote: "Public opinion therefore tends to look upon the constable as a symbol of oppression and restraint. . . . ." The Statement continued: "The policeman, it must regretfully be stated, has a bad name in India; he is accused both of tyranny and corruption". The people hated the policeman. In spite of it, the Government proceeded further in creating striking forces. The British wanted to create striking forces trained and equipped on military or semi-military lines. The result of such training given to police functionaries made them to look at their Indian brethren as enemies. The illiterate, underpaid, labour-class and ignorant policemen could thus behave to Indians as enemies. Hostility between the police and the people got multiplied as a result.

P. M. Stewart, an officer of the Indian police service wrote a book titled *Policing India* and he criticised the political employment of the criminal investigation department. The Government refused permission to publish the book. During 1925, a Provincial Police Committee was appointed in Punjab and about corruption in police service the Committee observed: "Bribery and corruption appear to be as universal now as twenty years ago, the only difference being that the increase in the wealth of the Province leads to the payment of larger sums". The Committee made many suggestions to improve the situation. The suggestions included increased supervision, less frequent transfers, encouragements of upright officers, punishment to those who involved in the Commission of misconducts, publicity of the action taken against corrupt officials etc. But, God alone knew how seriously and honestly the suggestions were implemented! An important recommendation related to honest recruitment of candidates to police service and a verification of their family background. Further, it was recommended to have an annual checking of the property acquired by the members of the service. Proper training with an emphasis on the development of desirable personality traits and inculcation of human values was insisted. The reluctance to enforce the suggestions paved the way for developing a culture of crime in police service.

On July 31, 1929, Sir David Patrie, the Director, Intelligence Bureau warned: "It is of atmost importance also that the admirable work performed in present trying conditions by the police should receive, not only the commendation of Government, but practical recognition which may help to make them feel that their work is fully appreciated". But, who was there to listen to such exhortations and warnings? The policemen became spiritless and frustrated. Such attitudes too paved the way for expressing perverted behaviour to people by policemen.

Freedom movement was getting more and more vibrant and the Congress Working Committee exhorted the policemen to treat the Satyagrahis and others engaged in the freedom movement as brethren and not as enemies. Nevertheless, the police became more aggressive and adopted a repressive attitude. In spite of the repression, the freedom movement continued with more vigour and vitality. The aggressiveness in police got encouragement from the British rulers and resultingly, the policemen became more brutal and wild animal-like to their Indian brethren. They involved themselves in indiscriminate brutality and merciless torture of men and women. Some research scholars attribute the present police strategies of employing torture on people indiscriminately to the obnoxious atmosphere which the British created for repressing the Indians involved in the freedom movement. The police are today accused of their indiscriminate use of force, torture, humiliating and degrading treatment to people in police custody.

Because of the indiscriminate use of force and torture on Indians by the policemen, hostility got developed between the people and the police. People took law into their hands and started attacking the policemen. Bombs were thrown at Sir Charles Tegart, the Commissioner of Police, Calcutta and to police stations/outposts etc. Inspector general of police,

Bengal and a superintendent of police were shot at in Dacca. The police became atrocious to people and the people, in turn, became atrocious to police. The Government encouraged the police to become more and more atrocious to people. The Governor of Bengal, when he addressed the police parade at Dacca in August 1930 said: "Your loyalty has stood firm against all temptations; every officer has testified to the unflinching courage, the unbroken discipline and the wonderful self-control, as a whole, has shown". This sort of encouragements further worsened the situation so much so that the police became more and more brutal, cruel, atrocious and wild animal like to their Indian brethren.

Hostility between Police and the People Worsens

The British considered the police in India as the servants of the Government and they caused them to commit atrocoties against the people of India. There was an equal and opposite reaction to police atrocities and the people reacted against. They could treat the police as enemies of the people. They committed crimes against the police as the police committed crimes against the people. In 1933, a delegation of India League prepared a report and the report read that the Government strategies to deal with the freedom movement included: "Wholesale violence, physical outrages, shooting and beating up, punitive expediations, collective fines on villages and seizure of land and property. The Government did all those through the army, police and jail functionaries. A situation emerged that the police could do anything only with the permission of the Government. People pelted stones on police if they could not do anything else. Protection of the police forces became a necessity then. Once, the Viceroy addressed a conference of senior police officers and said: "I take this opportunity of thanking you, Gentlemen, and through you all the officers and men of the police force for all that you have done for India during recent years. Since ...... April, 1931 we have gone through very difficult and stomy times. You and your men have had to bear the brunt of the attacks made upon Government, and many of you have no doubt at times felt apprehensive that the discipline and efficiency of the Force might be undermined by the constant attempts that were made to sap their loyalty, by the severe strain to which they were continuously subjected in dealing with subversive movements and communal disturbances and by the unjustifiable attacks that were made upon them for carrying out their bounden duty of maintaining law and order". The policemen/officers could not understand that all these were just games the Viceroy played to make the police more atrocious and cruel to the people of India. The police became more and more loyal to their white masters who did not bother much about the worsening of the police-people relationship.

The new Government of India Act received the Royal Assent on August 2, 1935. Lord Linlithgou who succeeded Lord Willington said to the policemen/officers in April 1936 that the welfare of the police would be at all times be his anxious care. The hostility between the police and the people got worsened day by day. In a clash between the police and the *Khaksars* in 1940 in Lahore, 34 persons and 2 policemen were killed and 63 others and a number of policemen were injured.

The police stood with the Government firmly and they were not concerned with people. The police mercilessly took action against the satyagrahis. Whenever the police got orders, they ruthlessly dealt with the situation. They showed no sympathy to their Indian brethren. Reports about the police performance from various parts of the country attested to the fact that they were loyal to the Government. Any measures taken against the sathyagrahis were brutally executed. The British authorities felt safe in police hands and they said that they had little cause for any anxiety. They were against the people of India—the Government felt.

There were *hartals*, protest meetings, processions and demonstrations all over the Country against police atrocities and the situation became critical. There were wholesale arrests of Indian leaders and the people became wild with rage. There were large scale firings by the police in many places. Each firing worsened police-people relationship. Necessarily, the widespread bloodshed in India put the British Government in many difficulties. In the meantime, the policemen in Bihar declared a strike and the Government employed British soldiers to put down the police strike.

India became independent on August 15, 1947 and Pandit Jawahar Lal Nehru then said: "We end today a period of ill-fortune". The police in India inherited a culture from their British past. Although, the police administration and the Government knew the situation well, nothing much was done to create a police service which was different from what it was in the past.

Police and Police Criminology in the British Past

It goes without saying that the police in India committed several crimes for centuries, but no scientific study on the causative or preventive or correctional aspects of this centuries old criminality was done at any time in the British India and earlier. Of course, some crackpot explanations about the etiology of crimes were given by individuals, commissions or committees from time to time. One can not blame anyone for not studying police crimes scientifically as the science of crime or criminology was not a developed discipline until recently. It is now not possible to say why the police in British India committed very many types of crimes. One could notice that dacoity was a heinous crime committed by people throughout the history of India and the police had to fight with the dacoits. How could they do so? They were illiterate or moderately educated. They were poor people who earned poor wages for the hard work they did. They were attacked and killed by people. They had authority, power and muscle strength. They used and misused them for many purposes. They violated the laws which they were to enforce and no one questioned them. Bentham's/Becaria's hedonism might have worked well to make them commit crime. Though various disciplines developed, no biologists, sociologists, anthropologists, psychiatrists, psychologists studied police crimes. Police were to obey the laws and enforce them. Then how could they be studied as crime-doers involved in the commission of crimes? That was unthinkable and that might be one of the reasons why criminologists ignored police crimes. In India, everywhere from east to west, north to south, the police committed almost the same types of crimes and therefore their crimes and criminal behaviour needed the support of a theory to explain police crimes. Criminologists did not conduct any serious studies for developing a theory to explain police crimes. The general theories of crime causation may not etiologically explain police crimes. Like white collar crimes, organized crimes, gang crimes, political crimes, nexus crimes, enforcement crimes, ideological crimes etc. , police crimes must be studied individually and their causes should be analysed separately. That did not take place for centuries in India and even now, the administers and academicians do not come forward to study police crimes. I consider the views and opinions of several commissions—both police and judicial—only as crackpot approaches and armchair explanations of police crimes. Lombroso spoke about born criminals and I do not know how far he could become successful in explaining police crimes! Police crimes have a distinct identity and the criminologist must study police crimes as he studies gang crimes, white collar crimes or enforcement crimes etc. The British did not study police criminality in India. It was nothing for them whose intention was to rob the Indians. Criminologists have studied gang crimes, crimes by or against women, juvenile delinquency, political crimes, crime syndicates, public order crimes etc. and have been trying to explain them. But police crimes and criminality had never become a topic of interests for criminologists. Some policemen/officers are recidivists and like pickpockets, they used to involve in corruption and corrupt practices. They torture people and involve in the commission of enforcement crimes including illegal detention, incommunicado interrogation and many types of nexus crimes etc. Nevertheless, their crimes were not made topics of research by the academic community.

Individual policemen were caught for their commission of crimes and in such instances, police used to conduct only individual investigation. Afterwards, the individual causes of crime may be found out. Resultingly, no theory of crime explaining police crime/criminals came out. Police crimes are seen everywhere—all over the world—at all periods during the history of the world. Police have been considered as a crime-controlling instrument and not a crime-committing agency. During the British past, the police were found to be susceptible to corruption, underworld interest, organized crimes, oppressive tactics etc. and necessarily, their operations under criminal conditions adversely affected administration of justice. Really, the enforcement of law suffered. The people of India, police administration, the Government and the individual police officers in British India knew that the police service was not an alert striking force to combat crimes. Crimes in India down the centuries, including the crimes committed by police functionaries, have been showing an upward trend. No statistical records were maintained officially in British India to know the extent and intensity of police crimes. Nevertheless, there have been observations and opinions on many kinds of police crimes. The enormity of police crimes was recognized long ago, nevertheless, the explanations offered to answer the "why" question of police criminality were not scientific. Recruitment of illiterate people, improper training, lack of promotion, lack of supervision, and similar crackpot theories could not answer the "why" aspects of police crimes. For example, today highly educated candidates are enlisted to police service, highly efficient officers supervise the subordinates, most modern training is received, promotion prospects are guaranteed and still many kinds of crimes, especially nexus crimes and enforcement crimes, corruption and corrupt practices, are reported from the police subculture. It goes without saying that the crackpot theories cannot/do not explain police criminality or increase in police crimes. The causes of police crimes have to be studied form various angles in a scientific way. For example, a man in police uniform becomes a supercharged person with potential readiness to commit crimes associated with the expression of aggression, with the acceptance of corruption money, with the interactions with nexus or underworld criminals and so on. The anti-social or criminal tendencies can develop in some candidates and then they become incapable of exerting self-control, of tolerating frustration etc. The climate of crime prevailing in the work environment may be responsible. People who are exposed to such situations may show extreme asocial trends in their personality which may imply a super-supercharged condition for deviating markedly from the norms of behaviour which the police ought to have.

After India became independent, the Indian police continued to function with the historical disadvantages which they inherited from the colonial past. There was no conscious attempt made to divorce the democratic police from the colonial police. Developments in the field of science and technology, growth of crime syndicates, Mafia operations and nexus criminals, political interference and pressures on police etc. have brought new dimensions in police crimes and criminality. Police often becomes a target of criticism and attacks from the press, people, politicians and courts. Nevertheless, a scientific approach in studying police crimes and criminality has not been undertaken in India. Sometimes, a journalist report or a mini-scale research on police brutality, corruption, involvement in political activities etc. may appear in the media and then people forget about them. The chapter that follows deals with police crimes in the independent India.

Police are the protectors of life and property. They have a responsibility. This responsibility flows from its very nature of as a community empowered to guard and protect life. In such a situation, there is no scope for custodial violence or concoction of evidence. This is the law enforcement that becomes selflessness and in such a position, corruption and corrupt practices do not have any place. Nexus transactions and collaboration with underworld criminals do not figure at all. Within the police culture, every person is accepted, respected and honoured precisely because he is a person and not a crime doer. Human rights must be respected. The police must work to ensure that the laws and institutions of the State in no way violate the life, but rather protect it and promote it. Nevertheless, death in police custody is reported! There must be mutual interaction and enriching communication between the people and the police. The people are not a useless burden. There exists a sort of covenant between the people and the police. There must be mutual acceptance and it can be ensured only if the police and the people obey the laws which are in force. Any violation, by either of the two, of the laws is a crime in every sense.

How was the police criminality in the independent India and why does criminality exist in police culture even after 50 years of independence? This is discussed in the chapter that follows.

References

1. Quoted from Anandswarup Gupta, *The Police in British India (1861—1947)*, Concept, New Delhi, 1979.
2. *ibid*
3. Quoted from '*A History of India*' by Michael Edwards, published in 1961.
4. Police, Progs. 241—243, July, 1911.

CHAPTER—5

Police Crimes after Independence in India

In British India, the police committed many types of crimes and they have been discussed in earlier chapters. There is a view that the police continued to follow the same strategies even in independent India. As soon as India became independent, an overwhelming majority of European officers opted for retirement and for obtaining compensation for their loss of career. Many Muslim officers went to Pakistan. Many Hindu officers and men in the N.W.F.P and Sind were allowed to migrate to India. Likewise many from other parts of India either migrated to Pakistan or remained in India. Thus, the police in India became a service managed and administered by Indians. Earlier, the Indian constabulary and subordinate ranks in police had to work under the white masters and invariably, the master-servant relationship between the British and the Indian police functionaries was found to be a cause of police committing crimes on Indian brethren. Then there was an explanation that the Indians had no option but to yield to the orders of the alien administration and to be loyal to them. The climate and the culture created and developed by the British for the free expression of police aggressiveness continued to operate even when India became independent.

Policemen/officers who were treated as Government servants were converted to act as public servants and were made to function under the Constitution of free India and the laws made thereunder. But, the change in the book did not have a corresponding effect in the field. The police were to function under the antiquated Indian Police Act—1861 and the

Acts enacted by State Governments in tune with the provisions of the Indian Police Act—1861. It took 25 long years for the Government of India to appoint a Central Committee on Police Training. In 1973, a Committee was appointed with Prof. M.S. Gore as the Chairman of the Committee. Prof. M.S. Gore wrote: "The popular impression with regard to non-registration and minimization of crime, complicity or connivance with the underworld, indiscriminate arrests and implication of innocent persons will have to be removed". What does it mean? It means that the situation was not changed even after 25 years of independence. "Connivance with the underworld" has now assumed more importance so much so that the films, papers, TV serials and research studies show them out to the people.

Gore Committee observed further that "to gauge the exact extent of corruption prevalent in an organization or at the various levels of hierarchy is difficult. As far as the police are concerned............, the dimensions of the problem continue to be large, nevertheless, indicates that the malice is difficult to eradicate. It would, however, be dangerous to develop an attitude that it is something which is inevitable and endemic". Professor Gore said so after evaluating the views expressed by a sub-committee of the conference of the inspectors general of police in India—1962. What does it mean? It indicates that there exists a culture of criminality in police.

The corruption and criminality in police did worry the British rulers. The Indian Police Commission: 1902-03 voiced against them. But, it was invain. The Delhi Police Commission said: "There should be a concerted drive to make it impossible for a dishonest person to remain in service. All complaints of corruption should be promptly investigated; and action against the guilty must be drastic whatever be his rank". Later, it was learnt that it was just a cry in the wilderness and nobody attended to it. The National Police Commission: 1977—81 said emphatically that corruption had gone wider and deeper. How many senior level police functionaries are accused of corruption, nexus involvement in crimes, unholy relations with underworld criminals and unscrupulous lawless law enforcement?—This is a hidden truth, nevertheless the fact remains that the truth is recognized all over the Country.

The more one reads the report of the Central Committee on Police Training, the more he becomes annoyed and irritated. The culture of crime and criminality continue to rule the police atmosphere. "As far as the thana police are concerned, however, the evidence before us seems to suggest that their image, by and large, is unsatisfactory. They are generally said to be impolite, authoritarian, professionally not upto the mark, dishonest and unsympathetic to the complaints and grievances of the people. They allegedly favour the well-to-do or the otherwise powerful sections of the community while poorly dressed citizens are either neglected or harassed". This observation was made by a Committee appointed by Government of India after 25 years of free policing in the Country and the certificate issued by the Committee was indeed frustrating. Crime and criminality within the police service seemed to be a more serious problem than the same noticed outside the police department.

Research Studies on Police in the Independent India

Researches conducted about police in many parts of the world would prove that a sort of criminality prevailed in police subculture. But, many researches did not look at the issue from a criminological angle. In a study conducted by Paul E. Smith and Richard O. Hawkins, they observed victimization by police in their country. They also noted a number of wrong-doings or misconduct by police. They spoke about police.criminality in low tone and the policemen themselves, therefore did not/could not think for a moment that they were committing crimes while they were enforcing laws.

In independent India, a number of studies were conducted mainly to study public opinion on police-citizen interactions and the people's appreciation on police work. In 1964, the Indian Institute of Public Administration, in 1965-66, the Indian Institute of Public opinion, in 1972, the Banaras Hindu University, in 1973, the Bureau of Police Research and Development, Ministry of Home Affairs, Government of India and in 1978, the Indian Institute of Public Opinion, New Delhi etc. conducted studies. All of them brought out the unsatisfactory image of Indian police, but none of them looked at the police misbehaviour from the point of view of a criminologist. Many individual research scholars too studied the police and one such study was conducted by Dr. Earayil and Dr. Vadackumchery. Their observations on police were published in the book titled Police and the Society (1985). I do not think that there is a need to discuss their observations here as they too were talking about custodial violence, employment of torture, filthy language/expressions, harassment to people, ill-treatment to citizens and all research scholars were talking the same thing time and again in different languages. A review of the research literature might show that the police in many countries and in India committed many crimes not only under the Penal Codes but also under many Special and Local Laws with immunity and status. In spite of the laws, police behaviour was regulated more by the customs which existed in police subculture and the customs contained law violations in many ways. The customs and traditions practised in police subculture were thought of as necessary and inevitable for the effective enforcement of law. Policemen thus became slaves of their customs/traditions which were crime-prone in many situations! Use of torture, for example, was thought of as an essential strategy to elicit confessions from the interrogated. There was the group support from police to commit illegalities in police subculture. The injuries thus caused and human rights violations thus committed were tolerated and encouraged.

Murder was, perhaps, the first crime recognized in primitive societies. But in police, whenever custodial murder took place, the police subculture made attempts to treat it as a suicide in the police lockup until and unless it was proved to be a custodial murder. For that, the people had to fight against the police. No police commission so far did or could evaluate police behaviour in such situations as crimes and they did not treat them from a criminological perspective. They did not analyse the causes of police crimes in depth. What they did was to make a surface analysis of police crimes treating them as mere misconducts. As a result, neither the administration nor the people dealt with them as crimes. The Commissions gave only a peripheral analysis of the causative aspects of police crimes and often took an advisory role in many situations. No outside force like the C.B.I./magistrates could process and investigate crimes whenever policemen/officers were involved. More often than not, departmental actions were taken treating police crimes only as misconducts. As a result, the crimes committed by policemen/officers became just departmental affairs to which many a time leniency was shown during departmental inquiries. This approach could not help to create a feeling among policemen/officers that they were committing crimes. The departmental inquiries conducted could not/failed to create any deterrence among the police functionaries and the crimes continued to be committed by policemen/officers.

In police culture, laws and customs existed side by side. The laws were in favour of the protection of human rights and dignity, nevertheless, the customs/practices were not always. The police behaviour (here the crimes police committed) ensured several privileges/advantages to the policemen/officers and in some cases to the suspects/detinues/arrestees/accused and so on. For example, the bribery and corruption guaranteed mutual advantages for the police and the suspects/detinues and so on. The police claimed that they were just enforcing the law, but in reality they did violate many laws which they were bound to enforce. No one had the courage to question them as the people thought that the police who represented the State were empowered to use force and violence on people. Use of force and violence were looked as legitimate acts of police and the police, down the decades, employed it indiscriminately. The people who belonged to the lower economic or/and social strata suffered the pain more than the affluent and the influential. The penal laws were not strictly enforced within the police society, rather were implemented among the people outside the police. As a result, two kinds of enforcement in law came into being—the police were not bound by the criminal laws when they enforced them and the people were.

Growth of Democracy and Democratic Values

There were many crimes which the police in the colonial past committed and the people under the British rule suffered. In a democracy, the people become the rulers and the police are the servants of the people (they were government servants in the British India). Any crime against the people becomes serious in a democracy, for the crime committed is against the rulers in a democracy. Torturing the suspects, employing excessive force on people by the police during a law and order situation etc. are not tolerated in a democracy. The opposition (political parties) makes them issues and the police become accountable. Even in the pre-independent India, the Police Act—1861 laid down the law: "it shall be the duty of every police officer primarily to obey and execute all orders and warrants lawfully issued to him by any competent authority". The same Police Act is in operation even today, but there is a difference and that is the democratic nature of police work. Regarding the policeman in a democracy, K. Krishnamurthi says: "As a member of a disciplined force in the midst of an indisciplined society, as a symbol of justice, as the visible arm of law, he has the supreme duty of earning the deep respect and love of the people by his integrity and devotion to duty while shunning the limelight of cheap and vulgar popularity[2]". Crime has no scope in such police work. But, the history so far of the police in the democratic India shows that the police involved themselves in the commission of many kinds of crimes. They did not make any attempts to mobilize a new culture of policing. Every policeman had an important role to play and together with the people they had to perform their duties. They ought to have behaved with an authentic ideals of policing a democratic society. They were to grow in respect for and service to every other person in society. But, they did not do so.

Take the number of private complaints filed by the people against the police before the courts of law, before the departmental authorities and before the Governments. Add to them the observations made by courts of law on criminal cases filed by the police and the same written by the courts while they appreciated the pieces of evidence and their genuine nature. Add further to them the news paper reports on police crimes and atrocities on people plus the unreported instances of police misconducts, misbehaviour and criminal activities including the nexus crimes, enforcement crimes and corrupt practices. It may give a part-picture of the quantum of criminality in police subculture. The National Police Commission: 1977—81 observed: "Police-public relations at present are in a very unsatisfactory state. While there are several reasons for it, police partiality, corruption, brutality and failure to register cognizable offences are the most important factors which contribute to this sad state of affairs. Police do in fact harass even those people who try to help them". The National Police Commission did not treat the disease from a criminological perspective, rather they tried to expose a part of police criminality in a mild way. In a study conducted by Alphonse L. Earayil and James Vadackumchery, it was brought out that even the police mhustache, police look, police language, police walk, police behavicur etc. were not commanding respect from the people. There was a sort of "social dangerousness" in such police tactics, behaviours and mannerisms. Quetlet (1796—1874), a Belgian statistician pointed out that crime was not something purely individual, but a mass phenomenon. In police, one could observe that the criminal behaviour exhibited by the police was a mass phenomenon. Concoction of evidence, torture of detinues, manipulation of records, corruption and corrupt practices etc. were seen as a mass phenomenon in police subculture. The National Police Commission: 1977—81 endorsed this view when they observed: "Unfortunately several police officers under pressure of work and driven by desire to achieve quick results, leave the path of a patient and scientific interrogation and resort to the use of physical force in different forms to pressure witness/suspect/accused to disclose all the facts known to them. . . . Nothing is so dehumanizing as the conduct of police in practising torture of any kind on a person in their custody".

The "police mustache", harsh look, angry eyes, inhuman faces, animal like behaviour etc. expressed by some policemen/officers were indicators of criminality in them. Cesare Lombroso spoke about identifying people having criminal personality form the physical anomalies seen among the criminals. Enrico Ferri and Raffale Garofalo accepted the biological determinism in criminal behaviour and Charles Goring disagreed with the findings as he could not find any statistically significant physical differences between criminals and non-criminals. I, for one, do not agree with Lombrosian concepts to identify policemen/officers who show criminal tendencies. While I may subscribe to the view that police criminality may be a mass phenomenon in democratic India causing "social dangerousness" in society, I do nct agree with the view of the Italian positivism that the criminals are atavistic in nature. While the police may show criminal characteristics in their behaviour, they do not in any way possess projected and pronounced physical characteristics which resemble atavism. If the policemen deliberatly handcuff a person in police custody merely to humiliate him, or is not releasing of an arrestee even in cases the bail can be granted, then the motivating factors must be identified not from the point of view of the Lombrosian atavism, but from other criminological perspectives. Why do the police show excessive severity and ruthlessness during public order situations? Can the explanations offered by Becaria, Bentham and Romilly give a satisfying answer to the question? The rule of law is that the implementation of la·v must be delineated by due process. But, does it take place in democratic India? Researches show that the rule of law is violated by the police themselves. The Report of the Central Committee on police training says:

"At the Police Training College, the trainees are taught to register all crimes as these were reported. In the district, they were asked to make a preliminary enquiry first and then record the F.I.R. after the preliminary enquiry which is entirely illegal". Why do they do so? What provokes them to do illegalities when they are supposed or bound to enforce the rule of law? The Central Committee did not evaluate such illegal activities from the points of view of criminology. The Committee further said: "They were told to forget scientific methods of investigation and resort to third degree though they were repeatedly cautioned not to take it to a stage when there might be an adverse medical report if the person subjected to third degree was medically examined". The question that needs an answer is: "Why do they resort to third degree methods when they know that they are against the law?" The criminal mind is expressed under the colour of authority, power and uniform. The strategies violating the law by the law enforcers become a subject or a topic of interest in police criminology. The Committee observed again: "In the district, they were told that bogus cases under section 190 Cr. P. C. were essential for a good statistical record although they had been warned against this in the Police Training College. There goes the list of malpracrices to which the new entrants to the service are introducted". I do not understand why the Committee used "malpractices" instead of "crimes" and the use of such light words mitigating the heinous nature of crime has often helped to give an impression to the police functionaries that they were not committing crimes. The police commissions, like the Central Committee on Police Training, too did not call police crimes by their proper names so much so that there exist no academic studies or scientific researches conducted to study the etiology of police crimes in criminological researches.

The Classical School of Criminology maintained the view that men were possessed of *free will.* They acted according to the pleasure they derived when they committed an act. O.K., in that case the policemen/ officers are to be treated as calculating animals and they do everything basing on the pleasure/pain they derive when they commit the acts. If they violate the laws which they are bound to enforce, it means that they get pleasure when they commit crimes. Necessarily, they do not experience pain and Bentham, Beccaria held the view that people did not commit crimes, because they were threatened with punishments that outweighed any gain resulting from their criminal actions. If the *free-will* and *hedonistic* theories of the Classical School of Criminology are taken to apply to police crimes, one may have to endorse the view that the policemen are not threatened with punishments when they violate the laws. I think that the policeman is little afraid of the punishments whenever he commits a crime. He has a safety feeling and it makes him to violate laws when he enforces laws. The hedonistic calculus does not work with the policemen as he feels fully secure when he commits crimes. His muscles, power, authority, uniform, police fraternity, awareness about the laws and punishments, pleasure etc. may give him a sense of security. Beccaria wanted that punishment to crimes should be prompt and inevitable. For police crimes, there is no prompt or inevitable punishment. According to Beccaria, it was the certainty of punishment that was more effective than the severity or cruelty of punishment. In police crimes, the certainty of punishment is not seen, rather, some of the police crimes become more a group activity than an individual activity. For instance, the informal arrests, illegal searches, prolonged detention in police custody, employment of torture, use of epithets/indecent language etc. are considered as group crimes of the police subculture. More often than not, such consensus crimes committed by the group are not punished with certainty. The police may get many advantages when they commit crimes, but such advantages become detrimental to the image of police in a democracy. The policemen/ officers who commit crimes expect certain advantages and the present system of police does not ensure a denial of the expected advantages produced by crimes and that has been one of the reasons why police crimes continue to exist in Indian democracy even after fifty years of freedom. In a study on police, it has been observed: "corruption can never prevail in a police station work unless there is a common consensus among the personnel working there. Hence, the subinspectors, sometimes, give a tacit approval for such practices [3]". Police Commissions in Delhi (1966—68), Bihar (1961), Madhya Pradesh (1965-66), Uttar Pradesh (1970-71), West Bengal (1960-61), Punjab (1961-62), Maharashtra (1964), Assam (1969—71), Tamil Nadu (1971), Rajasthan (1972) and National Police Commission: 1977—81 have dealt with police corruption and its consensus nature. The National Police Commission observed: "What the Police Commission said in 1903 would more or less apply fully even to the present situation. If anything, the position has worsened with more rampant corruption in police today with active connivance of numerous local dadas and unprinciples men in public life". Why think in this way? The houses of the directors general of Police in some States were raided on charges of corruption and corrupt practices. Corruption in free India has become quite common everywhere and the police may not be an exception. Corruption like cancer is a slow, but a sure killer. Likewise, corruption in police has created an impression among the people that police corruption is a sure killer of fair law enforcement and administration of justice. The *neoclassical* school in criminology made an attempt to link the individual crime-doer with the social world. The policemen too do the samething now and justify the police crimes as a part of the crimes seen in society. According to them, the police represent a cross-section of the society and precisely therefore the crimes seen in the society will be seen in the police too. But, critics on police crimes are of the view that the crimes in police are more than the same seen in society. After India became independent in 1947, the *salaried class* became more prominent. They became prominent because they found that they could misuse their positions to their advantages if they preferred so. Why? The reason was that India was democratic. The police too learnt that their authority and power were money and business for them and they could use/misuse, properly use/abuse their power in any way they wanted. New values came into being and the democratic police in India knew the ways of committing crimes either alone or along with politicians, other bureaucrats and underworld criminals. For example, in States were prohibition was enforced, the police knew well that alcohol was in high demand. Necessarily, an illicit production of hooch and an illicit distribution system sprang up. Organized bootleggers along with politicians and law enforcement machinery (which includes police) started to function. Crimes became inevitable and the police became nexus partners in the commission of crimes. Gangsterism, racketeering, syndicate-crimes etc. became crimes in which the policemen too were actively involved. A situation thus emerged in some States in India and the situation justified to undertake criminological researches in the areas of police and organized crimes/Mafia crimes/nexus criminality. But, so far, no serious studies were undertaken to learn the extent and intensity of police crimes *hic et nunc*.

Increase in Police Strength in Independent India

There was rapid growth in police strength after India became independent. An overwhelming number of new comers to police service created further problems and the training which was imparted to them was substandard and far away from being satisfactory. Even the objectives of police training were not specified and therefore, they were put in the terms of reference of the Central Committee on police training constituted by Government of India on November 10, 1971. Prof. Gore in his report on police training stated that "police training...... is currently in a state of general neglect....... the strength of the force has increased substantially in every State, but the facilities available in the institutions have not kept pace with this increase". Though the police claimed that they were imparting discipline to the new entrants to the service by giving an excessive overdose of parade, the fact remained that the so-named discipline did not or could not make them disciplined in life. They showed their muscle power and expressed emotions/suppressed vengeance to their supervisors on people with whom they interacted. There was no consensus on what should be the components of discipline in police. Different people in police had different concepts about police discipline and for many a total surrender to superiors' orders was the discipline for the police functionaries. They said: "obey first and then question" and that was discipline for them. Police in a democracy could not expect the people to obey the police without questioning the propriety of the orders. When the police is questioned even by the slighest non-verbal signal by the people, the policeman may get irritated. Consequently, he may exhibit aggressive behaviour to the one who questions the propriety. The task of a criminologist here is to specify more precisely what are the criminogenic conditions in police crimes. The new comers to police after India's independence were incorporated into the police subculture and they became a part in the subculture. Many made studies on specific types of crimes like white collar crimes, organized crimes etc. as they found such crimes having some special identity. But, as far as police crimes were concerned, researchers did not study them as a special category of crimes possessing special identity. The police commissions who studied many problems as per the terms of reference devoted their time to make recommendations for improving the police. Casually they spoke about the etiology of police misbehaviour and many a time, they advanced crackpot explanations and speculative interpretations on police crimes. Many members of the Commissions used to be retired/serving police officers who could not think about police beyond certain circumscribing limits. Hence, their recommendations were not aimed at reducing police criminality, rather were meant to improve the police system in the State/Country. The police in independent India have two functions—i.e., the functions of "peace officers" and "law officers". In both functions, the police have to use their discretion and it increases as the police functionaries come down in the hierarchy. Considerable skill is required in exercising the discretion particularly when arrests are made, when searches are conducted, when seizure is effected, when confessions are elicited. How can the police do them if they are not professionally trained in doing so? The truth and implication are that some functions of police are performed in an illegal way and they are not treated as police crimes. The rule of law insists that the police must perform their duties adhering to the rules and regulations. They have to do their job respecting the rights of individual citizens, but they do not do so. Why? When more policemen/officers are enlisted in police service, the learning was by apprenticeship. Duckling theory that a policeman learns to do his job while he is on the job got acceptance in India. Professional training was neglected and that was one reason for police criminality in India. No inservice training worth its name is offered in many States and that does affect the professionalism in police—say the critics. Characteristically, in this style of functioning, there may not be any reward for higher eduction. Seeing the deplorable situations, the Central Committee on Police Training suggested many refresher, promotion and specialized courses for all categories of police functionaries. But, National Police Commission found that the implementation of the Committee's recommendation was frustratingly slow in many States. The Committee suggested that every police training institution should have a research cell, but the recommendation has not been implemented in many States. Crimes against police, crimes by police and crimes committed jointly by police with others etc. are subjects of research interests. But, who cares? Police Act, 1861 did not say anything about police accountability to people for any crimes they committed in their functionings.

The human rights standards are very demanding in these days and yet the same Police Act—1861 has been in operation for the last one and half a century. People have expectations and the police have obligations and people do not expect police crimes. Statesman, Delhi (January 14, 1990) reported the result of a sample survey and it is seen that "the police are regarded by the public as power drunk, corrupt, immoral, without professional ethics and as agents of the ruling clique". The paper further reported that the police were in league with criminals. The ruling political party/clique misuses the police for narrow party interests and some unscrupulous politicians and policemen work together with criminal businessmen and commit nexus crimes. A noted jurist in India once said: "The police have increasingly become an object of ridicule and a source of threat to democratic governance and human rights[4]". The Amnesty International (1992) gives details of 415 cases of lockup deaths allegedly on account of police torture. The reports of the National Human Rights Commission give more details of lockup deaths that did take place in the recent past. If they are not crimes, then what are they? If criminologists do not study them, then who else must study them? Hence, police criminology must become a topic of research interest for police themselves. The response of the police to the study of police crimes has been far too inadequate.

Police Crimes and Political Development in India

Organizationally, the police are responsible to the executive branch of the Government in power, but in India, the day to day law enforcement functions are under the control of the judiciary to a great extent. The police have relationship with the political system and politicians in power. The police can be manipulated by determined ruling political interests and the experience hitherto proves that a pliable police force connive with the political parties/politicians to commit crimes. The *Freedom of Will* theory of the Classical School has no explanations to offer in such situations nor do the neo-classical and positive schools of criminology. The police are pressured to commit crimes and atrocities on people. Police activities relating to law enforcement come under judicial review and the police are accused of for their criminality in various ways. India has a free print media and it documents efficiently crimes committed by police (of course, with the views of the press in some cases) and the crimes by police have become too frequent to be ignored by the people, police themselves and the Governments. But, it seems that the response of the Governments, police and the people in general has been dilatory, uncertain and negative at times. Nevertheless, there were instances that the Government had taken police crimes seriously and initiated steps to prevent the crimes by enacting laws. For instance, gang rapes reported from police stations made the Supreme Court of India and the Indian Parliament to deal with them severely. The custodial rape was treated thus an aggravated offence punishable with very severe penalty. Yet, the Malayala Manorama (20-11-2000) reported a case of custodial rape by a very senior police officer in the State of Rajasthan. The Baghpat incident in Uttar Pradesh (1978), the Mathura rape case, the Bhagalpur blinding case, the Chirala (A.P.) lock up death case (1985), the Rajan murder case (Kerala), the Rashid murder case (Karnataka), the Nadiad assault case (Gujarat) are just a few instances which captured national and international attention in the recent past. No doubt, police brutality and use of deadly force have become topics of academic discussion, yet they did not give birth to a branch called police criminology. S. Venugopal Rao, a senior police officer once said that "it would be futile to deny that recourse to third degree methods in investigation is more common than admitted by the police." The Supreme Court of India in Ram Sagar Yadav V. the State (1985) 2 SCR 621 said that the police should not misuse their position for oppressing the innocent who looked to them for protection. Dr. N. R. Madhava Menon, Member, Law Commission of India writes: "If the police still become the willing tools of a corrupt executive government, the ordinary law can punish such officials. Of late, several policemen including high ranking officials have been prosecuted for serious crimes and in some cases, punished also. There have been court judgements awarding compensation to the victims of unlawful police harassment. Courts have started imposing personal liability on individual policemen instead of putting such burden on the State exchequer. Though it may tend to make policemen inactive in critical situations and thereby undermine efficiency of the force, it does convey the right message to officers that they are going to pay for their illegal actions even if they were only obeying orders of persons in government. Perhaps, such a development on personal liability may strengthen the hands of police to resist improper orders of politicians in Government". Ironically enough, one takes note of the fact that young people in good health are seen, sometimes, dead in police custody and the police, more often than not, claim such deaths to be suicidal. Upendra Baxi said once: "It is surprising to know that so many young people come to police stations to end their lives". He continued: "What is truly striking about India is the lack of respect for the rule of law not just by the people but also by those who make and enforce it[5]".

Crackpot Theories in Police Criminology

Thank God that I have not so far heard anyone talking about demenological instigation as the cause of police crimes. Nevertheless, a number of people, good-meaning citizens bring out a number of crackpot theories on police criminality. I have heard very senior police officers advancing crackpot theories to explain police crimes and to identify the causes of them. One explanation of police criminality is related to personality factors. Personality, the police administration thought to be the physique of the policemen/officers. A robust physique with proper development of muscles was the main consideration for recruitment. The administration did not pay any care to desirable personality traits in police recruits. Resultingly, it was hypothesized that people with strong authoritative and aggressive impulses could perform well as policemen/officers. Several studies conducted in the west demonstrated beyond doubt that policemen/officers valued obedience and self-control over their individual spontaneity, tolerance and lenience could work well in democracy[6]. But, such studies did not have any effect upon the recruitment of policemen/officers in India. In India, police personality or better "cop personality" meant nothing but a robust physique with violent personality traits. Those who possessed human qualities and desirable personality traits were considered as misfits to perform police duties. According to S. Venugopal Rao: "The situation in which police violence becomes manifest can be divided into three broad categories. First, there is terrorism and other acute and dangerous forms of ideological violence to which police response can be none other than that of counter-violence. To the second category belongs aggressive dissent which assumes ugly forms of violence and can be controlled only through force. In dealing with violence of these two categories, counter-violence is normative so long as it is regulated according to the law of land. However, with regard to normal day-to-day investigations, an occasional streak of violence emerges which is uncalled for and which no civilized society can accept. This is mainly due to overenthusiasm or pressure and influence of the complainants or equivocal directions from the higher echelons[7]". What has been observed hitherto was that one and the same policeman/officer did everything from anti-terrorism to serving of people in a human rights friendly way. He could not probably make distinctions between terrorists and ordinary law violators. Hence, he resorted the same aggressive tactics to both terrorists and common crime-doers. The complaint has been that there was no proper socialization within the police subculture. The occupational subculture of police thus became pregnant with violence and contaminated by torture of even innocent people. The character of some police work exhibited negative feelings and aggressive strategies to the members of the public. The police in India developed cynicism about people's motives. The people isolated the police from the community as they found them taking a hostile attitude towards them. Hence, the police felt that they should break the law to enforce the law. Over the last 50 years, the police in India have been doing the same thing and they, therefore, did not/could not conform to the rule of law. They did not scrupulously observe due process of law in their work. The courts, time and again, reminded them to adhere to the due process of law. "Judicialize" everything the police do—that became the need, urgency and necessity. The Supreme Court of India in D.K. Basu's case gave directives as to what ought to be done when the police took people in custody/arrested people. "A crime control policy" within the police department became the a necessity. The "Crime Control Policy within the Police" wanted to see the efficient, expeditious and reliable police service which was crime-free. Just recently, a sub-inspector was accused of showing disrespect to a deadbody of a woman alleged to have committed suicide. The news in the media reported that the allegation of the public was that the subinspector who went to conduct an inquest was drunk and was found lying near the corpse. Some people accused him of necrophilia. A senior police officer was deputed to conduct an inquiry and the paper reported that the inquiry proved that the subinspector did not show disrespect to the corpse. The general public were not prepared to accept the findings of the senior police officer. They demanded an inquiry into the allegation by an independent agency outside the State police and certainly it was the Central Bureau of Investigation. People said: "The Dog Does Not Eat Its Own Flesh" and therefore, "Ceaser's Wife Must Be Beyond Suspicion".

'Judicialize' the police—and that is the trend today. Rule of law was the philosophy earlier, but such a philosophy did not always guaranteed the "rule of justice". People wanted rule of law and justice. Today, the trend is seen more towards expanding and strengthening the concepts of rule of law and justice. People are given the right to counsel, the right to remain silent, right to be free from coercion when confessions are recorded, right to be medically examined and thus the police are pressured to become more transparent in their work. People have their dignity and autonomy. The police are bound thus to rework in such a way that the organizationally prescribed ends are fulfilled. They are not to employ questionable enforcement procedures to enforce law and administer justice. They are made accountable to what they do and are ordered to pay compensation to the victims of abuse of power and misuse of authority. Compensation is demanded and sometimes granted even for the use of profane and abusive language. Police overenthusiasm and concern with establishing their authority and pseudo-authority is questioned by the people and the press.

Police Corruption and Criminality

Police corruption and criminality are interrelated. Peter K. Manning writes: "Barkenders, shopkeepers and hotel clerks become, for patrolman, a resource that must be continuously serviced by visits and exchanges of favours. While it is apparent that this condition lends itself to corrupt exploitation by individual officers, even the most flawlessly honest policeman must participate in this network of exchanges if he is to function adequately. Thus, engaging in such exchanges becomes an occupational task that demands attention and time[8]". If this was what Manning observed in the United States, during 1970s, the situation has gone worse in India now. The police are blamed for corruption-money fixing, corruption-money splitting, corrupt practices, nexus crimes, enforcement criminality, payoff, kickbacks, sweet heart dealings, Mafia operations, contacts with underworld criminals and *goondas* and the list is endless. Policies and practices which are mutually beneficial and advantageous get developed and the allegation is that the enforcement system has been working efficiently and effectively with the help of professional, organized, convictional, traditional and white-collar offenders of all descriptions. The politicians-police nexus, politicization of police, policization of politics etc. have become matters of serious concern. The accusation is that many policemen and officers insist that all laws be enforced rigorously and vigourously against some people, nevertheless they do not insist that all laws be strictly enforced against them or against some in society. The police are blamed to take a "tolerance policy" toward the vices and crimes committed by some in society and selectively enforce certain laws against some people only if they find that it is to their advantage. Is it not a crime to do so? Criminologists may find fault with such selective enforcement, with such negative enforcement or with such tolerant enforcement. Many violations by police are visible and more and more police crimes become more and more visible in these days. Police corruption and their nexus dealings become more and more conspicuous now and according to some, the police perform their duties and enforce laws by encouraging and promoting crimes which they are bound to suppress. Police fencing crimes, criminals and their own crimes become a topic of interest for criminologists. Systematic violation of human rights and other penal laws by the enforcement/enforcing agencies comes under police criminology and lawless law enforcement. The people and experts can not follow a line cf least resistance to police corruption, crime and criminality. James T. Carrey says: "Where collaboration with organized crime is pervasive in a department it is supported by an informal social system that is at odds with legal statutues". Besides the high corruption in police department, one may take note of small bribes, mooching (receiving free items for favoritism shown), chiseling (free admissions to entertainments etc.), favoritism etc. in police works. Again, shopping (the appropriation of articles for personal use without making payments), shakedown (appropriation of items for personal use from a scene of search/crime), perjury (providing alibis for fellow colleagues in service for their illegal activities when caught), extorting money for advertisement in police publications, coerced purchases of tickets to police functions, street courts (settling minor traffic violations by cash payments without receipts), premeditated thefts by police functionaries and burglaries in blue" etc. are other forms of criminal behaviour[10].

Emergence of a new branch in criminology—i.e., police criminology—may be a need of the hour. Police crimes challenge the traditional explanations of criminality. Are the law enforcement officers who indulge in committing police crimes 'pathological'? What is the sociology of police crimes? What is the psychology of police crimes? What exactly are the criminogenic factors of police crimes?

There is an international and national thinking to make police crimes as special or separate crimes. This is an indication that there is the need for the development of a police criminology. For the rape, for example, committed by ordinary people, the law prescribes lesser punishment whereas custodial rapes are punished more severely than ordinary rapes. Torture by policemen is compensated whereas hurt by ordinary people are not necessarily compensated. Custodial death is followed by a judicial inquiry whereas the murder is not. When policemen are found involved in the commission of crimes, people demand for C.B.I. inquiries. When a policeman attacks a man, there is human rights violation whereas when the policeman is attacked, then there is no human rights violation. The postmortem of a person who died in police custody is videotaped and later examined by the Human Rights Commissions. Thus, a major preoccupation in criminology today is to develop a science of crime to understand police criminality. The law in action, the law in violation, the law violation by law enforcement agancies—all these assume a lot of importance. When a law enforcing group is studied by criminologists, then new theories of crime causation will come into being. They try to see that police crime is a function of who is enforcing the law, how those who are bound to enforce the law are able to violate the law and are capable of carrying on the commissions of crime with immunity and status. The theories explaining the causes of murder, rape, theft, forgery etc. can not explain police crimes. Likewise, the theories explaining criminal behaviour owing to mental disorders can not speak much about police crimes. I authored two books, namely (1) Police Enforcement Crimes and Injustice, (2) Indian Police and Nexus Crime. Certainly, they give a lot of details about police crimes and are perhaps the immediate reason for bringing out this title on *Police criminology and crimes.*

References

1. Paul E. Smith and Richard O. Hawkins, *Victimization, Types of Citizen Police Contacts and Attitudes Towards the Police,* form Police and Community Relations: Image, Roles, Realities, edited by Alvin W. Cohn and Emilio C. Viano, J. B. Lippincolt, Philadelphia, 1976.
2. K. Krishnamurthy, *Police Diaries, Statements, Reports, Investigations, Arrests etc,* Law Book Co., Allahabad, 1973.
3. Alphonse L. Earayil & James Vadackumchery, *Police and the Society,* Kairali, Trivandrum, 1985.
4. The jurist is Dr. N.R. Madhava Menon, see *Role of police in the Maintenance of Rule of law and in the Protection of Human Rights: Some Insights from Indian Experience in Democratic Governnance,* National Law School of India University, Bangalore.
5. Upendra Baxi, *The Crisis of the Indian Legal System,* Vikas Publishing House, Delhi, 1982.
6. Milton Robeach, Martin S. Miller, and John Snyder, *The Value Gap Between Police and Policed,* Journal of Social Issues, 27 (1971).
7. Venugopal Rao, S., *Police Administration,* Indian Institute of Public Administration, Delhi, 1982.
8. Peter K. Manning, *The Police: Mandate Strategies and Appearances* in Richard Quinney (ed.), *Criminal Justice in America: A Critical Understanding,* Little Brown, Boston, 1974.
9. James T. Carrey, *Introduction to Criminology,* Prentice Hall, Englewood Cliffs, 1978.
10. See also James T. Carrey, *op. cit.*

CHAPTER—6

Police Criminology: An Introduction

What is criminology? It is a study of crimes and criminal behaviour. This is a simple definition. Some criminologists may say that criminology includes the study of law-making, law-breaking and reactions to the breaking of laws. Earlier chapters showed how the police, by whatever name they were called in history, involved in law-making, law-breaking and reacting to the breaking of laws. How did they make the laws? They made their own law and tried to enforce them with muscle power? No body questioned them because they were afraid of them. History further showed that the police violated many laws which they enforced and they were not questioned by many. In a few instances, the violators were punished. History again showed that the police reacted to the violations of law sometimes violating the law by themselves. Thus the history attested to the fact that the law enforcers became law makers, law breakers and reactionaries to law breaking. Though they committed crimes of various descriptions from corruption to consensus crimes, and expressed criminal behaviours of many types from calling of epithets to concoction of evidence, no branch known as *Police Criminology* developed in the world. Why? If criminology includes the study of antisocial behaviour committed by the various crime-control systems, then the scope of criminology is indeed very wide.

A police subinspector was recently convicted for causing the death of a person illegally taken into custody and detained in a police lock-up. He was awarded life sentence. This particular sentence was newsworthy and the press, T.V., and radio published the news. The convicted 'police officer' met me a few years ago and told me that I must develop a branch called 'police criminology' and I asked him "why". He honestly told me that lack of knowledge in police criminology made him to commit a heinous crime which he would not have committed otherwise.

What was my response to his desire? Certainly, I could find a police officer—a murderer by act—requesting for developing police criminology. A law enforcement officer should not be a law violating person. But there he was and what made him to be so? He had the power and authority to enforce the law, but he abused his power and misused his authority to commit a crime—the crime of murder as defined in the Indian Penal Code. How many such murders take place in police custody? Official records show a statistics and human rights activists give quite a different statistics. What is the reality? The reality may be in between the two numbers. Whatever that be, the problem of crimes by police is a topic of interest for criminologists and people all over the world. If the criminologists do not scientifically study police crimes and criminal behaviours, then the police themselves may not think that they commit crimes and that is what the history tells us now. What is criminal outside the police station is criminal inside too; what is criminal outside the police uniform is criminal within the uniform too and what is criminal in police stations and within police uniform are criminal outside the police stations and police uniform. There exists a consensus in society on crimes and police crimes. The consensus position on police crimes is that legislations are required to define police crimes which are identified by the society. Enforcement crimes, nexus crimes, consensus crimes, conspiracy of silence, indifference, inaction etc. are identified as police crimes today. As shown in previous chapters, they are born and developed over a period of time. Nevertheless, no serious studies were conducted to analyse the causes of police criminality. Resultingly, there has been no effort done with the explicit purpose of demonstrating that there is a widespread demand for legislations to put down police crimes. A good number of people perceives police crimes as a problem today and the perception of the problem comes out through the press, court decisions, debates in the legislatures, public demands and small scale research studies. There is widespread concern among the people regarding the harmful effect of lawless law enforcement, lawless aggression, oppression, corruption, concoction of evidence, manipulation of records etc.

Questions a Criminologist Must Answer

Police is a law enforcement machinery. Law enforcement means and includes law violations. For example, the aggressive impulses in man—in the nature of man—account for a variety of crimes in police. What the police department can do is to check this aggressiveness in policemen/ officers. Some policemen/officers argue that aggressiveness is functional in police department. People are aggressive and therefore, the police can not but be aggressive. The counterargument will be that the policemen who are trained and are bound to be law-abiding cannot behave like the ordinary man on the street. There are boundaries that cannot be violated and no policeman can behave in a cruel, humiliating and degrading manner. He must be human rights friendly. There may be a set of supporting values in society and particularly in police subculture and they can not be/should not be linked with the criminal behaviour. For example, a rapist is a cruel man and he deserves to be treated cruelly. Some policemen argue that many rape cases go unpunished and therefore roughing up at police stations is the best punishment he can be awarded. Certainly, the argument is supported by the values maintained in the police subculture. How can this be accepted by a criminologist? A crime cannot be tackled or treated by the commission of another crime whatever may be the justification one may advance for rationalizing it.

Criminal values in the police reflect the values of a society as a whole, but in a somewhat distorted way—said a director general of police to me in a private conversation. What does he mean by that, I do not know, yet I know that no society accepts enforcement crimes or nexus crimes as pious acts. But the police are blamed for it. Which society accepts the nefarious activities of police who establish nexus partnership with nexus criminals? Aggressiveness or employment of torture is not the only crime the police are accused of. They are accused of corruption, corruption-money splitting, corruption-money fixing, nexus with Mafia/ underworld criminals, sweet heart dealings with politicians/political parties, misuse of authority or abuse of power etc. They are crimes and they are to be treated as crimes.

If crime is functional in a society, there is no meaning in having a police department—say some people. Policemen argue that no society can survive without crimes. There are many people who make a living just because people commit crimes. The lawyers, the judges, the police, the jail authorities, the priests, the teachers and so on live because there exist crimes in society. Police being a part of the society will or must have some crimes. The policemen further argue that the character of criminal behaviour is linked to the facilities provided for the police to commit crimes. The director general of police may commit crimes which a constable may not and vice versa, yet a criminologist may say that the director general of police commits all crimes which a constable may or can commit. Instances of torture or degrading treatment to the people may be more at the lower levels/at the police station levels; but a close scruting will show that the instances of torture and humiliating/degrading treatment are seen at the higher levels too. Allegations are plenty to show that the higher echelons treat their subordinates with utter disrespect and without showing due respect to human dignity.

No. I must think and say that man has both criminal and non-criminal potentialities, capacities, desires, inclinations, impulses, decisions and what not? Policemen/officers too have them. A criminologist sees that the given police system or subculture in police encourages the expression of a policeman's/officer's criminal inclinations. What does he mean by that? He thinks that the policeman can commit a lot of crimes and he can do so with his authority and power conferred to him by law. He can misuse his power or abuse his authority without any evil consequences afterwards. The members of the police service know that there exist nexus crimes in the department committed by them—from constable upwards—but a conspirancy of silence, approval, acceptance, encouragement make them to continue and live in the commission of crimes. Take another example. The members of the police service know that torture is employed in police custody. But here again, the conspirancy works well. A criminologist therefore asks: "What are the conditions which help the police to commit crimes?

No doubt, the given police system has a history of its own—and the history is centuries old. The police system inherited from the British past encouraged the expression of brutality, aggressiveness, torture, harassment etc. to people. The democracy and the interference of unscrupulous politicians in police affairs worsened the situation. The police inclinations to establish nexus contacts with the Mafia/underworld criminals further worsened the situations. The policemen enjoy a lot of advantages by their nexus transactions and sweetheart dealings with bandits of all descriptions. How is the subcultural situation in police to commit crimes? How is the distribution of opportunities to involve themselves in the commission of crimes? I think that the subculture is favourable and the opportunities are fine. The result will be commission of crimes.

There are a lot of legal norms which must be strictly adhered to by the enforcement agencies. But, history and experience show that they are not keen in observing them. The Indian Penal Code, Code of Criminal Procedure etc. lay down the norms of behaviour for the police. Nevertheless, the police functionaries are found to violate them. Why?

According to some policemen/officers, violations of the legal norms during the enforcement of law are a *sine qua non* for their group survival. For example, torturing a property offender becomes a necessary evil for the detection of crimes. If they do not do so, they may fail to detect the crime, recover the property lost and obtain a conviction. Resultingly, the people lose their trust and confidence on police. Hence, for them, commission of crimes becomes an inevitable and necessary evil for the group survival. But, criminologists may think in a different way. According to them, an uncontrolled police behaviour will cause more harm and damage than good in society. Hence, legal norms and regulations are essential for the group survival and precisely therefore, the police are not to violate the rules, whatever may be its advantages and success. The criminal laws which guide the police behaviour are the reflections of the general will of the people. What is the meaning of police violating the criminal laws for enforcing laws?

The police are conferred with certain privileges and rights and they are conferred only to administer fair justice and nothing more. Naturally, the laws regulating and controlling police behaviour may pose problems for the police to enforce laws in the way they want them to be enforced. There can be no general will of the people expressed authorizing the police to resort to oppression, torture or to involve in nexus criminality or enforcement crimes. Yet, the police do so. Why?

I find that the most important cause for the police to commit crimes may be due to the fact that those who have the authority of law want to retain their authority even to the extent of abusing their power and authority. They think that they have many privileges and rights and sometimes think too much that they have pseudo-authority as well. They exercise their authority and interpreted authority, pseudo-authority etc. Those who know that they are exercising their interpreted authority or pseudo-authority know fully well that they are violating the law. Such people want to retain their interpreted and pseudo-authority which may be abuse of authority or misuse of power. The laws which are enacted to control police behaviour certainly pose problems for them. They are powerful and there is no general will expressed permitting them to violate the laws which they must obey. Some vested interests may pressure the police to violate the laws for their favour. Such vested interests, the politicians, the affluent, the underworld criminals, the bandits and so on are powerful groups who enjoy enormous money power or authority to see that their views are enforced through the police. The police weigh the advantages and disadvantages and afterwards yield to their desires by violating the laws if they find that such a course of action is advantageous to them. Nexus crimes like bootlegging, corruption-fee fixing, kickbacks, payoff etc. are instances in point and the police stand to win. Police crimes become the inevitable outcome.

In police crimes, one may see a sort of consensus reached between the police and other vested interests. There seems to be a higher consensus relating to nexus crimes, enforcement crimes and political fiat-crimes than the same relating to informal arrests, illegal detentions and incommunicado interrogations. A consensus perspective will probably show considerable unanimity across various ranks and political forces. A conspiracy of silent understanding works in such situations.

Police crimes have been in existence for centuries. But no one, it may be stated again, has made attempts to study police crimes from a criminological perspective. Milder terms like informal arrests (instead of abduction/kidnapping), illegal detention (instead of wrongful confinement), indepth interrogation (instead of torture) were used to mitigate the seriousness of the crimes committed by police. The use of such milder and less harmful words were purposeful and certainly were the result of a conspiracy of approval of such despicable practices. Criminologists advocate the view that the criminal behaviour must be mapped before it can be explained. But, in police, there was no mapping of criminal behaviour. There was no explaining of police crimes. Everything was interpreted as necessary and inevitable for the enforcement of law—with some exceptions here and there to book some people as law violators. Afterwards, they were dealt with accordingly. But, such occasional dealings did not have any perceptible effect either in curbing down the police crimes or in curtailing their extent. Police crimes continued to dominate the police subculture. This approach could not make the people and authorities to know which aspects in police subculture supplied the quantum of crimes. They just thought that some individual policemen/officers committed law violations; but were ignorant of the 'real' criminal behaviour within the system. Statistics on police crimes may revral that the lower level functionaries are involving in law violations. They are often processed, chargesheeted and convicted or acquitted as the case may be. Police crimes, as they are understood today, are concentrated in the lower level functionaries because only their acts become visible to the people. Informal arrests and illegal detentions, incommunicado interrogations are very conspicuous so much so that the human rights activists take up the matter. But, what about the nexus crimes, enforcement crimes, kickbacks and payoff cases? They are less visible or invisible. The high level officials, politicians, nexus operators, higher-ups and the affluent control the State apparatus—as the allegation goes—and they see to it that their vested interests are protected. They do not get the 'labelling' as criminals. In fact, they cause more social harms to society than the lower level functionaries. Criminologists today are concerned with the extent and intensity of hidden crimes. They view the official statistics of police crimes with skepticism.

High level crimes are found to be well planned and patterned than the casual criminal behaviour. A torture in police custody may be a traditional crime in police sub-culture, but a nexus dealing with bootleggers is not. Both of them commit crimes. The nexus offender is motivated by his greed or acquisitive desires just like a corrupt official is moved by his urge to make advantages for his benefits. After India became independent, officials in Government service became more prominant. The salaried class could understand that they could misuse/abuse their power and authority for their benefits. Many became corrupt or found out means and methods to earn and become richer and more powerful. Even before India became independent, bribery was seen practised all over the Country.

Police Crimes as Seen by a Criminologist

Going through the history of Indian police, observations made by Police Commissions, opinions made by authorities and other individuals, reports of researchers, news in the media and what one sees in the police functionings, the crimes committed by the police may be—

1. Bribery, corruption, corrupt practices, corruption-money fixing, corruption fee-splitting etc.
2. Enforcement crimes like non-registration of F.I.Rs, registration of false cases, manipulation of F.I.Rs, perfunctory investigation, concoction of evidence, production of tutored witnesses and touts etc.
3. Enforcement crimes such as informal arrests, illegal detention, incommunicado interrogation, harassment and humiliation of suspects in police custody, resorting to degrading treatment and refusal to provide food for the detinue etc.
4. Use of torture, threatenings and coercion, unsettling of human mind, pressuring tactics, refusal to provide minimum human comforts, custodial violence and prolonged detention in clandestine places etc.
5. Custodial deaths, custodial suicides or causing situations for the detinue to commit suicide, custodial molestation of

women, custodial rapes, calling of epithets and filthy expressions, indecent behaviour and obnoxious tactics etc.

6. Nexus crimes such as collaborating with underworld criminals, neglect of duties, conspiracy of silence and inaction to facilitate crimes, booty sharing, sweetheart dealings, kickbacks, payoff, acceptance of grafts and other favours, misuse of authority, abuse of power etc.
7. Wilful omission to do the duties, showing partiality and favouritism, provoking, instigating, encouraging crimes and criminals, conspiracy of inertia, exercise of pseudo-authority, exercise of excessive authority and power, simulated encounters and human rights violations.
8. Misuse of vehicles and departmental resources for personal use, susceptibility to political pressures, vulnerability to illegal influences, undesirable friendship with the affluent, communal feelings, fanatical inclinations and parochial interests etc.
9. Disrespect to witnesses, complainants, members of the public, media personnel, ego-projections detrimental to fair administration of justice, frauds in T.A and *per diem* claims, manipulation of public money, misappropriation of property searched and seized etc.
10 Illegal searches and seizures, warrantless arrests, suppression of facts, suggestion of falsehood, substitution of untruth, causing of undue and purposeful delay, contaminating evidence, disrespect shown to articles and premises, harassment to the family members and kith and kin of the suspects, cruel and crude searches etc.
11. Misuse of police discretion, collection of incriminating evidence, violation of rules relating to electronic surveillance, interference in privacy, interceptions in correspondance, illegal surveillance, recording of involuntary and inadmissible confessions, illegal use of drugs, hypnosis, polygraph, brain fingerprinting or similar techniques during interrogation, unfair inducement to suspects, questioning of such unfair frequency, length or persistence as to constitute harassment to the interrogated, employing unfair methods which undermine one's ability to make a choice whether to make a statement or otherwise cooperate with the interrogator, questioning to obtain information not for use against arrested persons, denial of necessities such as water, medical attention, rest or physical

necessities to a person in custody, refusal to provide sanitary facilities to attend to the special needs of women and gender decency etc.

12. Indecency and lack of respect to juveniles and children, deception as to obligation to make statements during interrogation, making false promises, inducing a person by showing leniency to him or to people in whom he is interested, not allowing a counsel to be present during interrogation (not throughout the process of interrogation), unnecessary handcuffing, undercover investigation by deception etc.
13. Use of excessive use of force during law and order management, drunken behaviour in public, purposeful misinterpretation of law, making a non-cognizable offence into a cognizable one and vice versa, participating in festivities organized by vested interests, enjoying privileges which are not due to police functionaries etc.
14. Traffic law violations by police, giving false testimony in courts, purchasing provisions, edibles, liquor etc. without paying the price, misusing taxi-cars/private car for personal use or utilizing own vehicles, police vehicles and uniform for illicit business transactions/carrying contraband articles/doing binami business etc.
15. Use of illegal violence, mass-arrests, prolonged detentions, false encounters, brutal treatment of citizens, denial of Constitutional safeguards and civil rights, legislative protections etc. to people as a result of their political involvements in activities which are not accepted by the government in power. In other words, police participation in government sponsored political crimes including terrorism etc.

Police crimes—criminologists have not so far identified such a category in the study of crimes. They thought that police was an agency that fought against crimes and therefore they could not be considered as people committing crimes. For example, A beats a man. It is a crime under law. The police arrests A and beats him. It is then called custodial violence and no action is usually initiated against the policeman/officer. The question is: "whether there is a premeditation or malice aforethought for the constable to beat A". The answer is that a constable does not have it. Hence people consider the constable's beating as a necessary part of his job. When a policeman beats a man as part of his job, it is generally held to be justifiable. Then, what about custodial violence, in-custody rapes and murder in police lockup? Criminologists did not study such police crimes from a criminological angle. In-custody murders may be rare, but certainly they evoke a profound public reaction whenever they take place. Many in-custody murders may not be premeditated. Mostly, they are the end result of some personality clash between the interrogator and the interrogated or the accidental outcome of torture to obtain a pressured confession from the interrogated. Hence, some criminologists may call them "murder in the heat of passion". My casual study of the murdered in police custody revealed to me that the victim of in-custody murders were unknown to the policemen/officers in majority of cases. What I could gather from my conversation with police functionaries accused of in-custody murder/others who had first hand knowledge about some custodial murders might convince me that the "victim participated" in their murders—i.e., the victim seemed to be asking to be killed. The victim in certain cases had personality clashes or verbal attacks with the interrogated. In some cases, the victims simply refused to volunteer information about their involvement in the commission of crimes and the interrogators lacked sufficient expertise and skill to conduct psychological interrogation. The same principles might be applicable in the cases of custodial violence. However, the opinion was formulated after listening to the police versions only and to that extent, it might be imperfect.

Forcible rapes in police custody and there could be any number in Indian police history. Sometimes, they might be gang rapes. Indian police is male dominated and studies show that the atmosphere in police stations is fear causing. Women feel unsafe in police custody. India has passed a number of laws just to protect women form police crimes and to ensure their gender dignity under police custody. Studies on rapes further show that there exists rapist-victim relations in a good number of rapes. But, police rapes are found to be not the results of planning, but situational. The relationship between the rapists and the raped (victims) is non-existent. The women raped/molested by the police need not necessarily be loose women, although instances have been reported of raping women of bad character in police lockups. The relative isolation of police stations and the fear caused in women provide facilitating environments for sex-perverts in uniform. The age of the victim does not seem to have any effect on police rapes. 'Victim precipitation' and 'victim participation' are not found in custodial rapes. Nevertheless, some policemen think that a prostitute is an invitation to sex acts for them too and recently, some sex-workers in a south Indian State made attacks on policemen/officers who showed sexual perversions and indecency towards them when they were under their custody.

In India, the laws on rapes were amended to include custodial rape to be very heinous offence.

No doubt, custodial murder is seldom done for profits or as a part of a policeman's livelihood. Of course, torture in police custody may be linked to bribery or corruption. The speciality of police crimes is that the policemen/officers who involve in the commission of violent crimes do not see themselves as criminals. I have asked many policemen/officers to honestly tell me their feelings when they employ third degree methods or torture on people. They do not think or they can not think that they are committing crimes, rather they prefer to think that they are doing some holy acts fully justified by circumstances. Society does not give support to police atrocities or commission of violent crimes, nevertheless, it is tolerant to police cruelties to a certain extent. Proving the police power and showing the police authority may require frequent rehearsal of toughness and aggressiveness in police custody. The policemen usually do not have any guilt feelings and the victims often think that they are fated to suffer. Those victims who have committed crimes believe that they deserve to be roughed up by the police. They may show least resistance to police roughness and toughness. Police are inclined to think that their violent retaliation to criminals, suspects and the people are thus legitimized. I for one think that the higher rate of violent behaviour—atrocious behaviour—among the policemen/officers can be explained well in terms of a higher tolerance for their expression of violence shown by the police hierarchy and the people outside. They approve of police strategies in many situations. Nevertheless, people in large numbers come forward in these days raising protests against police atrocities and violence and the reaction has been more after the enactment of the Protection of Human Rights Act—1993. The policemen/officers are accused of treating criminals/suspects as people having no human rights. Policemen/officers who want to show or prove their authority/pseudo-authority, ego, paranoid personality etc. make attempts to humiliate, hurt, frighten, torture the people under their custody. In spite to the rising public protests to police violence, I am inclined to feel even today that the social/societal reactions to police torture and violence is mixed. They show at times a tolerating attitude and at other times an approving attitude. If a notorious *goonda* or a cruel rapist is violently handled by the police, the people may exhibit a tolerating attitude, but in no case of a murder in police custody, they show any such or similar attitude. Whenever the people see that a man is killed or a woman is raped in police custody, the reaction of the people tend to be quite harsh. Use of torture and other degrading treatment by police is universally condemned and the Convention Against Torture by the U.N. is specifically intended for that and prescribes victimological compensation. Police torture is considered to be socially threatening and is a crime in every letter of the word.

Nexus and Enforcement Crimes

Nexus crimes are sufficiently well organized and they can be pursued as a means to make exorbitant advantages for police functionaries. A State minister said that the principal employer of the enforcement functionaries is the Government, but it seems that a feeling has come into being among the people that the principal pay-givers for them are the nexus offenders like the bootleggers, Mafia criminals, criminal businessmen and so on. Traditional or conventional crimes like theft, burglary, larceny and robbery committed by people are punished in various ways from the ancient amputation of hands or death penality to imprisonment in contemporary India. Prisons in India are primarily used to house these conventional offenders while nexus criminals are honoured and respected.

Looking at the nexus crimes, we may note that they are calcutated and well planned. As mentioned earlier, I have authored a book titled *India Police and Nexus Crime* and I discuss various aspects of nexus criminality in that book. Nexus crimes require many decisions relating to amasement of wealth which can not be acquired legitimately. The planning—calculative component-in nexus crimes may be a sufficient justification for calling nexus crimes 'property offences' in police work. The abuse of authority/misuse of power by police, doubtlessly, gives confidence for the nexus neucleus to carry on his criminal careers. Nexus offenders mean business and police support insures safety. It is indeed difficult to estimate the extent of nexus crimes. For, the nexus offenders are not usually booked, arrested or prosecuted unless there is a demand for it and the demand is seldom seen. The salient characteristics of those caught for nexus transactions are, as a rule, rich, influential and socially placed on high pedestals.

Enforcement crimes may come under nexus crimes, but need not necessarily be so always. Enforcement crimes contain nexus crimes, but nexus crimes do not contain all kinds of enforcement crimes. Again I have authored a book "Police Enforcement Crimes and Injustice" and I explain in detail the various kinds of enforcement crimes seen in police service. There are a number of enforcement patterns which are professionalized, but they are not specifically recognized to be crimes under the existing penal laws. Enforcement crimes are committed during the course of police work. Sharp enforcement practices which are unethical and illegal come under enforcement crimes. Enforcement criminals are professionally skilled in avoiding detection and often the detection is very difficult, for, the people empowered to detect them commit such crimes.

For whatever reason, there exists some group support for nexus crimes and enforcement criminality. The personnel working in law enforcement offer support as they do not think, usually, that they commit crimes. They lack a criminal self-concept. Hence, generally, they do not withdraw from their crime career as the crimes insure many 'successes' in their life and profession. Social reaction to nexus and enforcement crimes tend to be indifferent or tolerant because of their low visibility.

Political Crimes and Police

Among the political crimes, criminologists put offences committed by governments or their agents against citizens who have political beliefs which the government in power does not accept. In such instances, the government in power and its agents violate Constitutional guarantees and civil rights legislations. Police are utilized by the government in power to effect the arrests of the political offenders and to detain them. The police are used for wiretapping to monitor conversations, intercept telephone messages, cease documents to conduct illegal searches etc. In some instances, the police may be pressured to kill people through simulated or false encounters and criminologists include such police activities too under political crimes. The police are blamed for resorting to unnecessary violence in civil rights demonstrations, political disturbances etc. Throughout the history of Indian struggle for independence, one could see police brutality on the sathyagrahis. The Jalian Walla Bagh tragedy was a case in point. Mahatma Gandhi himself wrote to the Viceroy on the 1st February, 1922 complaining against the "virulent type of repression that had taken place" in many parts of the country. The policemen assaulted innocent people, treated brutally those arrested and imprisoned and resorted to flogging of the Indians who fought against the British. Mahatmaji described such Government sponsored crimes as "official lawlessness" and "lawless repression". After India became independent, allegations are sometimes heard about Government sponsored terrorism and false encounters. The Report of the Committee of Concerned Citizens (1997—2000) wrote: "The Committee has been repeatedly highlighting this issue of encounters, precisely because it relates to extinguishing of human life and right to life by the Government itself—a Government which is expected to protect life and liberty under the

Constitution—and for which no recompense is possible. Such killings have become part of the State, consciously pursued and encouraged". The Committee continued: "Such fake encounters can no longer be considered as isolated aberrations or administrative miscalculations or termed as excesses or unintended transgressions of law by individual police personnel. They can only be perceived as the calculated and deliberate system response of the State which is adopting a policy of annihilation of individuals unable to comprehend a complex problem which is the result of inequity and denial of justice[1]". Many police officers/ policemen are found to be against political crimes sponsored by the governments. Studies conducted in United States of America about the police support to political crimes sponsored by the government in power show that the policemen/officers who have values against the illegal use of force against the political opponents do not generally offer support to such political crimes. However, in India, no such noteworthy studies have been conducted by anyone about police support to political crimes. If the police offer support to the use of illegal violence against political offenders, then they are mercilessly criticized by people who include neutral and civic minded people as well. The law enforcement officers and the government in power are blamed for taking lenient attitude to officials who commit crimes for the government. If at all some action is initiated, then the result is always predictable. Ultimately the charges are dropped and the policemen/officers are cleared.

Consensus Crimes and Police

The study of consensus crimes have thrust criminologists into a new area of enforcement crimes. In every law enforcement division, some crimes take place with the implicit or explicit consensus of all or majority of members. Corruption, corruption-money fixing, corruption-money splitting and many such illegal activities may be going on in a particular law enforcement division with the consensus of all or majority of the members constituting the department. Those who do not approve of such consensus-illegality may be taking a tolerating or indifferent attitude to such a culture of criminality. Employment of torture, third degree methods etc. in police is a crime and everyone knows about it. But no one resists to the use of such coercive and degrading treatment. Why? An atmosphere which must ensure justice and fair treatment to the suspects in crime must not be converted to a centre of torture and human atrocities. Torture is a human right violation, but the consensus—implicit or explicit—permits such inhuman treatment. Though the courts, researchers and police commissions, time and again, have spoken against such crimes in police subculture, they do not, it seems, treat them as consensus crimes. Whenever complaints are received about consensus crimes, action is taken, sometimes, against individual policemen/officers responsible directly for the commission of such crimes. The law says that omission to prevent a crime is an offence, yet action is not initiated against all responsible for not preventing the commission of such consensus crimes. Usually, the action is initiated, if at all necessitated, against those who are at the lower or lowest level of the hierarchy and as such the seriousness of the consensus nature of the crime is ignored or overlooked.

Consensus crimes refer to the acts/omissions of a department as a whole to the crimes committed while the individuals act in their corporate capacity. For example, a suspect is locked up without providing him sufficient cloths—in a degrading/humiliating way. This is done by an officer who is in-charge of a police station. Everyone in the police station knows that it is a crime, but no one resists to such behaviour. Criminologists tell such conspiracy of silence, tolerance, indifference, encouragement, connivance, promoting, etc. as factors responsible for the existence and survival of consensus crimes. Consensus crimes in police were recognized even before the Torture Commission—1855, but were not treated as crimes although provisions in law were made to punish the guilty. The laws were not strictly enforced and precisely therefore, a culture of consensus-criminality got developed in due course. Hence, the consensus-criminality has a history of many centuries. Now the consensus-crimes in law enforcement are discussed by criminologists as there exists a growing consciousness of the need to preserve and promote the changing/changed concepts of justice—the Equal Justice Under Law—and to protect the interests of everyone who deserves justice under law.

When crimes by policemen/officers were registered, then they may be investigated for administering justice to individual law violators, but in such cases, the protection of the interests of all concerned or affected were not taken care of. A group that is empowered to enforce law and administer justice can not and must not endanger justice by a sort of consensus—explicit or implicit—reached by it. The police as a group is again to protect the people as a whole from the law violators, but the police becoming responsible for violating laws is of bad taste. If so, a need for punishing consensus crimes too comes into being.

For those people concerned about protecting the human rights of citizens in furtherance of fair administration of justice, the State's role is also to prohibit all sorts of enforcement crimes including consensus criminality. The underlying principle is that all citizens should be ensured of justice and all citizens include the suspects, arrestees and detinues. Police is a monopoly service and therefore, the people do not have any means to obtain justice from other agencies. It being so, the people are fated to suffer the ill-consequences of consensus crimes. Police have an accountability and they are held responsible for what they do under the colour of their power and authority. If they resort to consensus-criminality, then it is a misuse of their power/authority. Some protective legislations (like the Protection of Human Rights Act—1993) are coming up to compel policemen/officers to apply stricker standards while they enforce law or investigate crimes. The trend is to impose strict liability on police for violating human rights.

Organised Crimes and Police

Organized crimes such as the 'syndicate', the 'Mob', the Combination are plenty in society. Sometimes certain policemen/officers become part of the organized crimes. How? For any organized crime to survive in society, the criminals need police support and legal assistance. Valachi from his researches affirmed that organized crime required the collusion of political and law enforcement support to exist and survive. Police might take a tolerant attitude to organized crimes and might get regular kickbacks for adopting a tolerant attitude—he observed. Studies conducted showed that there existed a mutually advantageous arrangements between the police and crime syndicates. The linkages between the suppliers of the vice through organized crimes and the police were well established in a good number of studies. The "payoffs" to police functionaries, the studies revealed, assured exorbitantly high profits to both the organized criminals and the police personnel. John A. Gardiner asserted from his studies that the price for the police tolerance to organized crimes might be too high since it involved the loss of police integrity and public contempt for law[2].

In connection with a hooch tragedy killing about 40 people in a south Indian State, a number of policemen/officers had been suspended. The reason for their suspension was their acceptance of payoffs from the bootleggers. The involvement in organized crimes by police had a notorious past. Many found that their involvement was their success in life and some saw social and economic development through participation in organized crimes. In the above hooch tragedy, according to (investigative) journalistic reports, many police and excise officials did become rich all on a sudden owing to their unholy nexus with the bootleggers.

Public Order Crimes and Police

Public order crimes may be prostitution, public drunkenness, illegal drug use etc. How many policemen/officers are involved in such public order crimes? There exists no statistics on the question. News paper reports show information about the drunken behaviour of policemen. The punishment rolls against drunken behaviour are many. People too subscribe to the view that the policemen drink. Films and T.V. serials show such behaviour of the policemen/officers and all can not be wrong. According to them, there is a widespread support for such behaviour in police subculture. People carry liquor to humour the policemen/officers for getting their things done. In police subculture, drinking among the upper middle class/higher class and top level is not even considered as public order crimes. The group reaction to public order crimes by policemen/officers is less severe than reactions to other types of crimes (e.g., embezzlement by policemen/officers) that take place in police subculture. In police, some believe that drinks reduce their stress and strengthen their bonds. There comes into being a sort of "fellowship" which may not be available otherwise.

Enforcement Crimes/Occupational Crimes and Police

Sutherland's '*white collar crimes*' and Vadackumchery's '*enforcement crimes*' are well defined and are known to many. Crooked practices may be seen in police subculture. Embezzlement, pilferage, hoarding of files and purposeful delay to cause anxiety and harassment etc. can be examples in point. The inventive geniuses for many kinds of occupational crimes may be, generally, men/officers who are well experienced in committing such crimes. In embezzlement, pilferage etc., the victim may be the government/people and the government may not have a face of its own. Embezzlers violate the positions of trust by stealing. They differ from pilferage. Even people around the offender may not know of the crimes committed.

Studies on the occupational crimes by police show that they get group support depending upon the kind of violations. Embezzlement of money—secret service fund—may not get group support. At the same time, embezzlement followed by sharing the amount thus taken may get some group support. Pressuring the complainants/petitioners to hire taxi-cabs for the policemen/officers to make a spot visit of the place of occurrence may get full support from the group. Thus, an embezzler may fail to get a group support whereas a pilferer may get it at times.

Those who ill-treat fellow citizens when in police uniform may be doing an occupational crime. There are any number of police ideologies which may sanction occupational crimes in police subculture. "Be sympathetic to people, but police must be police" and they mean that the police must be cruel, crude and animal like to create deterrence among the people. When such perverted ideas/verbalizations have been assimilated and internalized by individual policemen/officers, they make attempts to rationalize or justify their actions including occupational crimes.

Public reaction to some occupational crimes is found to be generally apathetic. Occupational crimes are often invisible to the public and many a time will be highly complicated or technical. The police hierarchy which must initiate action may be taking a lenient attitude to occupational criminals. The occupational crimes are usually not prosecuted and if they are committed by high ranking officers in the hierarchy, then they are not even known to many.

Thus, looking into various aspects of police crimes and police criminology, one may be inclined to think that crimes do take place in police culture, nevertheless, they are not treated as crimes. Why do crimes take place in police subculture? Why do some policemen/officers commit crimes? Why has not police criminology developed in spite of many kinds of crimes taking place in police culture? There are more questions than answers. And the police administration, there is an allegation, is not serious about the etiological aspects of criminality among the police functionaries. The chapters that follow deal with the etiology of police crimes. For, criminologists can not abandon the search for causes of crimes although the police administration may even subscribe to the view that the search for finding out the causative aspects of police criminality has been unproductive or purposeless in terms of its social utility.

References

1. Report of the Committee of Concerned Citizens (1997—2000), Hyderabad, 2000.
2. Joh A. Gardiner, *The Politics of Corruption*: Organized Crime in an American City, Russel Sage Foundation, New York, 1970.

CHAPTER—7

Sociology of Police Crimes

Enrico Ferri (Italy, C. 1884) spoke about the sociology of crimes, but he did not deal with the sociology of police crimes. At the same time he said that social conditions produced crimes of various types. The conditions under which the criminals lived and the pressures exerted by such conditions on people were considered as sufficient causes for the commission of crimes—the sociologists believed so. Ferri thought that the police could be a social factor for the causation of crime. But he was not referring to crimes by police, rather was concerned with crimes by people in society. Cesaro Lombroso (Italy, C. 1876) turned his attention from his atavism to sociological factors of crime and he found that various adverse (social) conditions encouraged criminality. Gustav Aschaffenburg (Germany) identified certain social causes of crime and criminality, nevertheless he did not say anything about police criminality. Police for them were a crime control agency. William Bonger (Netherlands, C. 1910) emphacized the economic determination of crimes. American criminologists prior to 1920 thought of social conditions as causes of crime. Afterwards and upto 1940, social disorganization was considered to be the main cause of crime and delinquency. In India, no noteworthy opinions, views or theories were proposed by anyone as the social cause of crime. For, criminology as a science was not known to Indians at that time.

Crimes and Police Crimes in India

All types of crimes under the Indian Penal Code—1860 were reported from all parts of India. In 1901, a total of 11, 21, 531 crimes under the Indian Penal Code—1860 and under various Special and Local Laws were reported in India. They were dealt with by police who concurrently committed a number of crimes. The Police Commission: 1902-03 noted them when they said that the police were corrupt and oppressive. It may be reiterated that the Commission was not at all interested to study police crimes—namely, corruption, oppression, torture, misappropriation of property, abuse of power etc.—from criminological perspectives. Nevertheless, the Commission observed that some social conditions and factors were responsible for police crimes (if at all one could call them to be so). The Commission found lack of eduction and training, low birth of the lower ranks, defective supervision, low pay and social status etc. were some of the causes of police misbehaviour and corruption. Police misbehaviour was considered as 'misbehaviour' and not crimes, for "*police crimes*"—the concept was not known to many then.

Social Causes of Police Crimes

We have information that the police committed a variety of crimes during the British past. But, we have little information as to how the social factors caused police crimes in India. Even in developed countries like the U.S.A., Germany, England etc., the relationship between social factors and crime was not clear during nineteen hundred and forties. Von Hentig (Germany), in his book *Crime, Causes and Conditions* published in 1947 wrote that social forces (social factors) had close relationship with crime and delinquency. According to him, unemployment, family discord, marital status, orphanhood, disorganized and deteriorated neighbourhood etc. could be the social forces of crime and delinquency. He did not claim that social forces alone (Ferri and Aschaffenburg did so) were responsible for crime and delinquency. "Criminal behaviour springs from the interplay of two groups of forces, the individual tendencies of human beings and the manifold forces operating from Without"—he believed.

Sociology of crime as a scientific discipline has a history of some decades in the west and the sociology of police crimes as a scientific branch in criminology is not yet born in India and elsewhere. Whenever crimes took place, people started telling some social forces as social causes of crime. For example, during 1866-67, people committed a number of dacoities, robberies and thefts and the causes for the crimes were attributed to the severe famine (during the same year) which spread all along the eastern coast from Calcutta to Madras. No scientific studies were conducted to establish the cause-effect relationship between famine and increase in dacoities, robberies and thefts. The findings were speculative in nature, of course with some justification in the social forces. Nevertheless, there was no answer to the question: "Under the influence of the same social forces on people, why 'A' alone committed dacoity and 'B' did not?" There were policemen who were corrupt and they extorted money from the dacoits, robbers and thieves. Policemen were paid monthly salary during the period of famine and yet they involved in extorting money from the dacoits, robbers and thieves? Why? Sociology of crime may not answer the question. Police officers who are paid well and placed high in police hierarchy are found to involve in nexus crimes and Mafia Operations. Why?

Social Factors—Forces in Police Society and Individual Policeman

An individual policeman works in the police department. The department has a work-atmosphere wherein crime may be reacted

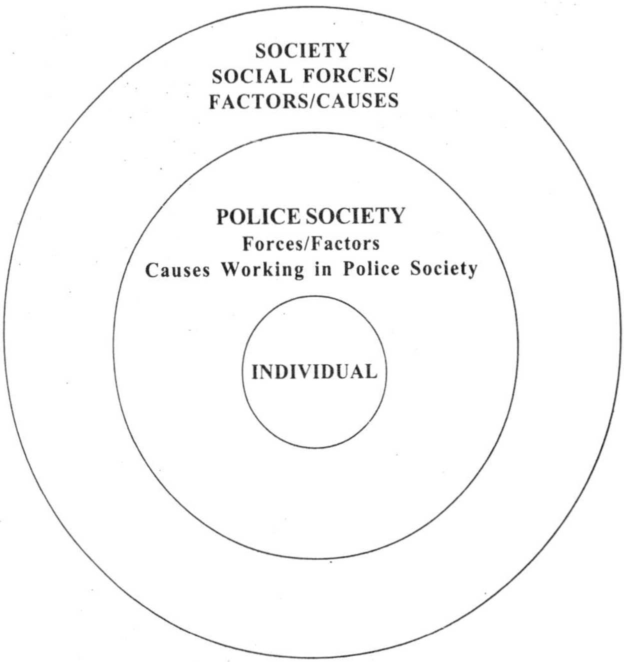

against or tolerated/encouraged/promoted. For example, in the case of corruption, the work atmosphere may be contaminated with a pro-corruption attitude. Or, take another example. In the work atmosphere, there may be an anti-torture approach. The individual policeman works in such atmosphere and some are influenced by the forces/factors seen in the work-atmosphere and some are not. It means that the social forces or factors *per se* do not make people/policemen to commit crime. They do not have any direct influence upon the policemen to commit crimes.

The police department (here, a small society within the larger society) works in a society. Take again the examples of corruption and torture. If the society is corruption-prone, then the police society too becomes corruption-prone. For, the police society is a part of the larger society. Again, if the society is against torture, then the police society too will be against torture. After the enactment of the Protection of Human Rights Act—1993, one notices a reduction in the employment of torture in police custody in India. I asked some policemen/officers to tell me the reasons for the reduction of police torture in lockups. According to them, the general awareness of the people that the police are not empowered to employ torture in police stations and the public reactions to the police use of torture plus the activities of the Human Rights Commissions and media make the policemen to have control over their aggressive tendencies. Whatever that be, the social factors in society has an influence on the police (a society within the larger society) which has an influence on the individual policeman. Some policemen fight against the social forces while some yield to the social forces that act upon them. In essence, the social forces have only an indirect impact upon people to commit crimes.

Police Crimes and Indian Evidence Act—1872

Section 24, Indian Evidence Act—1872 was about the irrelevancy of confessions before police officers. On January 30, 1872 Mr. Stephen presented to the Council and in the Bill, he introduced the oft-resorted police practice of inducement, threat or promise to the interrogated. They were offences under the Penal Code in India. But, how many cases were registered against policemen/officers who violated the law relating to the employment of coercion, threat and third degree? What were the social forces for the employment of such illegal tactics and methods? The evil persisted for centuries and the permissiveness in the work atmosphere permitted and promoted such despicable practices in police custody. Amidst such permissiveness and promotions, there are policemen/officers who never resort to such obnoxious practices. Why? Sociology of police crimes does not answer the question.

Ever since the Indian Evidence Act—1872 came into force, the policemen/officers have been demanding that the law ought to have trust on them. The society has appointed them to investigate crimes and the same society does not have any trust on them. What an irony! A lot of changes has taken place in society from 1872, yet there was no change or challenge to the provisions in the Evidence Act—1872 which treats the police as untrustworthy. The genesis of the provisions in the Evidence Act—1872 had its basis on the bad reputation and criminality which the police had in Indian society. To quote Anandswarup Gupta "the solution that was found was worse than the disease, for the law with regard to investigations and confessions, as finally established by the British in India created the vicious circle of law itself not trusting its enforcement agent and the enforcement agent being compelled to take recourse to improper practices to discharge his trust[1]". The sociology of crime—police crimes—does not answer the questions: "Why do the police violate law to enforce law?"

School of criminal sociology has some underlying assumptions and one most important is that unfavourable environmental conditions influence the individuals to commit crimes. "If confessions are not obtained or recoveries are not made, then the case is likely to be acquitted"—the policeman thinks so and therefore, he resorts to several foul methods to elicit confessions. The environments in police stations provide a conducive atmosphere to do so and the unfavourable legal environments compel him to have recourse to illegal strategies. Criminologists here argue that all policemen/officers do not behave alike under the same unfavourable conditions. Why? Then, they try to learn the social forces which pressure the policeman to violate the laws? They find that the pressure theory can not answer the question satisfactorily.

What was the pressure for the police to involve in the commission of dacoity in the past—to the blinding episode recently—to nexus crimes still later? A number of policemen/officers has been dismissed from service for their alleged involvement in the commission of various types of crimes down the centuries. In 1875, in connection with the rebellion in the Santhal Parganas, the police were accused of arresting people unnecessarily. In Gaya, some policemen were detected to have engaged in the commission of dacoities, mail robberies and other offences. Ultimately, a large number of them was dismissed. Some policemen were suspected to have established corrupt connivance with dacoits (among the Bheels) who were convicted in 1880. A commission who inquired in to the famine and subsequent lootings in Bombay during 1877 found that 40 policemen who belonged to the Railway Police were found to have involved in the plundering and looting of grains from the wagons. The policemen were subsequently prosecuted and punished. In 1890, a committee was appointed to investigate police affairs. The Committee found (1) undue delay in registering cases, (2) careless recording of the F.I.Rs., (3) omissions to collect evidence and send it to the courts etc. Certainly such practices led to miscarriage of justice and affected adversely the trial of criminal cases. Nevertheless, they were not treated as crimes by police. At the most, they were dealt with only as misconducts. If omissions to do a legal responsibility were crimes, then they were crimes. Another committee appointed in N.W.P. and Ouch in June 1890 found 'tyranny, oppression, corruption, fabrication and abuse of power and authority" in police. No one viewed them as crimes, rather tried to see only misconducts or misbehaviour on the part of the police. The sociology of crimes was not anybody's concern. The issue was considered only from administrative angles and the weaknesses of the police system or the defects of individual policeman/officer etc. were said to be the causes. This sort of lenient attitude and approach made the people and police to think that the police were not committing crimes. Moreover, the police could be held responsible only for misconduct or misbehaviour.

During 1896-97, there was a disastrous famine in the country. In 1896, there was an outbreak of plague in Bombay. The policemen then indulged freely in looting while they were on duty. They created panic and terror among the people. In 1899, 41.1 per cent of the chaukidari forces in Ranchi area were fined for misconducts[2]. Sir John Woodburn, Lieutenant-Governor of Bengal said on December 12, 1901 about the investigating system that: "it is dishonest and it is tyrannical". The Indian Police Commission: 1902-03 appointed by Lord Curzon in July, 1902 extensively dealt with police crimes, but the Commission did not call police crimes by their proper names, rather referred to them as misconducts or misbehaviour. The Commission pointed out corruption, corruption money-fixing, extortion of money by police, harassment to people, coercion, threatening of the womenfolk, dishonour to the people of low castes, acceptance of gifts/grafts, torture, gender indecent behaviour, degrading treatment to the detinues, informal arrests, illegal detentions etc. as misconducts. The Commission did not either analyse police crimes from the angle of the sociology of crime or from the angle of the psychology of crimes. The Commission could not be blamed for their analysis as the science of crime (criminology) was only an infant discipline when the report was prepared. The commission took a lenient attitude to police crimes. To quote the Commission: "There is, no doubt, exaggeration in the picture presented by some of the witnesses. . . . . . It is significant that a proposal to remove a police station from any neighbourhood is generally opposed by people. .... There are honest and efficient police officers at all grades, though they are represented as being very exceptional in the lower grades". What did it show? The lower grade functionaries in police were dishonest? If that was the reality, the situation was indeed very bad. Instead of blaming the police for their dishonesty and criminal behaviour, the Commission said: "neither do the Commission forget that much may be said in excuse for the misconduct of the police in the generally indifferent attitude of the people in respect of crime, in the encouragement of corruption by the readiness with which the people offer illegal gratifications, and in the low pay and poor prospects of the police service". The Commission, it seems, had a soft corner towards police crimes although they said that "honourable exceptions and mitigating circumstances can not efface the general impression created by the evidence recorded". The Commission did not propose initiation of prosecuting policemen/officers who committed offences. Instead the Commission affirmed: "There can be no doubt that the police force throughout the Country is in a most unsatisfactory condition, that abuses are common everywhere. ...." The Commission, as said repeatedly earlier, failed to look at police crimes from criminological perspectives. The result has been that the police continued to commit crimes in various ways. For, there was no analysis of police crimes from a legal or criminological angles. In 1907, the number of police officers dismissed in Bengal for misconduct was many. 179 men were dismissed. 148 officers and 1623 men were punished departmently. 15 police officers and 155 men were convicted by courts for various offences. Almost 10 per cent of the total strength had to be punished for various offences. In 1911, Government of India became concerned with the crimes by police. Government wanted to frame definite rules for conducting inquiries into complaints against police. Still, the Government used the word "malpractices" in police and not "crimes by police". In the case of ill-treatment of people by police, the Government thought of instituting prosecution against police officers/men. The Bombay Rule on the subject was: "directly, an accused person is placed under arrest, the investigating police officer shall, as the first step in the police investigation, ask him whether he has any complaint to make of ill-treatment by the police and shall enter in the case-diary the questions and answers. If an allegation of ill-treatment is made, the investigating officer shall there and then examine the prisoner's body, if the prisoner consents, to see if there are any marks of ill-treatment and to record the result of his examination. If the prisoner refuses to allow his body to be examined, the refusal and the reasons therefore shall be recorded. If the investigating officer finds that there is reason to believe the allegation of ill-treatment, he shall, at once, so far suspend the investigation on which the prisoner has been arrested as to forward the prisoner with his complaint, the record of corporal examination, any other evidence available, and, if possible, the police officer implicated by the prisoner's complaint, to the nearest magistrate having jurisdiction to enquire into the case".

Although the Government thought seriously about police crimes, the records show that the prisoners, more often than not, did not make complaints against police officers/men. They were afraid of ill-treatment and further torture by police officers. Moreover, there was no certainty about actions and prosecutions against policemen/officers in such cases of complaints.

Criminologists ask the question: "Why torturing in police?" Torture in custody was made an offence under the Indian Penal Code—1860. But, torture continued. Police was a power and the individuals caught by the police were powerless. Did the society tolerate torture by police in their custody? No. Yet, the police employed it and the use of torture forced the Government to enact new rules against torture. Nevertheless, the rules were not abided by.

Anomie and Police

Emile Durkheim introduced the concept of 'anomie' which meant "a state of lawlessness"—a state of "novmlessness or a lack of regulation". The history and evidence in hand proved that a state of anomie—normlessness—prevailed in police since its inception. They violated the laws which they were bound the obey and enforce. Anomie was characterized as an absence of rules by Durkheim and in every case, it indicated social disorganization. Durkheina believed that normlessness was one manifestation of the underlying process of disorganization.

Was the police in India disorganized?—or—better, was the police in India in a state of disorganization? The police have been involving themselves in the commission of various types of crimes and certainly the police crimes indicated anomie in police organization. The supervisory officers were blamed by all police commissions so far appointed for their lack of effective supervision of the subordinates. Researchers found fault with many social conditions which caused anomie in police service. Many rules were made time and again to make the police law abiding. Perfunctory investigation, callous indifference to complainants/witnesses/informers, gender indecency, lack of supervision, use of third degree methods etc.

were just a few characteristics or manifestation of disorganization (anomie) in police department.

Robert Merton had further elaborated 'anomie' and introduced the concepts of 'conformity, innovation, ritualism, retreatism and rebellion to explain deviant behaviour. In police, one may take note of the fact that there has been a conflict between values and norms. No attempt was made to have a clarity on values and norms. As a result, the individual policeman/officer got confused. Administration of fair justice was a value and the norms to achieve such a value were in the statutes, rules, regulations etc. which ought to have guided the police. But, they did not, instead some policemen/officers became their own rule and measure. Resultingly, police crimes came into being. Torture, corruption, concoction of evidence, illegal arrests etc. became institutionalized and the history manifested that the police subculture considered them as approved ways of behaviour. However, there was disjunction between the larger social goals and the parochial police goals. The society resisted the means the police adopted to reach their goals, but the society did not become successful always.

Robert Merton argued that "*conformity*" did not lead to deviance. Here, one had to resort to legitimate means and did the police do so? The pamphlet "Police Reform" published by Dinsha Edulji Wacha from Allahabad in 1911 referred to the police as "the rotten organization which purported to protect life and property and detect true crimes". The pamphlet spoke about the 'anomie' in police department and Merton's '*conformity*' had nothing to do there. The pamphlet said further that the constables were mostly from the labour class, were mostly illiterate, were having no clear notion about morality and necessarily, such a state of affairs would bring anomie (lawlessness) in any society. The same situation continued even after India became independent and no "innovation" (as Merton would say) could be introduced in democratic India. *Innovation* for Merton was the adaption and the police in India too wanted to become a police service in a democracy. However, they continued to follow and at times invent illicit means to reach their goals even after India became independent. Corruption, torture, calling of epithets and nexus dealings etc. continued to be seen in police subculture. In short and in reality, the police in the democratic India did not adopt (innovation) to a value system that was human rights friendly. Anomie continued to persist in police subculture.

The Indian society wanted the police to behave strictly in accordance to the approved means, and not in an arbitrary way. The police commissions, courts, people, press and laws insisted the same, but not successful always. Why? The police in democratic India continues to abide almost compulsively by the hitherto practised or followed institutional norms which were oppressive and people unfriendly. Even before 1907, there was a move to enact a new police Act for India. But the British could not do so owing to political reasons. Surprisingly and frustratingly, no Police Act has been passed in India after her independence in 1947. The Indian Police Act—1861 (some states had passed their Police Acts exactly in tune with the Indian Police Act—1861) continues to rule the police. According to Merton in *ritualism*, people approve of the means, but not the goals, In Indian democracy, police could not approve of the democratic means as they had to operate under the provisions of the antiquated Police Act—1861. Resultingly, they rejected the democratic goals and means and continued to commit police crimes as they used to do in the past.

In *Retreatism*, Merton said that the people rejected the cultural goals and institutionalized means of achieving them. In *rebellion*, one could see a rejection of the cultural goals and institutional means. It differs from retreatism in that the condemnation was not strictly desired. Did the police reject the cultural goals in policing the society? No, they did not. They accepted the goals, but rejected the democratic and people friendly means to achieve the goal. Police crimes became the necessary outcome there. Many did not think seriously of the institutional means and goals of police in a democracy. What were the values the police had when India became independent? They did not have any values which were different from what the British police had. What were the special means which the police adopted when they switched over from colonial rule to the democratic rule? They did not go for any special means. The result was that police crimes which existed in the British rule continued to flourish in the democratic rule as well. A few observations about the police crimes in Indian democracy by Shaw Commission of Inquiry may illustrate this further:

Detention of Man Chand under MISA and registration of a case under DIR in 1975, detention of Dr. Karunesh Shukla under MISA in 1976, detention of Shri. Virendra Kapoor, of Vaid Guru Dutt, of Prabir Purkayastha and so on reported in the interim Report II of Shah Commission of Inquiry are instances in point. The Commission has brought out the use the MISA against ordinary criminals. To quote the Commission: "The Commission views with anguish the evidence of patent collusion between the police and the Magistracy in denying the citizens their basic freedoms by arrests and detentions on grounds which were now admitted to be non-existent or deliberately invented. Even when the slender legal remedies were attempted to be resorted to by the aggrieved citizens, these were considered sufficient provocation for incarcerating them on fabricated or non-existent grounds".

The Shaw Commission spoke of (1) large scale fabrication of records, (2) arbitrary or unlawful execution of law, (3) non-accountability of police officers to any public authority, (4) political considerations in police work, (5) subverting the rule of law by police authority, (6) politicking by police, (7) susceptibility to political whims and fancies of the ruling party, (8) fraudulent creation of legal facade etc. etc. Criminology deals with all of them as crimes and must find out the etiological factors and preventive strategies.

Cultural Transmission and Police Crimes

Cultural transmission theories in criminology focuses on the development of a criminal culture in specific settings. They also look into how does criminal culture communicates its patterns. In police, patterns of crime are culturally transmitted and there exists ample evidence to prove the same from the period of Torture Commission—1855 and before. The same patterns of crimes have been repeatedly seen for centuries in India and the patterns take new shapes and forms in these days. Shaw and Mckay noted that weak social organization permitted the development of a delinquent system whose values competed with the conventional one of the larger society. Police was or has been a powerful community within the society. They enjoyed a lot of power and authority. Some of them exceeded or misused or abused their powers or authority for securing personal gain or for securing advantages to other individuals/organizations and they did many things for administering justice or in the pretext of administering justice. A culture containing perverted values got developed and in such a value system, torture, illegal detention, arbitrary arrests, corruption, concoction of evidence etc. were justified. The British wanted an oppressive police and a culture got developed in India and the culture did not allow the police to act on behalf of the people as a whole. They acted for the British Government in power and the significance of their accountability to the people was overlooked. The culture continued to dominate police work even after the independence of the Country. To quote once again the observations of Shaw Commission: "Forging of records, fabrication of grounds for detentions, antedating of detention orders, the callousness with which the request of the detinues for revocation of orders of detention or even parole were ignored—in short, the manner in which a large majority of these persons were incarcerated for the only fault, namely, dissent or suspected dissent from the views of the centres of power, should be a warning to every thinking man as to how an Act initially intended to serve an extremely limited purpose to deal with the misdeeds of a special category of persons can be given such a wide and comprehensive application so as to embrace all sections of the population to penalise dissent". In the history of Indian police, similar strategies are seen adopted in many other areas of law enforcement. As early as in 1890, a committee appointed to study, *inter alia*, the existing system of and methods adopted in the investigation of crimes found that the police abused the word "truly" in section 161, Code of Criminal Procedure. The section related to the examination of witnesses during investigation. Police officers pressured witnesses to adhere in courts to the statements put into their mouths under circumstances in which the witnesses were helpless to say anything other than what the police told them to say. The police threatened them telling that prosecution for perjury would be initiated if they did not yield to police desires. The abuses were so many so much so that the word "truly" was later omitted under section 161 Code of Criminal Procedure. Whenever the police could manipulate law to their advantage, they did so without any consideration shown to administration of justice. This kind of culture has been transmitted from generation to generation until at last, as some critics might say, a criminal subculture emerged in police subculture.

Edwin H. Sutherland brought the concepts of favourable-unfavourable definitions of crime. In a nutshell, he said that those subgroups that approved of criminal behaviour would have higher violation rates than those subgroups that looked at crimes unfavourably. Police have a patterned set of values and the values have travelled a long way. Look into the reports of the police commissions appointed from the British period till date. The words like oppression, torture, corruption, concoction, crude behaviour, illegal detention, manipulation of records etc. are repeatedly used. Many judgements, media reports, people's experience, cultural programmes and real live situations endorse the same. They show that a culture favouring definition of what is unlawful has been in existence down the centuries. The police subgroup appears to condone such kinds of unlawful behaviour. In such a culture, the new entrants socialized by the police may be inclined to accept such values. The new entrants get opportunities to commit illegal acts with immunity. Coupled with it, there is the absence of departmental and social control. Resultingly, the new entrants to the police subculture may act out what they have seen, heard and experienced or have been taught. The police subculture favours criminal acts and behaviour.

Opportunities and Police Crimes

Police as the law enforcement agency gets any number of opportunities to violate laws with immunity. The police can take a person into their custody and employ torture. Police may interrogate a suspect in isolation and that facility itself is an opportunity to employ torture on the interrogated. A policeman working in the police computer centre does not accept corruption money from the members of the public, for he does not get opportunities for the same. He is not in a position which helps him to violate the law. The director general of police may not manipulate a F.I.R. If at all opportunities are available in plenty, one may not commit crimes if the subculture is not favourable to him. For example, many political leaders are interrogated by police, but there comes no allegation that they are tortured by the police. Why? The reason is that the police subculture favours torturing of people who are in the low socio-economic strata of the society. Central Committee on Police Training and National Police Commission had pointed out this fact in several places in their reports. A scantly dressed man on road is a suspect for a policeman and a person who is a political orphan may be a victim of police torture. The culture in police is not against such behaviours. A subculture is a powerful force and is ever present in the police. I have heard police officers claiming that police torture, concoction of evidence, manipulation of records in certain situations/cases are *valued* behaviours in police subculture. The culture accepts such behaviours as appropriate and are accepted as proper by the police subgroup.

I consider police crimes as crimes committed by the powerful on the powerless. Hence, they are called acts of abuse of power and misuse of authority. Police culture as seen today permits such abuses and the police gets a lot of opportunities. This is seen in the simple shouting at people by epithets to nexus or Mafia crimes committed by individual policeman/officer as the case may be. The individual policeman/officer knows that he is committing a crime when he does so, yet he commits. It is not necessary that all who wear a police uniform indulge in police crimes. There are psychological and moral determinants of police criminality and they will be discussed in the next chapter. Yet, the "criminal traditions" existing in police subculture may provide opportunities to commit crimes and justify them.

Low Class Culture and Police Crimes

Policemen for centuries in India came from law social and economic backgrounds. In many correspondences during the British past, one may take note of the fact that the illiteracy, low socio-economic background and lack of self-esteem of the police constituting the constabulary were blamed to be some of the major causes of police deterioration in India. A certain categories of crimes—e.g., use of filthy language, acceptance of petty privileges and bribery etc.—are connected directly or indirectly to the illiteracy and low socio-economic background of the lower level functionaries. Just examine the values of lower-class culture. I must think that some of the crimes committed by policemen come out of the lower class culture to which they belong. Low class people use vulgar language more often than those who belong to the higher class. I do not think that they have a feeling that they are using obscene language when they speak in that way. Such words, expressions and manners come out of their lower class culture. Policemen in the British past were low paid Government servants. They were enjoying the status of labourers. The officers during the British regime were paid slightly better, but certainly poor in every sense. The higher and the highest echelons in the police had exorbitant salary. Necessarily, the disparity in pay, allowances, emoluments and perks between the lower and higher ranks make them desperate in life. The lower rank has a culture and every member of the lower rank desires social and economic mobility upwards. They can not go up through the legitimate ways and therefore they have recourse to illegitimate and illegal means to go higher and higher in economic status. Corruption, corruption-money fixing, corruption-money splitting, acceptance of graft/illegal remuneration etc. thus come into being. Every rank wants to go up to the next higher rank. Corruption, Mafia involvement, nexus criminality etc. lead many to affluence and influence. For some police officers, all behaviour is valued and they say that the police commit crimes because they can not commit crimes otherwise. A constable can commit crimes as a constable and not as a director general of police. A constable may create a witness in a criminal case whereas a director general of police may have monthly kickbacks or payoff from nexus criminals or crime syndicates. The lower level policemen, middle level police officers and the higher/highest level police authorities work together and they mutually see many of the crimes committed by everyone. In doing so, individual policemen/officers may aspire to achieve and acquire many human comforts, but do not get them as there are roadblocks. If that is the case, then police crimes may come into being. Man has the need and the man who commits crimes for gain is one who has the greed. The policeman is not an exception here. If one has the greed and he wants to make income, then he may involve in nexus transactions or may show low-class culture, namely, toughness, arrogance, rudeness, smartness and the like. They commit crimes after crimes and become better and richer. At the same time, the society accepts conventional images more highly than police criminality.

Culture Conflicts and Police Crimes

Society's cultural norms and the cultural norms practised and perpetrated by the police culture conflict each other. For example, use of epithets is a disapproved behaviour in the general culture of the society. The use of vulgar language may be an accepted norm in the police subculture. In any case, the norms in the two cultures conflict each other. Corruption and corrupt practices may be an accepted norm in police sub-culture, but they are not so in the general culture. Criminalization of police and police crimes are closely connected with the cultural norms the police has. Police culture in different countries may be different and may conflict each other.

The people and society reacted sharply to some of the criminal culture seen in police service. During the freedom struggle in India, the police were involved in wholesale arrests of the Congress leaders and the people reacted vehemently against the police actions. Even today, people react to police strategies when they realize that the police behave rudely with people just for satisfying some politicians or political parties in power. Shaw Commission found police officers who—

> "may have simply acted in compliance with the orders or instructions given to them"
>
> "may have carried out the instructions a little zealously than others"

And the orders were illegal and instructions were unlawful. After the internal emergency (1976-77), the public reactions to police atrocities and crimes in democratic India were unimaginably vehement. Society reacts to police crimes. The news media becomes critical to police crimes and they capture and hold public attention further. The police is an interest group and they organize their values. They have their own values in the investigation, prevention and control of crime, management of law and order, V.I.P. security, intelligence collection etc. In their value system, they adopt several strategies which are against the values which the society has. These values conflict each other. The police values may be based on gain, prestige, status etc. and the larger society may not accept such values.

Police Structure and Police Crimes

Has the police structure to do anything with police crimes? No scientific studies were conducted to know the relationship between police structure and crimes. Police has a pyramidal structure with the policeman at the bottom and the director general at the top. It is a hierarchy. The lower rank is subordinate to the higher rank and there is rigid and strict disciplinary control. Police Discipline, Inquiries, Punishments and Appeal Rules are in operation in many States so much so that strict disciplinary action can be initiated against the lower ranks for any misconducts without any difficulty. Though the Police Act says that subordinates are not bound to execute the illegal or unlawful orders of their superiors, the law in practice becomes different from the law in the book. Disobedience of orders is not possible in many situations. Some policemen/officers complain that they will be pressured to obey the superiors' orders which may not be always legal or lawful. Resultingly, police crimes may come into being. Frank Tannenbaum and William Bonger spoke about facilitating environment as an explanation of criminal behaviour. Accordingly, the structure of the police hierarchy and rigid disciplinary controls which the higher ranks have on the subordinates provide a facilitating environment not only to maintain peace and harmony in society, but also to commit police crimes, particularly torture, corruption and concoction etc. No crime can survive longer in police unless the hierarchy favours it. The police structure may create criminals and it is more so in simulated encounters, false registration of cases, employing torture on suspects etc. Crimes in police subculture are the manifestations of a pervasive police structure. The pervading police structure may act upon individual policemen/officers and provide a prevailing climate of motivations to commit crimes. The police structure theory has a defect and that is: "Why don't all policemen/officers living in the same police structure become police criminals?" The question is answered by sociologists. They bring some processes involved and according to them, these processes explain the differential reaction of policemen/officers to their environment.

Process Theories and Police Crimes

Gabriel Tarde (1843—1904) said that a man learnt crimes just like others learnt a trade through training and association with others. Imitation, he said, was the process by which people committed crimes. He put forward some laws of imitation and according to him, they were the basis for the causation of crimes. I think that Tarde's imitation may be a factor influencing some people to commit crimes. In any case, it can not be the only factor.

Tarde thought that man had the tendency to imitate another and this imitation was in proportion to closeness of one's contact with the other. In police crimes, no doubt, the imitation works. Police personnel work in closeness and certainly, one imitates another in certain situations. However, it can not be said that everyone imitates another in all kinds of police crimes. Tarde, however, did not speak anything about the importance of identification and suggestion in committing crimes. People have a tendency to identify with others. The identification can be with individuals, 'isms and values etc. If the police values are to achieve the goal by any means, some policemen/officers may resort to any foul/criminal means to reach their goals. Inculcation of values plays a role here and the values must be inculcated by people having an upright conscience. Policemen/officers may identify with individuals whom they take as their role models. If the role model is one who exhibits criminality, then the individuals who identify with such a role model may commit crimes.

Like identification, suggestion too works as a powerful factor in the commission of crimes. The suggestions can be from the society or from other individuals. The suggestion can be conscious or unconscious. There can be autosuggestions as well. A corrupt police officer may emit suggestion and a policeman with a weak ego structure may become a prey to such suggestions. Relative deprivation may be a powerful suggestion to one who feels so.

Differential Association Theory and Police Crimes

Earlier, the views of Edwin H. Sutherland were discussed. He is known for his differential association theory. He speaks about the criminalization process and the salient points of his theory are:—

1. Criminal behaviour is learned, or stated another way, criminal behaviour is not inherited. I differ from Sutherland's view as I find that learning may be one of the several ways a person studies how to commit crimes. As far as police crimes are concerned, the learning process is just one among the many processes.
2. Criminal behaviour is learned in interaction with others in a process of communication, verbal and non-verbal. What about the first crime which man committed in society? Adam and Eve violated God's commands and the cause for the violation of the divine law was, as the Bible says, devil's instigation and man's innate deprivity. I agree with Sutherland that the process of communication may be one of the several ways

people learn to commit crimes. As far as police crimes are concerned, each crime differs from the other. When a policeman/ officer decides to manipulate a record or concoct an evidence, he does so, sometimes, in isolation and for the first time in his life. An intelligent policeman/officer creates crimes and I believe that there is no need to teach a man how to commit crimes. He commits them unless he is controlled by an external or an internal or both forces.

3. The principal learning of criminal behaviour, Sutherland says, occurs within intimate personal groups. According to him, impersonal agencies of communication such as movies, newspapers etc. play a relatively minor part in the genesis of criminal behaviour. Intimate personal group is something which is not clear. Because of transport and communication, the world has become very small. Man learns through several ways—even through internet, satalite communications—and Sutherland's view that impersonal agencies of communication play relatively a minor role in the genesis of criminal behaviour is not acceptable. News papers, films etc. are not impersonal agencies of communication. As far as police crimes are concerned, there are crimes which are committed in extreme isolation and no intimate personal groups may teach such crimes. Planting evidence on a scene of crime secretly may be a police crime which no intimate personal group can teach. An element of creativity comes here.

4. Sutherland speaks about the learning of criminal behaviour and according to him, the learning includes—

(a) techniques of committing the crimes—sometimes complicated, sometimes simple—and

(b) the specific direction of motives, drives, rationalizations and attitudes.

His arguments are equally applied to all types of learning. I find that no one can commit a crime as he is taught or as he has learnt. Every crime is a new crime and no criminal generally wants to be detected. If one wants to avoid detection of crimes, he can not and does not reproduce a crime as he has learnt it. In police crimes, particularly in concocting evidence and in manipulating records etc. there is a court to study and scrutinize the evidence produced with the help of learned lawyers. Hence, the techniques of committing crimes must be unique in every case.

5. For Sutherland, the specific direction of motives and drives is learned from favourable or unfavourable definitions of the legal code. As far as police crimes are concerned, there are many crimes in which the policemen/officers are not concerned with the favourable or unfavourable definition of the legal codes. The police have to register cases, detect criminals, investigate crimes and in so doing they commit crimes and that is what is seen in the manipulation of F.I.Rs, recording of false witness statements, registering false cases and what not? The policemen/officers repeat their crimes like a recidivist and they are not caught as offenders/criminals. Whenever the people who are to register, investigate and detect crimes commit crimes, all the theories put forward to explain other types of crimes committed by people outside the law enforcement cease to have any validity.
6. For Sutherland, a person becomes delinquent because of an excess of definitions favourable to law violations over definitions unfavourable to violations of law. "Favourable or unfavourable to violation of law"—this is not an issue of serious concern for the police. For, they enforce law. They interpret law. They decide the favourable/unfavourable aspects of laws and their violations etc. All these theories are applicable to crimes committed by people outside the police department. Abuse of power and misuse of authority, use of muscle power and employment of third degree methods etc. of police can not be treated as crimes just because there is a favourable definition of law for its violation.
7. Differential association may vary in frequency, duration, priority and intensity. Police department deals with crimes and criminals. Police crimes take place in an environment pregnant with crimes and their investigation and detection. In such an environment, frequency, duration, priority and intensity have no meaning and relevance. Policemen/officers get ample opportunities to involve themselves in the commission of various types of enforcement crimes, nexus criminality and crimes of traditional nature.
8. According to Sutherland, the process of learning criminal behaviour by association with criminal and anticriminal patterns involves all of the mechanisms required in any other learning. Admitting that learning is a process in police crimes, it may be accepted that it is not the only process[4].

   Sutherland was not dealing with police crimes or enforcement criminality. His theory would account for crimes in other areas other than police crimes. Personality factors and opportunities are important in police crimes. He just asserted that criminal behaviour was determined in a process of association. But he did not explain the process in clear terms. Instead, he said that criminal behaviour was determined by the quantity of the contacts with criminal patterns—i.e., the relation was proportional—the greater the number, the higher is the rate of contamination. What about the personal and social differences in resistance or immunity to contamination? According to Sutherland, all are equally vulnerable. The degree of exposure to criminal patterns decided the fact whether or not one escaped or succumbed to crimes. All policemen/officers exposed to corruption and corrupt practices do not/need not become corrupt officials. At the same time, they are always exposed to various types of crimes committed by people and the members of the police service. If contact and frequency, intensity and duration etc. of the contact with criminal patterns/ criminals decide the crimes, then the policemen/officers have no option but to become criminals. Every policeman/officer gets enough opportunities to meet, mix and mingle with criminals of all descriptions. Nevertheless, it does not mean that they become criminals and commit crimes which the people in society do commit.

Crimes by People and Crimes by Police

There is a lot of difference between the crimes committed by people and the crimes committed by police. When a murder is committed by a man, the police have to register a F.I.R. When a F.I.R. is registered, the police may manipulate the F.I.R. in such a way that the murderer is convicted or is acquitted as the case may be on the basis of the manipulation in the F.I.R. Doubtlessly, the police commit a crime here when they manipulate the F.I.R. Usually a murderer is not a recidivist whereas the manipulator of F.I.Rs is. Police crimes are repeated and recidivism may be seen in police crimes and criminals. Gabriel Tarde, Edwin H. Sutherland, Williiam Bonger and so on do not talk anything about the recidivism in police service. They deal with crimes committed by people and not by the members of the enforcement machinery. Tardian imitation, Sutherland's differential association etc. are not of much use to explain police crimes and criminality. Police crimes can not be accounted for in terms of contact with others who indulge in criminal patterns. Police crimes are committed, sometimes, entirely alone or in secret and rarely reveal or expose them to their friends, subordinates or superiors.

Self Concept and Containment Theory

W.C. Reckless and Simon Dinitz proposed self-concept and containment theory to explain crimes and criminal behaviour. Their theory holds the view that if an individual possesses a favourable self-concept, then he is directed toward law abiding behaviour. Otherwise, i.e., unfavourable self-concept, he is directed toward delinquent behaviour. How far does the theory explain police crimes? How to measure the self-concept of police officers? No studies were conducted in that area. I have interviewed many policemen/officers with an intention of understanding their self-concepts. I have found them justifying many police crimes, rationalizing police criminality and glorifying police officers who were notorious in committing police crimes. I have found only a very few policemen/officers who admitted police crimes as crimes. Some reluctantly admitted the fact that police did commit crimes while they enforced the law.

'Society needs a police force which commits police crimes'—that is what some police officers argue when they justify police criminality. 'Every society gets a police force it deserves'—they substantiate their arguments further. Policemen too are a part of the society and therefore the policemen show the same and similar character of the members of the society. When the society itself is criminal, there is no meaning in going after police criminals—they argue further. Amidst their arguments and counter arguments, I could observe that they admitted the reality that police crimes were a reality from the time the service was instituted. The reality continued from its inception and is still continuing.

Confusion on Crimes and Labeling of Police Crimes

Society and policemen label a person who commits a crime as a criminal. When the same act is committed by a policeman, then he is not labelled as a criminal. For example, when a man is forcibly taken into custody by another man, then the act is called abduction. When he is confined in a room, then the act is labelled as 'wrongful confinement. Likewise, when a man who has not committed a cognizable crime is taken forcibly by a police officer, it is called 'informal arrest' and when he is detained unlawfully in a police station, then it is called "illegal detention". Why? There is a double standard in approach to one and the same act. One act is branded as a crime when it is committed by a man on the street whereas it is not called so when it is committed by a policeman/officer. Police initiate prosecution in the former case and no prosecution in the latter case. Why? The police do not measure the same act using the same scale. Instead of initiating action against the policeman/officer for the crime he commits, he is glorified. The police filter out the same act in different ways. It is the police who decide whether or not a particular action should be treated as a crime. The penal laws do not have much to do in such situations. The criminal act of a person, irrespective of the fact that he is a policeman nor not, must be taken to decide upon the nature of the offence.

When a man is beaten on the road by another man, a case is registered against the offender. When a man is beaten in police custody, no case is usually registered. When a record is manipulated by a man, a case for forgery is registered. When a record is manipulated during the course of investigation, it is called "strengthening the evidence" for a successful prosecution. Torture under police custody is known as 'depth interrogation'. Criminologists show how the police can manipulate crimes to their advantage? Obviously, the law does not justify such actions, justifications and discriminations. What the police do are not the crystallization of the general will of the people, but the result of the perverted way the police look at their own crimes and crimes committed by people in society.

Human rights movement in India—before and after the passing of the Protection of Human Rights Act-1993—and its demands for justice exerted a powerful appeal on the police, people and authorities to look at police crimes as crimes under the penal laws. Public litigation societies and individual citizens took police crimes to courts of law. After India became independent, people approached the courts with private complaints against the police for many things they did in the name of law enforcement or in the pretext of law enforcement. The courts of law accepted the complaints and took cognizance of police crimes. After 1993, the human rights laws got more acceptance and recognition with the enactment of the Protection of Human Rights Act.

Today human rights activists go after police crimes and try to get compensation for any human rights violations. Nevertheless, other types of police crimes and enforcement criminality remain to be unattended. Police crimes are:—

1. Abuse of power, arbitrary arrests, attack on innocents etc.
2. Bribery.
3. Corruption, corruption-money fixing, contamination of evidence etc.
4. Detention in illegal custody, detinue harassment, humiliating detainees etc.

5. Encounters—simulated, epithets in police language etc.
6. Falsifying records, false entries, false arrests, fake evidence and false witnesses, fist approach etc.
7. Graft, acceptance of favours, privileges, concoction of evidence, coercion, making of false promises etc.
8. Haphazard way of investigation, hurried closure of cases, half-hearted police work etc.
9. Interrogation in depth, interviewing indecently, indecent language at the public etc.
10. Justice delayed, judgements made without evidence, justness overlooked etc.
11. Kickbacks, payoff, degrading treatment, disgraceful dealings, oppression, overlooking of just administration etc.
12. Laying of false evidence in courts, illegal searches, ignoring of evidence.
13. Mooching, manipulation of records, manhandling, muscle power showing.
14. Nexus criminality, enforcement crimes, collaboration with underworld criminals etc.
15. Organized defiance to authority, police strikes, omissions to do the duty legally bound to do.
16. Partiality, parochialism, prejudices shown during law enforcement.
17. Questioning in an unauthorized way using questionable methods—by unqualified/underqualified interrogators.
18. Responding negatively, indifferently and culpably to people's needs.
19. Sweet-heart dealings, susceptibility to political pressures and the affluent in society.
20. Trickery employed for getting a conviction, thefts of seized articles from a scene of crime/search etc.
21. Undercover surveillance in an illegal way, underhand dealings for miscarriage of justice etc.
22. Venemous dealing with people involved in communal riots, political strikes etc. and victimizing the powerless and the defenceless.
23. Witnesses—tutored, false, disinterested—produced for defeating the prosecution cases.
24. Yielding to pressures, parties, 'isms', 'ologies', vested interests etc.

25. Zealous and overzealous enforcement of law violating human rights.

The conventional style of studying crimes and criminals has focused on the crimes committed by people outside the police and law enforcement machinery. Criminologists ask questions mainly about their crimes. They ask the policemen, the law and themselves the question: "who is a criminal?" And they get an answer to their question that a criminal is a person who violates the law and the person so doing is outside the police. Today they ask the question: "Who is a criminal in police?" The answer to the question gives the extent of police crimes. They ask further question: "Why do the police commit crimes?"—"What are the crimes usually committed by the police?"—What way can the society prevent police crimes?" The question and answers to the questions give birth to a new branch in criminology and it is nothing but Police Criminology.

Police Crimes and their Effect on Society

Not much has been done to date to study the impact of police crimes on society. Police crimes do make the people to lose their trust and confidence on police. 34 years ago, a Christian priest was arrested for allegedly murdering a woman. The Sessions Court convicted him for death. The High Court acquitted him as found not guilty. Today's paper brings a news that the real murderer of that woman was a different person and a clean confession made by the children of the killer to the priest has raised a number of questions on police crimes including the nature of witnesses produced by the police to see that the priest was convicted by the Court of Sessions.

Any research study on police hitherto conducted, though does not speak of police crimes, does give a negative view on many of the police doings. In earlier chapters, the views of the committees and commissions on police were exposed to some extent. One does not find significant differences between the police crimes during the pre-independence period and post-independence period. The police crimes which were in existence during the colonial rule continue to exist in the democratic India today and that too after 50 years of freedom. In some areas like nexus crimes and encounter crimes, the picture has become darker. Police officers who are caught for crimes and human rights violations are more negatively evaluated by the people than those who are not caught. For example, corruption in police is accepted by the society, but a police officer caught for corruption is negatively evaluated. People avoid them as criminals. When a single policeman/officer is caught and punished for police crimes, the entire department and all personnel working therein are viewed as criminals. On the other hand, when a teacher is caught and convicted for an offence, the people and society do not look at all teachers in the teaching community as offenders. Each policeman is a legion and the social reaction to police crimes is generally against all personnel in police department and not against a particular individual caught and convicted for the alleged crimes. The negative evaluation is always followed by negative consequences.

The policemen/officers who admit that they are involved in the commission of many types of police crimes admit further the society's disapproval of police service. The way they see themselves is the way people look at them. Police is considered as a crime control apparatus and they are also viewed as a crime committing apparatus. Crimes are seen as a normal part of the police community. The police have power and authority, but they misuse the power/abuse their authority and people call their acts as crimes.

Some policemen/officers maintain the view that police crimes can never be eliminated since they perform an important social function. When the people see the atrocious and animal like policeman, they become afraid of the police and the fear caused by the deterrent policeman is sufficient to effect control on crimes. Police crimes thus become necessary and inevitable for social welfare. However, the advocates of that school of thought do not say anything about nexus criminality by police officers or police collaboration in Mafia crimes/underworld criminals or involvement in corruption and other corrupt activities. The impact of police crimes on society is very much detrimental to the functioning of the police system in a democracy.

Every individual policeman/officer, precisely by reason of his power and authority is entrusted the duty to administer fair justice. Hence every threat to just justice administration must be necessarily felt in his very heart. But police crimes, like any other crimes in society, cause alarm and anxiety among the people. Whatever is opposed to fair justice administration such as arbitrary arrests, nexus crimes, enforcement criminality as well as disgraceful enforcement of law is an infamy to police and to democracy. Sociology of police crimes may not be able to offer a full explanation to the emerged and emerging crimes in police service. Yet, we may say that all police crimes are caused and there may be several causes behind each type of police crimes. The causes behind corruption and corrupt practices may be different from the causes behind employment of coercion and third degree methods. The reasons behind nexus crimes and enforcement criminality may be different from the reasons behind misappropriating valuables from the scene of crime/search. Mable A. Elliott and Francis E. Merril speak about multiple causation theories in juvenile delinquency. According to them there is no single predisposing factor leading inevitably to delinquent behaviour. I think that the causes of police crimes are many and my analysis of individual instances of police crimes confirms the fact that there are not less than six or seven factors which influence a police officer/policeman to indulge in police crimes.

A policeman has his inherited and acquired qualities—both good and bad. He works in a situation and there will be the pressures of the situation and the weakness of the social order. The inherited and acquired strengths/ qualities of a policeman/officer help him to withstand the pressures exerted by the situation. A policeman/officer who has the strength of character can steer his course without deflection even in the façe of very powerful external or situational or sociological pressures. Nevertheless, if the policeman/officer is supercharged with ego-weaknesses and emotional disturbances he may drive himself off course owing to the situational pressures/sociological factors. The situations a policeman may have to face with are social, economic, departmental, political, health, familial or anything of similar nature. If he has no qualities and strength of character in him, he may resort to police crimes to manage the situation. The weakness of the system may help to accelerate the expression or criminal tendencies in a policeman/officer. The disruptive impact of the police organization may be a factor in police crimes. Hence a criminologist studies both the predisposing and precipitating causes behind police criminality. The history of police in India does not provide a good background for a crime-free police culture. The post-independence history too is not favourable to a crime-free police culture. Moreover, there is the personal disorganization which is different from the social disorganization within the police department. Of course, personal disorganization may result from the social (here, the police departmental disorganization) disorganization. Throughout the history of Indian police, one takes note of the fact that the people and the governments take steps and measures to correct the police when disorganization comes into being. Police commissions/committees are appointed and they suggest remedial measures. Organization—disorganization—reorganization and that is the continuum and the social situations which create an environment for the police to indulge in crimes can be corrected provided there is a will for the same.

References

1. Anandswarup Gupta, *The Police in British India: 1861—1947*, Concept, Delhi, 1979.
2. Anandswarup Gupta, *op. cit.*
3. Anandswarup Gupta, *op. cit.*
4. Edwin H. Sutherland, *Principles of Criminology*, 4th ed., Lippincott, Philadelphia, 1947.

CHAPTER—8

Psychology of Police Crimes

The Crime in India—1998 published by the National Crime Records Bureau, Ministry of Home Affairs, Government of India writes: "To take a person in custody is to limit his freedom. Taking advantage of such a situation, the custodian may attempt to commit crime on the person under custody. Individuals come under the police custody for various reasons like arrest, police remand or even where the custody *per se* is unauthorized. Most prevalent crime in police custody are: "assault of various types, rape and murder[1]". Though the National Crime Records Bureau say so, they do not analyse the causes of police crimes or suggest remedial measures. However, the Bureau call such acts custodial crimes. Custodial crimes are as old as organized policing in India, but no serious studies on the psychological causes of custodial crimes were ever conducted. Is there something called "the *criminal mind*" of the policeman? Though custodial crimes have been reported throughout the Country down the centuries—from Torture Commission—1855 and before—no one was sent for any psychiatric examination. Even in the blinding case or in the crude custodial rape of Maya Thyagi, the policemen were not subjected to a psychiatric examination. In the notorious case of Rajan murder or in any other cases of custodial violence, no psychiatric examination was/is proposed. The question is: "Are the police crimes the result of a particular type of mind possessed by individual policemen/officers?"

Psychologists have not devoted much time to study the psychology of police crimes although a lot of psychological researches were conducted to learn the psychology of crime and criminal behaviour. Prior to the development of more scientific theories on the psychology of crime, people believed in demonology, innate depravity, exorcism etc. *Trephining* was practised during the stone age and it was meant to allow the evil spirit to go out. Flogging and other forms of corporal punishments were given to banish the evil spirits, Witchcraft too was seen during the later part of the fifteenth century. All of them were based on superstitions and unscientific or prescientific explanations of crime and criminal behaviour. Psychology of crime, as a scientific discipline, developed only in the beginning of twentieth century and therefore it is quite understandable that the Torture Commission—1855 did not think seriously about the psychology of police torture and other degrading treatments. The Indian Police Commission: 1902-03 and even the National Police Commission: 1977—81 did not consider the issue of police crimes from psychological angles. No psychologist—not even a criminologist was seen in the Commissions.

Psychological Theories of Police Crimes

Henry H. Goddard said that people who possessed a high I.Q. were law abiding. According to him, law grade mentality was the greatest single cause of crime and delinquency. Whenever the police functionaries in the British India were found to have involved in the commission of crimes, to have proved their inefficiency in detecting crimes, to have manifested criminal tendencies in their duties, then they were blamed to suffer from low intelligence. In 1867-68, the inspector general of police, Bengal region pointed out that the "weak point" in police was the want of intelligent, well educated police officials[2]'. Eversince, the lack of intelligence, illiteracy and lack of education etc. were time and again brought out as the principal cause of their misconduct, indiscipline, inefficiency, ineffectiveness, failure etc. in their police service. Are we right, agreeing with Goddard, to say that the low I.Q. level of the police functionaries is the most important single cause of police criminality? I do not and can not agree with Goddard or other committees/commissions who made similar observations. Senior and very senior level police functionaries are detected to have involved in many types of crimes—both traditional and modern including nexus crimes—and that alone is enough to disprove Goddard's theory on crimes.

By the beginning of twentieth century, psychologists succeeded in developing relatively objective and reliable techniques for measuring, describing and comparing the test responses of a large number of people. By the help of Simon—Binet scale, the scientists attempted to differentiate the I.Q. level of the criminals to that of non-criminals of all ages. After the World War I, researchers proved that low I.Q. level had little or no significance in crime caution.

Crimes committed by police may be calling of epithets to participation in crime syndicates/nexus criminality etc. and therefore the I.Q. level does not have anything significant to do with police crimes. The I.Q. level may decide how well they will be able to commit crimes—rather than whether or not they must become criminals. Factual evidence shows that police officers well qualified academically are caught for corruption and corrupt practices; for employment of torture and other degrading treatment. They exhibit higher intelligence than many other types of offenders. If only a police officer has a high I.Q., he will be able to concoct evidence in criminal trials or manipulate records for a successful prosecution.

Dispositional Theories and Police Crimes

Physique and certain psychical dispositions were related and in 1926, Ernst Kretschmer authored a book titled "Physique and Character". According to him there were *asthenic* (leptosome), *athletic* and *pyknic* types among the people. *Athletic* had developed skelton and muscles. *Asthenic* was a long and skinny individual. *Pyknic* was small and round. Kretschmer associated a type of temperament with each body type. The *athletic* body type and *asthenic* body were related to crime and delinquency. The British recruited robust people with good physique and muscle growth as they wanted an oppressive police force in India. They were given physical training and thereby strengthened their muscles. Intellectual instructions were not seriously given and thus no proper socialization of police was meaningfully ensured. Perhaps, the mental disposition to employ torture, violence etc. in custody was due to the athletic body type of the policemen. William H. Sheldon measured the physique and compared the body type to temperament. He found a high correlation between physique and temperament. He classified people into ectomorph, endomorph and mesomorph. Mesomorph was the athletic type. Glueck studied on Shedon's classification and found that mesomorphy was stronger among the criminals and delinquents. Of course there were criticisms against Kretschmer's, Sheldon's and Glueck's observations. Yet, the fact remains that the police even today prefer to recruit *athletic* body type and more researches are required to confirm the fact whether or not the athletic body type of the lower level functionaries have anything to do with the custodial torture of the people under police custody. I for one think that the physique, the athletic body type and the muscle of the police functionaries provide a psychological disposition to have recourse to violence and related behaviour patterns.

H. J. Eysenck and a few other researchers argued that extroverts were less easily socialized and were more likely to show criminal behaviour. Police service is a man oriented service and necessarily many police functionaries are extroverts. They can not be introverts. Psychologists argue that adequate socialization becomes essential for a person not to show criminality and criminal behaviour. The complaint against the police functionaries is that they are not adequately socialized during their induction training period. Some say: "A *man* goes to police training centres and returns as a *policeman*" and they mean that a man without proper/adequate socialization. Researches are required to establish the relationship among police training, socialization and police crimes. The Central Committee on Police Training writes: "Training is a conscious effort to impart, improve or increase knowledge and skills and to develop attitudes and values of an individual in a desired direction".

Instinct Theories and Police Crimes

Man is an animal—but with a difference, i.e., he is a rational animal. Both men and animals have instincts and they express them. Animals express them as they want and men express them if they are not controlled. In any case, some criminologists believe that every human being is a potential criminal. When man is compared to animals, man is more aggressive than animals. He is more destructive and dangerous. When man's instinctual energy is thwarted by some external forces/environmental roadblocks, then his aggressive drives may be expressed if not controlled either by an internal force or by an external force (in some cases by both).

Aggression can be expressed in many ways—directly or indirectly, physically, verbally, vicariously etc. Use of torture, abusive expressions, epithets, harassing the suspects/their dependents, humiliating people or committing human rights violations etc. may be the expressions of aggression which are not controlled. Because of the muscle power and strong physique, some of them express their aggressive drives as they want them to be expressed. This is seen from the inception of police force and even now when the police force has been converted to a police service.

Uncontrolled expression of the instinctual drives means lack of proper socialization and maturity. I have a number of case studies relating to policemen/officers who expressed uncontrolled instinctual drives—namely aggression and I have specially taken note of the fact that they suffered childhood frustrations and neglect. Their socialization at home and school has been inadequate and did not have proper cultural development. They did have physiological maturation, but not psychological and moral maturation. Resultingly they expressed their uncontrolled passion, eruption of aggression drives, disobedience, violence etc. Psychologists may further argue that the police discipline becomes a myth and one does not see it when police express aggression and destructiveness when they interact with people or materials. How can the police become rebellious and express their uncontrolled passion if they are properly disciplined and adequately socialized?

Psychologists engaged themselves and concentrated upon criminal behaviour from evaluating the personality factors of offenders. The 'trait approach' attempted to find out a consistent and relatively stable and constant picture of the inner structure and mental functioning of an individual so that one can very well predict another's behavioural patterns. The personality trait psychologists presume that one can very well predict the behaviour of a certain person at a given situation through his traits. Then a question arises: "What are the specific psychological traits which make a policeman/officer to be crime prone?" I have conducted some studies and attempted to observe the projected personality traits among police functionaries. Evidence in hand proves that a policeman's/officer's behaviour varies markedly from situation to situation, from problem to problem and from role to role. There is differential treatment of offenders and differential law enforcement. Moreover a policeman shows changes in his behaviour when the performs his special roles in a given situation. A policeman who becomes aggressive when he is performing his duties as a person in the general executive branch changes his behavioural patterns when he works in the intelligence wing. He makes adjustments to the changing realities. The major difficulty, as I observe, with the trait approach has been the powerlessness of the static components or constructs to anticipate the complex variability of police responses. I do not think that there is any relationship between the personality traits of police functionaries and the crimes they commit. I can not say that the personality traits of policemen/officers cause police crimes. My studies do not indicate whether the criminal behaviour of police personnel is the result of certain personality traits in them. The personality traits observed among policemen/officers are seen in all people and therefore I can not isolate a single personality trait/group of personality traits in policemen/officers not found among other people.

Then a second question is asked and that is: "What do psychological traits do in criminal behaviour? I observe that the personality traits among policemen/officers do not ordinarily determine whether or not a policeman/ officer must commit a crime, rather they determine how he may function as a criminal if he commits a crime. For example, a policeman/officer who has a projected personality trait like immorality can decide how he will function as an immoral man in case he commits a crime. Similarly, the dishonesty, aggressiveness, insincerity in a policeman will not make him to commit a police crime, rather such traits will decide how he will function as a criminal in case he commits a police crime. There are instances in which corrupt policemen/officers investigate corruption cases. Such officers need not become corrupt when they investigate corruption cases. If they decide to become corrupt, then they will be corrupt to the maximum.

Conscience and Police Crimes

Hans Eysenck says: "Propensity to crime is universal, but is held in check in most cases by a given person's conscience". What about the conscience of a policeman? The conscience is not formed one day, too soon. It is not formed after a recruit has been selected for police training. The 'conscience', as Eysenck says, is essentially a generalized set of conditioned responses built up during childhood and adolescence. According to him, the 'conscience' is expected to be underdeveloped either through a failure of social and family conditions to provide the proper means of developing it or through innate weakness in the person concerned of the mechanism involved in the elaboration of conditioned responses. If a recruit who comes to police training has an underdeveloped conscience, he is, in all probability, to involve in the commission of crimes. If the policization is inadequate, he is certain to commit police crimes without any guilt feelings or prick of conscience. However, no research studies were conducted to know the development of the human conscience among those who commit police crimes. What I have observed may be of some relevance here. Policemen/officers who indulge in the commission of police crimes generally do not feel guilty and precisely therefore, it is presumed that they suffer from an inadequately conditioned human conscience in an upright way. Once a clinical psychologist administered a test to a batch of police trainees and he found out that some of them suffered from an underdeveloped conscience. I do not know the validity of the test he administered, yet the fact remains that there is the need to screen candidates with an adequate development of human conscience in them for police job.

Psychoanalytic Theories and Police Crimes

Sigmund Freud (1856—1939) introduced the concept of '*unconscious*' and emphacized that all human behaviour was motivated or purposive. According to him, man has urges, ideas, desires and instincts. They are basic to man, but he represses them as the morality does not permit their naked expression. They are natural 'drives' and they come naturally. For him, the original nature of man is 'assertive and aggressive'. All people have criminalistic tendencies. This is the reason why socialization becomes essential for human beings. During the socialization process, man learns to control his criminalistic tendencies. Resultingly, he develops strong and effective self controls. If his socialization is adequate, he does not commit crimes. If at all he commits crimes, he feels guilty for what he has done. Socialization takes place during infancy and childhood and an improperly socialized child does not develop an ability to control his instincts and impulses.

A policeman/officer who becomes aggressive or who employs torture in his work is one who has not developed adequate self-controls. If he does not feel guilty when he does so or commits a crimes, it means that he had an improperly socialized childhood.

For the psychoanalytic school, the human personality consists of three elements. The *ego*, *superego* and *id*. *Id* is the reservoir of urges, desires, drives and instincts. The society's dos and don'ts form the *superego*. Superego is otherwise called the *human conscience*. The ego makes attempts to achieve an acceptable balance between the *id* and the *superego*.

Whenever a policeman commits a crime, it means that the development of the superego is inadequate in him or he had such an *id* energy in him that he can not but commit the crime. Hence, psychoanalytic school believed that an inadequate formation of the superego or an overeffect of the *id* complexes causes crimes. In police, the superego already formed during the infancy/childhood is further developed by adequate policization. If the policization too is inadequate, there is all likelihood for a police officer to indulge in the commission of crimes and it is very high particularly when the police officer's superego formed during his early childhood too is inadequate or weak.

Alfred Adler (1870—1937) developed the concept of *inferiority complex*. According to him, some people suffering from an inferiority complex commit crimes just for getting the attention of others. Applying his views on police crimes, one may say that police crimes, to some extent, are the results of inferiority complex which policemen/officers suffer from. This explanation may be more correct in the cases of nexus criminality and other sweet heart dealings to make exorbitant profits by means of committing crimes. They want to become richer very soon and the richness may help them to compensate their sense of inferiority. The explanation is valid in the case of corruption and corrupt practices, in participating in gang activities and the activities of underworld criminals and in becoming susceptible to political pressures and to the pressures of the affluent and the powerful. Those who commit police crimes are recidivists. Carl Gustav Jung (1876—1960) popularized the concepts of extrovert and introvert which might explain police crimes which have the characteristics of recidivism.

Psychoanalytic school speaks about the overdevelopment of ego and its relationship with the commission of crimes. In police, during the initial stage of their training, a lot of tough training methods are resorted to. The police subculture permits such a hard physical training. Resultingly, some become aggressive, rough, unyielding, cruel etc. and they express such traits when they interact with people. Owing to the misconception relating to the development of human personality, some police trainers think that effective policing can be ensured only if the ego of the trainees is overdeveloped.

Identity Theories and Police Crimes

What is the role which must be played by a policeman/officer in society? If a policeman/officer does not have a clear picture of his role as a policeman/officer, he suffers from an identity crisis. The identity crisis well be typified by '*role diffusion*' or an acute lack of ability to decide upon the role a policeman/officer must play in a society. Erikson explains the importance of the identity crisis, role diffusion etc. in the commission of crimes. The policeman who drinks, who is indifferent in his work, who is lethargic and does not care the people etc. commits police crimes and Erikson's views on role diffusion may explain such criminal behaviours better than many other psychological theories.

Distorted perception of self and lack of self-esteem may cause police crimes. Police uniform, power and authority make some to think too much about themselves and they develop distorted perceptions of their selves. Such people may exercise authority which they do not have or may show pseudo-authority. It has been noticed by me that policemen/officers who commit police crimes, generally, have a low opinion about themselves and about those who commit similar crimes. They have contempt of them and others. They suffer from low-esteem and self-hatred. They curse their uniform and their authority which they have abused/misused.

Psychiatry and Police Crimes

Do the policemen/officers who commit police crimes suffer from any specific mental disorders? No studies have been conducted to know the truth and no policeman/officer who is detected to have involved in the commission of police crimes is usually sent for any psychiatric examination. It seems that there is virtually no psychiatric or neurological disorders that have not been linked in one way or other with crimes. Psychiatrists believe that every crime is causally related to some mental diseases. If so, police crimes too are related to some mental disorders. Researches conducted give contradictory findings. Some studies show a high correlation between crime and mental disorders. Recent studies prove that a good majority of the law breaking people are normal individuals and they do not suffer from any psychoses, psychoneuroses etc. Paul Schilder, H. Warren Dunham and M.H. Erikson and so on hold the view that crime and mental disorders are not intimately connected.

I have not conducted any serious researches to know the cause-effect relationship between mental disorders and police crimes. Nevertheless, my close observations of some policemen/officers who indulge in the commission of police crimes make me to affirm the fact that it was difficult for me to establish the cause-effect relationship between mental disorders and crimes. At the same time, I observe that a policeman/officer can not perform his work as a policeman/officer if he is a psychiatric or neurotic patient. But he does his work well. Corrupt policemen/officers perform their duties very efficiently and so do those involved in the commission of nexus crimes and enforcement criminality. Many police crimes are to be executed very intelligently and to presume that all those policemen/officers are psychotic or psychoneurotic may be against factual evidence and reality. Just as any skilled work requires a high degree of personal adjustment, so does the police criminality. Seen in this perspective, the relationship between good psychological adjustment and police criminal behaviour may often be complimentary rather than reciprocal. The police officer who catches a policeman committing police crimes handles the calculating criminal with considerable apprehension and caution than he does with the neurotic or psychotic. Hence, I notice that police crimes and mental disorders are contrasted rather than equated. At the same time I have observed the policemen/officers who commit police crimes showing symptoms of psychopathy. Before discussing the relationship between police crimes and psychopathy, it may be necessary to deal with the theories of moral development and police crimes.

Theories of Moral Development and Police Crimes

E.M. Foder found that delinquents had a defective moral development compared with non-delinquents[3]. How is the moral development of the police functionaries who commit crimes? I have found that different policemen/officers have their own concepts about morality. One senior officer told me that legality and morality would not go together. Another officer said that police had to see that they did every thing legally and morality had nothing to do with legality. A third officer held the view that there was nothing called legal morality. A fourth one endorsed the view that morality was subjective and a fifth one affirmed that morality was nothing but lack of opportunity. All said and done, police crimes had a morality and a person who had an upright formation of a moral conscience would withdraw himself from committing police crimes.

Policemen/officers want to achieve their goals. But barries come in between them and their goals. In such situations, they feel frustrated. The drives in such motivated individuals, sometimes, make them to opt for illegitimate means to achieve their goals. When a police officer interrogates a suspect, he may create barriers so that the police interrogator can not get a confession from him. He feels frustrated and in such a frustrated mood, he may have recourse to aggression which may be a human right violation. Morality or moral sense of the police officer may exert little or no influence upon his behaviour.

Psychopathy and Police Crimes

Are the policemen/officers who commit crimes psychopaths? A psychopath is a person who is free from neurosis, psychosis or mental defectiveness. He knows the consequences of his behaviour, but does not have any inner feelings for what he does. He justifies and rationalizes his acts. He is not deterred by punishment[4]. Criminologists have found that psychopaths would appear in excessive numbers in criminal population and I endorse the same view as far as police crimes are concerned. Many who commit police crimes lack guilt feelings and are not afraid of punishments. They rationalize/justify their crimes under many counts. All policemen are not psychopaths, but most of those who commit police crimes are found to be psychopaths. Psychologists and psychiatrists have delineated various categories of psychopaths, but for them only one category is a criminal psychopath. A criminal psychopath thinks that his act is really warranted, reasonable and justified. Many who employ torture, participate in nexus criminality, concoct evidence etc. think so. They do not establish warm and interpersonal relationships. They suffer from a lack of superego conscience. They have ego centricism. A policeman with a psychopathic personality and who involves in the commission of police crimes is certainly a symbol of the failure of the justice system, police organization, democratic set-up and the society.

Attribution Theory and Police Crimes

"*Other people in police service do, it then why don't I?—why cann't I?*" The criminal policeman thus finds satisfaction in explaining away his criminal behaviour by *neutralization* or by *rationalization* or by *justification*. The rationalizations/justifications/neutralizations may be in different ways. They may attribute their criminal behaviour to the political set-up, to the poor salary, to status consciousness, to the economic conditions or to any such factors. The rhetoric may be good, but the reality is different. Those who say so may ultimately say that they are crime prone and that is the reason why they indulge in the commission of crimes. They find it extremely difficult to convince themselves with their arguments although they may be able to convince many others with their hollow arguments.

Relative Deprivation Theories and Crimes

A director general of police had a personal scooter and he used it for his personal journeys. Others who were occupying higher positions in the hierarchy started murmuring against him and even accused him of showing behaviours less than his dignity and status. He said that he could not maintain a luxurious life with others' money and illegal income. Such people are exceptional in any service. A study proved that people who had relative deprivation committed police crimes and involved in nexus criminality. They compare their position and income with those who occupy similar positions/higher positions and compare them. They feel desperate if they are not able to come closer to others in comparison. The relative deprivation, psychologists say, has a strong motivational force to make money through illegal/immoral ways. A luxury seeking wife at home, some children who are prodigal and so on may worsen the situation. Instances are not rare that policemen/officers who have faced such existential situations have committed suicide.

Inflated Ego and Paranoid Feelings

Megalomania is a type of delusion in which the subject considers himself possessed of greatness. He thinks that he is justice incarnate and he may think that he is everybody and everything in police administration. This is an abnormal case, but there are cases of lesser intensity and degrees. They may have delusions of grandeur and ego inflation. A person with an ego inflation may commit atrocities when he learns that his ego is hurt. Instances are there that policemen in groups have gone out of the camp to attack people who have misbehaved with a fellow colleague of theirs. The inflated ego is a cause of muscle-crimes and other types of behaviour which causes injury to people.

In paranoid personality, the person affected becomes hyper-sensitive, rigid, unwarrantedly suspicious etc. He often has an exaggerated sense of self importance. He wants to show that he is always right and others are wrong and has a tendency to blame others and to ascribe evil motives to them. Policeman/officer who enjoys a lot of power and authority conferred to him by law is a curse and burden if he is affected by a paranoid personality.

I am O.K.; You are Not O.K. Attitude

Power and authority which the policeman/officer enjoys by virtue of law help him to silence people in many occasions. An attitude of "I am O.K.; you are not O.K." taken by some policemen/officers becomes a root cause for many types of police crimes. Police crimes were not considered as harmful acts to society by the policemen themselves, instead they treated them as necessary and inevitable for the larger interest of the society. For example, a tutored witness was considered as a necessary evidence to get a conviction in a criminal trial. Although many courts pronounced acquittal verdicts on the basis of unbelievable and tutored witnesses giving testimony, no criminal actions were initiated against those who produced such tutored witnesses. This sort of lenient attitude gave an impression to law violators that they could afford to do anything with immunity. The collective reaction to police crimes was weak and it helped only to multiply enforcement crimes by police. Criminality by police got acceptance and the police started to behave as "I am O.K.; you are not O.K."

The Police Bureaucracy and Police Crimes

The police in India has a bureaucratic structure. The bureaucracy insists efficiency and enviable output in police actions. More often than not, individual policemen/officers can not ensure speedy efficiency if they perform their duties strictly in accordance to law and the procedure established by law. Skolnic in this context writes:

"The police in democratic society are required to maintain order and to do so under the rule of law. As functionaries charged with maintaining order, they are part of the bureaucracy. The ideology of democratic bureaucracy emphasizes initiative rather than disciplined adherence to rules and regulations. By contrast, the rule of law emphasizes the rights of individual citizens and constraints upon the initiative of legal officials. This tension between the operational consequences of ideas of order, efficiency and initiative on the one hand, and legality, on the other constitutes the principal problem of police as a democratic legal organization[5]".

Certainly, the police is in a dilemma and policemen/officers experience acute mental tension in such a psychological milieu. The bureaucracy wants quick results and the bureaucratic demands impose pressures on individual policemen/officers. The higher-ups in police headquarters may make telephone calls repeatedly—again and again—so much so that the subordinates may be forced to have recourse to all sorts of means/methods—fair or foul—to reach the goal. Accordingly an individual policeman/officer may violate the civil and legal rights of the suspects. On the one hand, the laws want to protect the rights of citizens and on the other hand, the police bureaucracy in a democracy pressures the individual policeman/officer to behave in an unlawful manner. In such a psychological and administrative set-up, police crimes become an inevitable outcome. In all democratic countries, therefore a number of laws has been framed to restrict and control the authority of policemen/officers.

Conflicts between Laws and Police Bureaucracy

Laws are made to control the police and the irony is that the police themselves violate the laws. Detection of crime and criminals is an objective of police bureaucracy. But how? The police must do it only as per law and procedure established by law. As an easy cut to detect crime and criminals, the police may employ torture indiscriminately and harass the kith and kin of the suspects etc. Can they do so? If they do so, they commit serious crimes and their strategies constitute blatant violations of law. During the internal emergency in India (1976-77), the police involved in the commission of large scale atrocities and crimes. In order to effect the arrests of people, the police in some States made a master copy of the grounds of arrests and then cyclostyled them for arresting anyone whom they did not like or they were pressured to arrest under instructions from the centres of power. After the period of emergency, many policemen/officers had sleepless nights and many police departments established policies aimed at reducing those forms of police crimes and misconducts. Police bureaucracy can not and must not come into conflict with the rule of law. A police bureaucracy must conform to the legal system. It must enforce and implement policies within the framework of law. According to Bernard Cohen . : . "..... police organizations have systematically violated the law, but this may be due to a malfunctioning bureaucratic structure or to external factors[6]".

Police Subculture, Police Psychology and Police Crimes

The police alone possess the exclusive and monopolistic authority to exercise legitimate physical and lethal force against the citizens. Precisely therefore, they can misuse their authority or abuse their power; precisely therefore, the police have a psychological advantage over others in doing so. Allegations are there that the police get money for torturing people and also for not torturing people! The police subculture is an informal collectivity of police functionaries whose work routinely brings them together into situations where they may use their power or misuse their power or use their authority or abuse their authority. The police subculture thus consists of a mixture of law enforcement and law violations. The same policeman/officer who enforces law violates the law. He registers cases against corruption and corrupt practices while he himself may be a corrupt individual and thus one may enumerate any number of examples to picture the police subculture. Police subculture has a psychological effect upon police crimes. Police subculture is a product of certain conditions inherent in the police work and the subculture may vary to some extent, from country to country and from time to time.

Police Fraternity and Police Crimes

Professional fraternity may be seen in all professions and among all professionals. They share the same experience. Policemen having trained on the same parade ground and having exposed to the same training and work situations have got a better chance to develop consciously or unconsciously a police fraternity which may be used or misused by them for their advantage. Corruption money-splitting may be an example of this sort of fraternity being misused.

Police bureaucracy may insist to do everything as per law and procedure established by law. But the police culture may not, as the rules in books can not be the rules in practice. Hence the police subculture develops many strategies which may be informal, but realistic for attaining the organizational objectives. The strategies developed by the subculture may be fair or foul and thus there exists a tension between the bureaucratic laws and subcultural strategies. The demanding public and the press too put several restrictions on police. The Legislature, makes laws for the police to observe. But the Legislature, people and the press usually do not take into account the different and various situations faced by policemen in reality. Generally, the different situations encountered by the police are of such a variety, uniqueness and complexity that the rules enacted by the Legislature can not be enforced as they are. The police subculture may violate some such rules and then the society and people are not found prepared to tolerate the police with understanding. Here too there exists a tension between the police subculture and people's demands. Police organization wants to call them '*police force*' while the people in society want to call '*police service*'. There is a lot of difference between the two. The National Police Commission: 1977—81 has been criticized by well-meaning members of the public for its constant and continuous use of the words 'police force' instead of 'police service' throughout the reports. The use of the words 'police force' has a psychological impact upon the members of the service to use their muscle power on and often—and sometimes when the force is not necessary at all. On one side, the police have a lot of rules and restrictions on the use of force and on the other side they are called 'police force'. Certainly, the "police force" may employ violent force on people and the police subculture may permit the employment of such violent forces on people. The people may resist the subcultural patterns and strategies and the members of the 'police force' will be addressed as 'police butchers", "mad dogs in police uniform", "police monsters" etc. Perhaps a change in the concept may create a corresponding change in police attitude and police crimes. Police force may be converted into a police service.

Legal Force, Necessary Force and Police Brutality

People are not against the police using legal force when situations arise. But they are against the use of unnecessary force. A person who resists an arrest must be subdued. The necessary force legally permitted may be used. The use of such necessary force is not called to be a police crime.

Having come to police custody, some policemen employ custodial torture on a person in his helpless and defenceless condition. This is objected to by the people as the use of force is unnecessary and unwarranted. Often such an attitude comes from the perverted notion about police force. Perhaps an initial use of some legal and necessary force was allowed, but the continuation and escalation of the same is in violation of law. It is no doubt a police crime.

Police brutality means brutality by the police just because they wear the police uniform. The policeman/officer abuses his position and exercises violent force for no reasons or for personal reasons. This type of police behaviour is little different from the routine violent behaviour of ordinary citizens or worse than their behaviour. Custodial violence, rape, harassment etc. are diabolic in nature.

Working Class, Violent Force and Police Crimes

What is the reason why are the constables recruited primarily from the working class—with less eduction? One reason for such a recruitment is that the administration knows well that the constables coming from such working class background will not hesitate to use violent force. If they are given hard physical training, then they may develop a brutal mentality. Whenever they face frustration during the training period—particularly on the parade ground—then they have no option but to repress their emotions/surcharged emotions to the frustrators. The repressed emotions may have to come out for reestablishing their disturbed homeostasis. Often, they can not express them as they are under rigid disciplinary control in police training institutions. In such situations, they may resort to aggression and I have observed the aggressiveness among police trainees. They make verbal attacks on their instructors or curse the situations. They may transfer their aggression to less powerful areas and psychologists say that the use of filthy language, torture on the helpless, violence against the defenceless etc. can be traced back to their frustrations and repressions during their training period or afterwards. This is otherwise called the transference of aggression.

Studies show that many constables to police service come from lower-class background—i.e., working class—and their educational achievements are not enviable. The officers at the lower level are found to come from a better economic class, but their educational achievements are not covetable. The police subculture thus is comprised by persons from lower—or—middle (a little less or above) backgrounds and they take up the job as they find the job as a means of upward mobility. They may become corrupt to earn more and many police constables opt for joining the general executive branch from battalions even overlooking their seniority and one of the motivating factors is to earn an extra income from their job. A police constable was candid enough to say that he used to get Rs. 60 everyday and he did not know from where the money was collected. A system worked very well and in such an established system, he could not but yield to the prevailing custom. He was afraid that he would be branded a "black sheep" if he objected to the system.

Studies conducted on American police proved that senior and very senior level police officers resorted to violence and involved in many other malpractices. The study proved further that police work for them was a means by which they expressed their need for violence through a more sophisticated structure and legitimate channel. I think that the study could be of great validity in India too. A person who has violent tendencies can transform it to a respectable force if he wears a police uniform.

Middle level, senior level and top level police officers are blamed to establish nexus with criminal businessmen, criminal politicians and underworld criminals to make their job more lucrative for them. One of the reasons for establishing such criminal nexus is the opportunity which those officers get to make a sophisticated structure a means for making exorbitant income for them. They may harass or create problems if the nexus criminals do not yield to their desires. The police have power and authority and together they make heavens on the earth.

A question is asked always by many from all walks of life. Why do the police come always in the picture when nexus crimes—such as bootlegging, gambling, prostitution etc.—are detected? Police alone are permitted to use force against citizens. They can fight against any evils in society. They are given power and authority under all penal laws to initiate action against any type of criminals. No enforcement agency enjoys such powers as the police enjoy. Police organization is indeed huge and their members are given special training even in the use of weapons and firearms. All these factors create and strengthen solidarity among the members of the police service. Socioculturally, the police are considered as a force which may utilize violent force if they are not attended to. This makes them to involve in a number of crimes which other law enforcement functionaries cannot commit if at all they want to.

Group Cohesion and Police Crimes

There is group cohesion in police. Each one is a part of a '*whole*' and each one has no existence without the '*whole*'. People are afraid of individual policeman/officer as they know that he is a part of a '*whole*'. The 'whole' has got strength and force. The '*whole*' is a force and the force is a form of behaviour which, once initiated, is difficult to be controlled. Legitimate force, necessary force, unnecessary force, illegal force, minimum force, police brutality—all these belong to the same family and only a hair-splitting difference exists between two types of forces. Police know the difficulty and they know that it is to their advantage that such a difficulty exists. This too is a reason for police crimes. They can make a non-cognizable crime into a cognizable one and vice versa. They can argue for "mistake of fact", "doing in good faith", lack of malicious intentions etc. They can plead for immunity and they can practise many such crooked ways during law enforcement. They are crimes but crimes do exist. A defensive reaction reinforces the unique solidarity exhibited and expressed by the police subculture.

Personality of Police Officers and Police Crimes

Earlier the relationship between personality and police crimes has been discussed. The same is not again elaborated here; nevertheless, the fact remains that there takes place behaviour modification in people. People behave in a particular way not because they want to behave in that way but because they have no option to behave in any other way. Again people behave in a particular way, not because they have a belief in what they do, but because they have opportunities to behave in any way they want. The police enjoy unique authority and power. They know that corruption, corrupt practices, use of torture etc. are forbidden by law. They also know that these forbidden acts can be done with immunity under police uniform. In the role of a police officer, one can do many things which he can not otherwise. Exploit the opportunity and cash the situation. A director general of police was once accused of accepting Rs. 40 lakhs to save a culprit in a criminal case. True or false, police officers get opportunities to commit illegal acts in a legitimate and legal way. Their uniform has a glamour and they can exercise a lot of discretion for or against somebody. Police authority is a monopoly and so does the misuse/ abuse of police authority. To question police authority, misuse of power, abuse of discretion etc. are difficult and time consuming—are laboursome and expensive—are painstaking and troublesome. The police functionaries know them well and they know further that the people are helpless before their mammoth authority. They know what they commit are crimes. They know further that the police crimes have become legitimate when they are committed with a police uniform. After wearing a police uniform, a police officer calls epithets and talks foul language. He interprets his behaviour as legitimate and necessary for the larger interest of the society! He employs violent forces and a form of behaviour which he never expresses in his life becomes a legitimate behaviour when he wears the uniform. He releases his repressed feelings and emotions under the colour of his uniform and authority (pseudo-authority). Some police officers behave in an unbecoming way just to maintain his membership in the police subculture.

The subculture has framed certain rules which are crime—prone and the policeman has no option but to follow the rules. Police subculture may even encourage torture or corruption. It may censure police brutality and the police hierarchy may impose rules against corruption which may be rejected by the police subculture. Psychologists feel that this too may be a cause of police crimes.

Psychology of Current and Contemporary Police Crimes

The crimes which the police committed during the nineteeth century were different from what they commit today. India is a democracy today and precisely therefore the socio-political and administrative conditions are different from what they were in the colonial rule—in the British raj—in the imperial administration. At that time, the policeman (constables) had no contacts with top level administrators. But today, the lowest level police personnel can have frequent and close contact with the highest level politicians. Together they can manage and manipulate many things. They can just ignore the formal administrative hierarchy. Informal channels of communication have developed. Police associations are functioning in full swing and the allegation is that there is politicization of police and policization of Politics. There is another stronger allegation too and that is: "there is criminalization of police and policization of criminals". A third allegation is that there is criminalization of politics and politicization of criminals and the criminals and politicians need police help, support and patronage to succeed in their endeavour. Studies conducted may prove that the allegations do not come from vacuum and they are not altogether baseless.

In democratic India, the opportunities to commit crimes are plenty and one sees Mafia crimes, crime syndicates, racketeering etc. and all of them require police help. As said elsewhere, I have discussed the unholy relations between the police and organized criminals in my book *Indian Police and Nexus Crime.* Today, India is in the line of liberalization, privatization and globalization etc. and in such a scenario, crimes too have better scope in many areas. The police will have more opportunities to involve themselves in the commission of crimes. People want police support to run their business of gambling, tender flesh trade, nexus transactions, *goondaism*, crime schemes etc. and the policemen today realize that their authority, power, uniform, time, inaction, lethargy, overaction, negligence, indifference, political affiliation, *nexus* contacts etc. are time and money for them. Their muscles, lathies, guns and show of them can bring luxuries and cash to them. Today, there exists a number of important considerations which determines effectiveness, conduct and reputation of the police. They know that their success depends on many factors other than strict enforcement of law. The success of police work today has become a matter of interpretation and precisely therefore, on the perception of individual policemen/officers. In such a mental situation, crimes in police uniform may become a way of life for some. In fact, there exists a climate of widespread acceptance of crimes by policemen/officers. The acceptance of crimes (e.g. corruption, corruption-money splitting, corruption-money fixing, nexus crimes, enforcement criminality etc.) in police can in some way be explained by the multiplicity and gravity of today's *acceptances* of such crimes in society outside the police department. Society's acceptance of crimes can certainly mitigate the seriousness of police crimes and police responsibility over them. Police crimes, corruption and nexus criminality etc. are fostered by powerful social, cultural, economic and political currents which encourage an idea that police uniform is a means to achieve individual success in life. A uniform which must ensure public safety, care, protection etc. is considered by individual policeman/officer as a means to achieve his parochial interests with the support of vested interests. A kind of conspiracy for commission of crime by vested interests with the help or show of police uniform prevails in the socio-political and psychological melieu. In such a melieu, the individual motivations to crime must be studied. The definition of police crimes has become a major problem today. For, what is defined as traditional crimes in the penal codes has become traditional crimes only for the ordinary people and no more to the vested interests, politicians, businessmen and so on. For them, they are only human acts to be ignored by the enforcement agencies. Hence, anything done by police to promote the vested interests of the powerful and of the affluent is rewarded. They need policemen/officers of all ranks and therefore they recruit men and officers from all levels in the hierarchy. More about the criminology of police crimes is discussed in the chapter that follows.

References

1. *Crime in India: 1988*, National Crime Records Bureau, Ministry of Home Affairs, Government of India, 1999.
2. Anandswarup Gupta, *The Police in British India: 1861—1947*, Concept, Delhi, 1979.
3. E. M. Fodor, *Delinquency and Susceptibility to Social Influence Among Adolescence as a Function of Level of Moral Development*, Journal of Social Psychology (1972), 86: 257—260 and in relation to the positive relationship between conformity

and moral development, H. D. Saltzstein, R.M. Diamond and M. Belenky, *Moral Judgement Level and Conformity Behaviour*, Development Psychology (1972), 7: 327—336.

4. See Henvey Cleckley, *The Mask of Sanity*, C.V. Mosby and Co., St. Louis, 1941. See also, Cleckley, *The Psychopath: A problem for Society*, Federal Probation, 10 (October-December), 1946.
5. Jerome H. Skolnick, *Justice Without Trial: Law Enforcement in Democratic Society*, Wiley, New York, 1966.
6. Bernard Cohen, *Police Theory: New Perspectives*, from *Criminology in Perspective*, S.F. Landan (ed), Lexington Books, Toronto, 1977.

CHAPTER—9

Criminology of Police Crimes

Police crime is a reality—a reality that existed since law enforcement in whatever form came into being. But the crime was not recognized as such until recently. The Crime in India, of late, published by the Ministry of Home Affairs, Government of India provides a full chapter on *police crimes*. It means that police crimes are now recognized as a reality and the criminologists are developing a new branch 'Police Criminology' in criminological literature.

Organized police is of recent origin in the world and of still recent in India. Ever since organized policing has come into existence, crimes of various types and categories were committed by them and sometimes they were detected to have committed the offences. But, as indicated elsewhere, the crimes by police were not treated as a special or specific category of crimes. Resultingly, no special or specific theories relating to police crimes were formulated by criminologists, sociologists, psychologists and so on. In spite of the crimes committed by police from time to time, the police continued to exist and survive as an agency created for detecting crimes, preventing and controlling them. Police as law violators never captured even public attention as the people were overenthusiastically interested to maintain them as defenders of law enforcement. Greek philosophers of the fifth century B.C. asked the question: "What is the philosophy of law and law enforcement?" The enduring principles of law enforcement (policing the society) were accepted by humanity and wherever or whenever the sacred principles violated by the enforcement agencies, crimes came into being. But the legal philosophers were not found to be concerned with the etiology or prevention of law violations by the enforcement officials themselves. The philosophical-legal thinking of the past has been a force for the law enforcement and it continues to be so even now. The philosophical-legal thinking of the past (or of the present) did not care much to explain why law violations took place during law enforcement. Lawless law enforcement has been a reality but has been viewed as not serious even by the contemporary criminologists.

Police crimes and police criminology which we have discussed at length in the previous chapters show that the police themselves were not concerned with the philosophy of what they did. They behaved, sometimes, in the way they wanted. As time went on, people enacted certain new laws by the help of which they wanted to control the police with penal sanctions. The Indian Penal Code—1860 and the Code of Criminal Procedure—1862 had some provisions of law intended to control police behaviour during investigation. The provisions of law thus enacted did not and could not control the police as there were no enforcement agencies appointed to see that the police enforced the law as per law and the procedure established by law. The framers of law and legal philosophers sought to construct some provisions to control police behaviour and not for effectively enforcing them. They wanted just to prove to the world/people that policing was something which must be legally and fairly executed. They wanted to give a rational basis for policing and tried to formulate general theories for the effective enforcement of law. They did not do anything more than that. One major cause for the violations of law by the police has been a lack of clear understanding of the philosophy of policing among the police functionaries.

Institution of organized policing was for the people. Police, no matter how efficient and effective they are, must be reformed or abolished if they are not just and fair to people whom they serve or are bound to serve. This idea did not go into their mind as the administration was not keen in inculcating that idea to them. Every individual—no matter he is a citizen, a suspect in a crime, an accused or a criminal—has some inviolable rights and the police can not and should not override such rights. The rights which the people have or ought to enjoy are not subject to the calculus of police interests. Rights to life, liberty, equality and dignity are sacred rights and the police are not to deny the enjoyment of such rights by abusing their power and misusing their authority. Informal arrests, illegal detention, custodial violence, calling of epithets during law enforcement are injustices and crimes. Police philosophers may argue that an injustice is tolerable only when it is necessary to avoid a greater injustice. But in police work, such situations are rare, if not non-existent. In any case, unfairness and injustices committed during informal arrests (abduction), illegal detention (wrongful confinement), custodial violence (torture) etc. are not tolerated. They are not or ought not to become subjects of bargaining and arguments. The international community condemns such injustices and unfairness by any law enforcement agencies.

The people and the police have entered into a sacred contract and the contract was that the police would enforce law in accordance to law, equity and good conscience. The police would enforce law as per the procedure established by law. It is for doing so the society pays salary for them. The salary is paid only for the work lawfully done by the police. The society is not to pay a single paise to anyone who enforces the law unjustly and unfairly. Why should the society pay salary for the crimes the police commit or for the *goondaism* they show? The police system was established for the mutual advantage of the people and the police. Whenever the police execute law in an unfair manner through commissions and/or omissions, then there is a violation of the terms of contract. Resultingly, a conflict arises between the people and the society. Whenever a policeman/officer commits a police crime during law enforcement, he is concerned more with his interest than anything else. He may make fortunes or may express his instinctual energy. He may then interpret that he is doing things for the larger interests of the society and it is only an interpretation of his act and not the reality.

What is the meaning of concocting evidence in a criminal case or producing tutored witnesses during a criminal trial? Are they not crimes to do so? What is the advantage of entering into *nexus* transactions? Such acts may further the interest of the investigating officers/police officers and nothing more. What is just in such situations? Fairness in policing will take away all subsequent criticisms and allegations against police functionaries. It is for this, the procedural laws are enacted and the manner in which they are to be enacted is taught. The manner in which the procedural laws are to be enforced is decided only by the fairness in dealing with issues, events and individuals. Fairness in policing means that the police are rational and objective in their approach and assessment. The police do not have any vested interests and they protect the interests of others affected by law violations. If the police do not have any vested interests, then it goes without saying that arbitrary arrests and indepth interrogation after arrests cease to have any relevance in the philosophy and practice of police work. Morality and moral judgements have a greater importance and influence in policing as the enforcement of law must be conscientious, reasonable, prudent and diligent. With this philosophical background, I wish to discuss the criminology of police crimes in this chapter.

Criminology of Police Crimes

Under Chapter 13, on Custodial Crimes in CRIME IN INDIA—1988, the Ministry of Home Affairs, Government of India writes: "Custodial crimes which include death in police custody has drawn attention of public, media and legislature over the past many years. Even the Human Rights Commission has taken serious note of such incidents". The number of deaths in police custody for the years 1995 to 1998 is as under.

Reported Custodial Deaths in Police Custody during 1995-1998*

Sl. No.	*Year*	*No. of Reported Custodial Deaths*
1.	1995*	31
2.	1996	49
3.	1997	40
4.	1998	46
	% Change in 1998 Over 1995	48.4 %
	% Change in 1998 Over 1997	15.0 %

Date for 1995 not furnished by Bihar, Gujarat and Meghalaya

**Source:* Crime in India 1988, Ministry of Home Affairs Government of India.

As compared to the year 1995, the year 1998 recorded an increase of 48.4 per cent in custodial death cases. The increase from 1997 to 1998 was 15.0 per cent. Custodial deaths, if they are murders by police, mean that an agency established for protecting the lives of the people becomes the killer—the annihilator of human life. The policemen/officers responsible for the murder of the people in their custody probably would not have killed them if they were not policemen/officers—if they did not have police power and authority. The investigation conducted on custodial deaths proved that 90.90 per cent were true cases.

People who are taken into police custody are tortured to death and the theories of criminology so far proposed can not answer the question: "What is the etiology of murder in police custody?" Demonology may say that it is the devil who kills a man in his desperate conditions in police custody. If so, the devil must be brought out and current criminology concentrates on it? "Causing death" of a person in police custody can never be considered as a form of criminal justice administration or law enforcement—even when the intention is to ensure justice to crime-doers. Rather, it runs completely counter to the philosophy of policing which is meant to protect human life. Any sort of torture is a disregard shown to the inviolable dignity of human beings. Whenever the policeman/officer does so, he ceases to be a human being entrusted with justice administration and becomes a means which, under the guise of administering fair justice, actually harms people.

At the time Lord Maccalay drafted the Indian Penal Code, he was unaware of custodial rapes and that too under police custody. But today, the Indian Penal Code under section 376 (2) specifies immediate punishment. In cases of custodial deaths, the Indian law requires a mandatory inquiry by the Magistrate into the cause of death[1]. Custodial rapes are awarded very severe punishments and the law treats it as a very serious offence. National Crime Records Bureau says: "rapes in police custody is seen as a stigma on the law enforcing agency by the citizens. Police which is a primary agency for ensuring the safety of women, children who are downtrodden is not forgiven by the society if they themselves get involved in rape cases, that too in police custody. The number of such cases reported for 1995—98 at all India level are:

Incidents of Custodial Rape in Police Custody during 1995—1998*

Sl. No.	*Year*	*No. of Reported Custodial Rape cases*
1.	1995*	6
2.	1996	6
3.	1997	6
4.	1998	4
	% Change in 1998 Over 1997	-33.3 %
	% Change in 1998 Over 1995	-33.3 %

Note:- *Date for 1995 not furnished by Bihar, Gujarat and Meghalaya for 1995—1998 by Daman & Diu.
**Source:* Crime in India 1988, Ministry of Home Affairs, Government of India.

The data furnished by the National Crime Records Bureau gives some details only on custodial deaths and rapes. The inalienable rights to women's dignity is questioned or denied on the basis of muscle strength in an isolated condition. The rape in police custody is the sinister result of abuse of power which is not resisted by the victim as she is defenceless and helpless. The woman in police custody is made a subject to the will of the stronger. Police power and muscles become factors leading to the destruction of sex values and dignity. How can the police claim to protect the life and dignity of people when they themselves commit human rights violations?

Look at the complaints received against the police: Crime in India—1998 gives details on them.

Number of Complaints Received Against Police during 1996-1997

Year	*Number of complaints received*	*Number of cases registered*
1996*	36624	2214
1997**	123523	2276
1998**	88628	3242

* Excluding Bihar, Daman & Diu and Delhi
** Excluding Daman & Diu

The complaints against the police are those filed before the police authorities. There are private complaints filed before the courts and complaints preferred before Human Rights Commission, before the Government or before the Women's Commission etc. The figures relating to them are not available. Police departments may institute departmental inquiries when complaints are received. In 1996, the department initiated 14527 departmental inquiries. During 1997 and 1998, they were respectively 12357 and 8506. During 1996, a total of 291 magisterial inquiries and 319 judicial inquiries were held. The figures for magisterial inquiries for 1997 and 1998 were 326 and 213 respectively. The same for judicial inquiries for the two years were 460 and 562 respectively.

According to the National Crime Records Bureau, "during 1998 as many as 1645 police personnel were sent for trial against whom complaints and charges were framed. During the period, 148 police personnel were acquitted and 66 police personnel were convicted. Further, the NCRB'S report says that during 1998, minor punishments were awarded to 21103 police personnel and major punishments were given to 3709 police personnel. On the basis of the departmental inquiries, 828 police personnel were either dismissed or removed from service at all India level in 1998. The number of police personnel dismissed/removed from service was 488 and 1063 for 1996 and 1997 respectively. 2204 and 3105 police personnel were awarded major punishment respectively for 1996 and 1997. They were 21426 and 22230 for minor punishments during the year.

What do they indicate? They suggest that the crimes and misconducts in police must be studied with a research mind. The issue is one which must be answered by a theory and not at all by a departmental, magesterial or judicial inquiry in individual cases. Philosophy of policing does not contemplate crimes by police and more recently, the police are blamed by the public and media for their unholy nexus with criminal politicians, criminal businessmen, criminal bureaucrats and underworld criminals and so on. Enforcement criminality, nexus crimes, kickbacks, payoff, corruption-money splitting, corruption-money fixing, participation in underworld activities, sweet heart dealings etc. appear in news media along with the names of low, middle, senior and top level police functionaries. True or false the allegations are, the news captures public attention and necessitates an indepth criminological inquiry to find out the root causes of the malady.

Crackpot Theories on Police Crimes in Criminology

Police corruption was always pointed out as a cause of crime and criminality in society by western and eastern criminologists, theologians, philosophers and well meaning members of the public even in the beginning of 19th century. But they did not analyse the causes of police corruption. It seems that they took it for granted the existence of police corruption and found that police corruption could only multiply crimes in society.

Police commissions appointed in India from time to time—including Torture Commission—1855 analysed the extent and intensity of police misbehaviour. None of them treated police misbehaviours as crimes as the National Crime Records Bureau has done it, of late. The police commissions hitherto advanced some crackpot theories about police crimes as their interest was not to study police from criminological perspectives.

Emile Durkheim was perhaps one of the earliest thinkers who presented a theoretical framework for aggressive behaviour. He was not talking about police crimes. Nevertheless, his theory could be applied to police crimes particularly when they committed violent crimes. Police, from the time of British Rule in India was a cohesive group and a coercive weapon of the Government. A cohesive group would in all probability use repressive laws and the police in India too did it. Emile Durkheim endorsed this view and Bernard Cohen writes: "the application of violence serves several useful functions for the police. First, it provides summary punishment to the criminal, especially in situations when the court may be excessively lenient. Second, it attempts to deter the criminal as well as others from committing the same or similar acts. Third, it serves to protect the police from injury and harm. Finally, it strengthens police solidarity and cohesion, while at the same time reaffirming who the real criminals are". Criminologists ask the question: "Whatever may be the lofty objectives of employing violence, can the police go to the extent of killing a human being in police custody?" No, they can not and should not. Yet they do and why? Commissions of inquiry are appointed in individual cases and they, more often than not, bring out the precipitating factors and special motivating forces to commit a specific crime by individual police officers. Any number of commissions are appointed in all States and no commission has ever dealt with police crimes from criminological angles. In custodial rape cases, a number of commissions has suggested very severe punishment, quick investigation etc., nevertheless none of them has ever dealt with the issue as a criminologist would do it.

What is the meaning of police committing crimes to deter people and other criminals? Commission of crimes by police has never deterred people from committing crimes. It has helped them to take precautions against the commission of crime. A crime causes another crime and never will it prevent or control crimes! For example, police corruption causes further corruption and crimes. It will never ensure peace and harmony. The fear that the police will employ torture will compel people to humour the police so that they escape from torture. In order to get police support, people take introductions and recommendations. The crimes that come out of a crime committed by police may be many. Today, the police are blamed to have unholy nexus with criminal politicians, unscrupulous businessmen and underworld criminals. If so, one can more or less imagine the magnitude of crimes committed by the nexus partners. Criminology of police crime is concerned with the totality of crimes.

William Westley, a researcher in police crimes argued that the main reason for the police to utilize illegal forms of violence was to defend and improve their social status. This might be true in America where the standards were different. In India, the use of violence and torture could never improve the social status of police officers, rather could bring down their social status. People look at a brutal police-policeman with a contempt and nickname him as a wild animal. In India, police resorted to torture for deterring the people so that torture was a means of many to make some earnings under the colour of their uniform. I have observed that many policemen/officers withdraw from torturing people as they grow older and older. There is no evidence to show that the more torture one employs, the more social status he gets.

After the enactment of the Protection of Human Rights Act—1993 in India, the use of torture/violence in police custody has certainly come down. But, allegations of police nexuses with criminals, Mafias, criminal politicians and so on have gone up. Certainly, when one pattern of crimes goes down, another pattern of crimes may come up. If torture was a source of income in the past, then corruption by way of torture must be substituted by another crime for making an equal or more income. Nexus criminality or various other kinds of enforcement crimes may be the substitutes for torture in police custody. William Westley's findings that the police could defend their social status by committing torture on people too were equally unacceptable. No one can defend his social status by way of committing crimes. According to him, "the police employ violence to persuade the public to respect their occupational status". No, that is not true. Criminological studies on police crimes give different explanations and findings for police criminality and status.

As seen earlier, besides custodial deaths and rapes in police custody, there were 123523 complaints against police during 1977 and 88628 during 1998. They were the recorded complaints received by the police authorities. The actual strength of police during 1998 was 1020171 in India. It shows that the problem is indeed very severe. The estimated population in India for 1988 was 970900000 and the total number of crimes registered under the Indian Penal Code/Special and Local Laws was 6180996. What does it show? It shows that the complaints against the police outnumber the crimes recorded in the whole country. During 1998 one observes that the percentage of crimes was 6.37 of the total population and the same of the complaints against the police was 6.37 of the total strength of the police in the country. During 1977, the percentage was higher than what it was for police for 1998. William Westley says further that the courts do not adequately punish the police offenders and this lenient attitude taken by the courts make them to violate the laws with immunity. They are found to utilize unnecessary force for ensuring informal control over certain criminal behaviour of the people. The methods employed by the police become a subject of criticism and the objectives achieved by the use of such illegal methods are forgotten. In other words the police give expressions to their criminal mind to fight against the criminality in society. For example, the police may take the kith and kin of the suspect to pressure the suspect to surrender before the police. This has no justification in law and the same is a violation of law. How can the people tolerate such violence against the innocent especially to women and children of the suspects in crime? An unjust exercise of power and authority can not legitimize police actions whatever may be the advantage received by the society. It is a violation of the contract between the police and the society. Criminologists study the issue from this angle and the scandalous enforcement of law and the reckless tampering of the human rights of people can not be treated as a part of duty of the police functionaries. The statistics provided elsewhere in this chapter shows that many departmental, magisterial and judicial inquiries conducted against the policemen/officers end in the awarding of minor or major punishments. Human Rights Commissions, of late, award compensation to the victims of police crimes, abuse of power or misuse of authority. People and the police till recently did not consider their illegal acts as "crimes", paradoxically they treated such violations of law as their "rights" to the point that the society and the State must accept them as necessary for the effective enforcement of law.

Police Discretion, Bureaucracy and Police Subculture

Discretion involves a decision. Discretion can be exercised basing on objective facts in a given set of circumstances or at the will and pleasure of the person exercising discretion even ignoring the objective facts. Human values and morality consciousness play a role in the exercise of discretion. Researches show that police exercise formal and informal discretion. Arrest is discretionary. A police officer may arrest a person if that is necessary. The police bureaucracy, rules and laws give specific guidelines for the arrest of people. If that is the case, a police officer may not have any discretion in effecting the arrest. Once a person is arrested, how to deal with him? The arresting officer has a lot of discretion there too. Here comes the need of applying informal discretion. Studies show that the lower level functionaries exercise more of informal discretion and the higher level or top level functionaries exercise formal discretion. The officer who exercises the informal discretion can, sometimes, ignore the guidelines given by higher authorities while they issued orders on the exercise of formal discretion. Once a director general of police issued an order stating that all telephone calls to police stations must be reciprocated by "good morning, good afternoon or good evening" as the case might be so that the caller at the other end felt pleased at the response from the police stations. The police staff at the station house had no discretion but to answer the telephone calls by "good morning, good evening" etc. What happened later was that the staff in police stations responded as per the instructions from the police headquarters but with a tone of voice that would invariably displease the caller at the other end. The staff had the power to exercise an informal discretion as they wanted and they exercised it without showing any respect to the callers by giving wrong non-verbal signals. The nature of police work, particularly at the field level or operational level, is such that the personnel at the cutting edge level can exercise their informal discretion in a human rights unfriendly manner. Members of the police rank and file may misuse their discretionary power which may lead to incalculable and irrational behavioural patterns. Instances are plenty to show that the informal discretion exercised by the members of the police hierarchy have caused irrepairable damage to the image and reputation of police department. The police behaviour in such situations are evaluated as inappropriate and objectionable. Informal discretion exercised in an inappropriate way may be a signal to others for bringing graft, illegal gratification, corruption-money etc. Some policemen/officers want to project an authoritarian ego to people and give an impression that they can do a lot of harm to anybody if they choose to do so. Such people may purposively show negative personality traits when they interact with people. They may express inappropriate discretion to frighten, harass and humiliate people. Criminologists ask the question: "Why do the police behave the way they do?"

Sometimes, the police take a decision not to set the law into motion even when they see a cognizable crime committed in front of them? Why? In a recent case, a girl was subjected to non-stop rapes by several men over a period of six months. The *relay rape* became a sensational issue through the media and a case was registered and investigated. Nearly 40 people were convicted by the court and the court made very damaging comments against an inspector of police who refused to register the case when it was reported. Ultimately, the inspector was placed under suspension and departmental proceedings initiated against him. Was it not a crime to refuse registration or criminal cases when they were reported? Such refusals may not be visible to the society. They may not be even known to the higher ups or to the courts of law. An officer's discretion and decision not to invoke the law, not to investigate the case, not to detect the criminals may be motivated by considerations which are illegal. In many cases, the officer doing so may not have to suffer the consequences of the miscarriage of justice. There may be cases in which bribery or corruption does not play a role. The lethargy or inaction of the police officer may be the prime factor for not setting the law into motion.

In many jurisdictions, gambling, prostitution, bootlegging, nexus crimes may be in full swing and the police officers may be aware of them. But, they ignore them or become partners in such underworld activities. They may receive regular payoff or kickbacks in such cases. By conniving with the criminals in operation, they make fortunes and the media in these days bring any number of such instances. Some police officers say that they do not initiate action against such organized/syndicate criminals because they are helplessly handicapped to set the law into motion. For them, such crimes come within the *no enforcement areas* of policing.

Earlier, mention has been made about politicisation of police. Differential treatment of politicians may take many forms in law enforcement. Politicians of the ruling party may be favoured while the politicians of the opposition may be arrested or may be subjected to very serious action taken against them when they are not involved in the commission of any offence. Such allegations are often seen in the media. This quite obviously is improper. Sometimes, it so happens that the laws which are not generally enforced are enforced purposefully to put the politicians of the opposition in trouble. Many a time, the politicians of the opposition are at their wit's end as they are incapable of defending themselves or of producing adequate proof of discrimination against them. This sort of unequal enforcement of law expresses the criminal mind of the enforcement machinery and their political affiliations. The police apply here a double standard and accept it for their personal advantages more than political advantages. If at all cases are registered out of pressure against the politicians of the ruling party, some police officers investigate the cases perfunctorily and see that they escape punishment.

Sometimes, it so happens that police officers decide to harass the politicians of opposition. Characteristics of such harassment may be seen in shadowing them and watching their activities. The purpose is just to annoy them and thereby preventing their freedom to move about. Harassment is generally of extremely low visibility.

Symbiotic Relationship between Criminals and Police

Recently in a south Indian State, the diaries of a bootlegger was seized. The diary contained the names of top level politicians, police and excise officials. On interrogation of the bootlegger, it was revealed that his policy was to pay top personnel in police, politics and excise as much as necessary to keep them happy and quiet. He also said that he used to pay something to everybody or as many people as possible to implicate them in his bootlegging business and to keep them from talking loudly. The range of payoff thus went from a weekly/monthly salary to police officials to a festival bottle for their personal drivers. Regular payments to higher officials, holiday and birthday gifts to their wives and children etc. were the means by which the above said bootlegger purchased protection from law enforcement against him.

The symbiotic relationship between police and syndicate criminals can be (1) nonfeasance (failure to perform a required duty), (2) malfeasance (the commission of some act which is positively illegal or unlawful) and (3) misfeasance (the improper performance of some act which a man may properly do). All the three—namely nonfeasance, malfeasance and misfeasance-are crimes in every letter of the law and the criminologists study them from many angles.

Nonfeasance means the omission of some acts which ought to have been performed. The officials tolerate all illegal activities of their *nexus* partners and underworld criminals who keep up their protection payments. The officers involved see to it that they cautiously receive the payments from trusted partners and that there is no evidence to show that they receive payoffs. They present reasonable explanations and excuses for their inaction, lethargy and omissions. They ignore the illegal activities completely or they are told to ignore them by their superior ranks. When complaints are received, they conduct a ritualistic raid and that too after giving sufficient information in advance and thus they whitewash the syndicates activities. They don't utilize their legal powers to prevent nexus criminality and organized crimes. Why?

Malfeasance means the performance by a public official of an act that is legally unjustified or harmful. In connection with a political convention, some policemen/officers pressure people to contribute liberally to the success of the convention or to provide vehicles for transporting political party men for the convention. People honour police requests/demands expecting favoured treatments. Likewise, some pressure the rich and the affluent to provide vehicles for their pleasure trips or to visit their kith and kin or to arrange picnics for their relatives. They dine in hotels without payments or stay there without paying rent. They receive edibles, gifts, presents etc. from mill owners, shop keepers and so on. If they are not crimes, then what are they?

Misfeasance is the wrongful performance of a normally lawful act.

Courts of Law and Police Crimes

Judgements pointing out and criticizing the crimes committed by police are numerous. The courts all over the country make attempts to discipline the police and control them. Some trial judges do acquit the accused because they have been dealt with by police in ways which are improper and illegal. Criminologists think that the acquittal does not mean much unless the police officers who are responsible for the acquittal are not dealt with properly. "Unfair detection techniques" by police are not favoured by courts. Once a few women constables—dressed well—were sent to bus stations and railway platforms with instructions to give signals to men signifying their intention to go with them if they were prepared to entertain them. The intention of the police functionaries was to catch hold of eve-teasers and those who molested women in public places. Thus, many boys were entraped and the press reported the police strategy to take into custody the eve-teasers in the city. People commented at it "indecent strategy", "unfair techniques" and "illegal methods" etc. Police methods certainly were unfair and improper. The zealousness of these neatly dressed women constables extended beyond merely being in a position to give signals and included a number of techniques whereby the accosting was given by the women constables and not by the eve-teasers. The police officers were not to spend money from the exchequer for this sort of law enforcement—said a journalist on the occasion. The propriety of these police practices is criticized.

About the enticement of homosexuals, Donald J. Neman gives an example. He writes: "A psychiatrist who, on court order, has seen many homosexual defendants for diagnosis, notified the court of what he feels is the typical operation of the vice squad in such cases. The arresting officer goes to a public rest room or to some other location which is frequented by homosexuals. Upon seeing a potential defendant, the officer will stare or smile or will even affect feminine mannerisms. While urinating, the officer will handle his genitalia in such a manner as to excite or arouse the interested defendant. The defendant then will make an oral proposition which results in his arrest". A judge who apprised the police technique said that the practice was 'atrocious, appalling, horrible and miserable'. The accosting by policemen or women police is an expression of criminal tendencies.

Overzealous police officers resort to several such techniques. In order to catch hold of people who smoke cigarettes or beedies, police officers in plain cloths go to cinema theatres and start showing cigarettes, offering them to people, asking for matches etc. People view such police techniques as improper methods. Smoking cigarettes in theatres can be stopped by other effective methods and the police must not waste their manpower for such useless works. They have plenty of other works which are more serious than these sorts of minor violations. Unwise allocation of police resources and manpower is improper and unnecessary. Petty crimes or crimes of such nature are not usually contested or the judgements are not generally appealed against. This weakness must not be exploited and the attitude of any police officer to exploit the weakness of people is nothing but an expression of his criminal tendencies.

Police have cultivated sources of information and some of them are ex-criminals or those who commit crimes. Police show leniency to them and they may take it for granted that they thus get a licence to expand their own operations. Instances have come to notice that the police give permission to some such 'criminal' informants to commit a limited number of property offences and earn an income for the information they have supplied to the police. In some such cases, the policemen/officers establish clandestine understanding to part with a portion of the booty they thus make through their criminal activities. If at all the police are forced to initiate action against such favoured criminals, the charges against them are commonly reduced to lesser ones.

The observations made against the police for the obnoxious practices employed by them are a legion, and once an Allahabad judge branded the police as an organized group of criminals. Of course the observation was objectionable for the police. In the judgement against the observations of the judge, the Supreme Court of India upheld the view stating that there was a lot of truth behind the exaggerated version of the Allahabad Judge. Some courts have noted that the police registered false cases against innocent people and they arrested people for offence which they have not committed. If nothing was possible, the police used to register a case against people who were informally taken into custody and they did so just to protect their interests.

Affluence and Police Crimes

There is a view that policemen/officers become corrupt not because they are starving, but because they want to earn more. Top levels in police become corrupt not because they were less affluent, but because they want to accumulate wealth over their affluence. Affluence, say criminologists, is a drug and has drug effects on the affluent. Many develop a sort of dependence on the drug of affluence. Or why did a top level police officer misappropriated Rs. 10,000 per month from the Secret Service Fund entrusted to him?

Man has his "physical needs". He has "moral needs" as well. Physical needs may be looked after by affluence. But moral needs cannot be. Only a "moral conscience uprightly formed" can control the moral needs. There is an affluence of law which can be properly used or misused by police.

Those who misuse their power or abuse their authority for satisfying their physical needs suffer from a moral collapse/decline. Their moral conscience is not uprightly formed. They register false cases and manipulate records. A director general of police who was alleged to have abused sexually a girl (the girl committed suicide subsequently), registered false cases against her brother and harassed him very cruelly so that the boy did not venture to raise allegations against the director general of police. After several years, a case for sexual abuse and abetment to suicide was registered against the director general as ordered by a court. The investigation proved that the allegation against the director general of police was not baseless.

Police stations have a number of files dealing with a variety of crimes. The police stations keep a number of criminals of various descriptions. The station atmosphere is contaminated with talks, discussions, conversations relating to crimes and criminals. The station premises are filled with many vehicles and articles connected with crimes. Any officer/man working in such an environment will be pregnant with notions, ideas and concepts relating to crime and criminals. He thinks more about crimes and criminals. The affluence of an atmosphere containing crime and criminals exerts some sort of influence on him to become crime-prone. A poet has sung that a person who lives in darkness starts loving darkness. He may not be able to tolerate light. Likewise, any person who lives in an atmosphere pregnant with an affluence of crimes and crimes will, in all probability, start loving crimes and commission of crimes. He develops a pro-crime attitude and shows crime-prone behavioural patterns. An inspector general of police once told me that his main work was reading files relating to crimes. After reading the files for several days—different files—different crimes, he started to develop an attitude in favour of crimes and criminals. He further said that any police officer who lacked a moral conscience which was uprightly formed, probably, would develop a crime-prone attitude in due course of time. I think that the way of life, values, characteristic pattern of behaviour, attitude etc. which policemen/officers develop while they are on the job may be a product of a distinctive cultural system which prevails in a police station atmosphere. Evidence available may show that a culture which prevails in a police station is not only a culture that fights against crimes and criminals, but also a culture that tolerates crimes including corruption, torture, concoction of evidence, manipulation of records, enforcement criminality and nexus crimes. The culture that is seen in police is one which favours law enforcement in an atmosphere which violates moral and legal norms. They can not go together. Hence, between a law-abiding and non-law abiding culture, there arises a difficulty for police personnel to decide on where exactly they stand in relation to these two mutually conflicting values and classes of activities. Between the two perceived alternatives—i.e., law abiding and non-law-abiding—a policeman/officer has to work and necessarily a policeman/officer develops an attitude which favours an overt commitment to the law-abiding alternative and a convert commitment to the non-law abiding alternative. Criminologists think that this is one major cause of police crimes in society.

People are afraid of the police. The police have a deterrent effect on people. Police have power, physical strength, authority, manpower, resources, masculinity, bravery and precisely therefore the people treat the policemen as "tough ones". The policemen too want to show their tough nature by expressing no "softness" to criminals unless they are pressured by forces which are above them. Each policeman wants to show his "smartness" in his job and he has an inclination to adopt fair or foul means to establish his "smartness" which involves the capacity to achieve special status for him. In such a culture, police crimes may be seen unless they are checked by powers which are above the smart policemen/officers. Policemen/officers who demonstrate their smartness through unfair and illegal methods must not be encouraged—must not be accorded prestige and status for what they do. "Toughness" and "smartness" are encouraged if they ensure success but without evaluating the nature and quality of the "toughness and smartness" thus expressed. This is found to be another cause of increasing police criminality—say criminologists.

Motivation of Criminal Behaviour and Police

The members of the police service are fully aware that they are violating the law when they do so. They also know the law violating nature and culture of the service. The question is: "Why do they commit crimes?" The most general answer is that their crimes are motivated by their desire to achieve ends which are valued by them and their culture. Torture is motivated by a desire to obtain a confession through short-cut methods and the strategy is valued by some in police service-is tolerated by many in police service and society outside. But, torture is disvalued by law and the culture all over the world. It is considered as a crime everywhere. Once a police officer was asked to answer the question: "Can you perform your job strictly in accordance to law—with the statutes you have?" He candidly confessed that he could only if everyone wanted to administer fair justice. But, many did not want it. Hence, the laws were violated whenever one could. The motivation to commit police crimes comes from many sources and a single policeman/officer can not fight against the forces which operate on him.

A Wrong Vocabulary of Police Literature

Section 76, Indian Penal Code—1860 reads: "Nothing is an offence which is done by a person who is, or who by reason of a mistake of fact and not by reason of a mistake of law in good faith believes himself to be bound by law to do it". Section 79, Indian Penal Code—1860 reads further: "Nothing is an offence which is done by any person who is justified by law or who by reason of a mistake of fact and not by reason of a mistake of law in good faith believes himself to be justified by law, in doing it". They are wrongly interpreted by some policemen/officers to get immunity from criminal liability for the crimes they commit. How many criminal cases registered by police are referred as "mistake of fact?" and the number of such cases may reveal the extent of referred cases. The "techniques of neutralization" proposed by Sykes and Matza may be introduced to explain the police crimes in "mistake of fact" cases. Technique of neutralization is the *process of reasoning* in which a policeman/officer justified his act even when he knows that he purposively commits an offence under law. He has a wrong *vocabulary* about "mistake of fact", "mistake of law", "good faith" etc. If he has a different vocabulary, then he may not commit such acts. The policeman/officer may engage in deliberately violating the laws and register cases against innocent people, but his action is then accompanied by reasoning or by filing of a false final report. The law says that an individual is not culpable and therefore not punishable legally if his act shows an absence of criminal intent. Research studies show that this loophole in the penal law is the most exploited provision accompanied by a rational interpretation. During 1998, a total of 2151160 cases under the Indian Penal Code—1860 were registered for investigation. Out of them, 118018 cases were referred as the charge found false/mistake of fact/ law etc. and such a large number of referred cases is of bad taste. A criminal case means physical and mental pain to many and has penal significance for the accused, waste of money for the public exchequer and loss of manpower/time for the police department. Rationalization and reasoning do not/cannot take away the criminal content of police actions if they are initiated purposively to put the suspect/accused in mental agony and victimization. Criminologists may call such rationalizations and reasonings "senseless". They find rationalization and reasoning as the prime motive when cases are registered. Sometimes, the registration of cases for *expost facto* rationalization/justification may be the result of some conspiracy between the police and vested interests. Such actions may be "acceptable" to the legal system, but may be a crime for the larger society. A denial of responsibility after rationalizing the whole action is no excuse for the law enforcement machinery. Criminologists may say that the rationalizations and reasoning out comprise a significant component of Edwin H. Sutherland's definition "favourable to the violation of law" in police service. The police cannot deny the effects of injury caused to people by their actions.

The criminogenesis of police crimes may be of interest to many. No scientific study has been so far conducted to look at police as a group of people committing law violations. Monastic criminality theories—sponteneity, possession, rationality, external forces, internal mechanisms—did not speak about police crimes and criminality. Though studies were conducted on organized crimes, white collar crimes, political crimes etc., the scientists were found to neglect lawless law enforcement, enforcement and nexus crimes by enforcement agencies themselves. Pluralistic theories too did not deal with police crimes. Police have been fighting against crimes and criminals. The emphasis given to police as fighters blinded many to look at them as violators. Even "integrative theories" did not deal with police crimes. The chapter that follows, like the present one, discusses the crimonogenesis of police crimes form different angles.

References

1. See Section 176, *Code of Criminal Procedure*—1973.
2. William A. Westley, *Violence and the Police* in Norman Johnston *et.al.* (ed.), *The Sociology of Punishment and Correction*, Wiley, New York, 1962.

CHAPTER—10

Criminogenesis of Police Crimes

Police have principally to control/prevent the commission of crimes. For this the British recruited rubust people who were not well educated. They were given hard physical training and certainly, they had the courage and self-confidence to deal with many situations. How did such a robust force take up the responsibility of investigation of crimes? Investigation of crime was an intellectual exercise and the rubust physique or hard physical training had nothing much to do with investigation of crimes. In some countries, law and order functions are done by police officers who do not investigate crimes. Crime investigation is a separate branch and it does not have anything much to do with law and order. Criminologists feel that police crimes can be reduced if the police is bifurcated into two, namely, (1) law and order and (2) crime investigation. They must be kept in water tight compartments.

Differential identification—i.e., the law and order policeman views him as a detector and investigator of crime and criminals or vice versa—is found to be a cause for police crimes. A crime investigator identifies himself with a law and order policeman when he investigates a crime or interrogates a suspect. He plays a dual role, but does not show appropriate personality traits when he performs his different roles. When he is interrogating a suspect in a crime—may be the real criminal—a criminal identification occurs in him as he is directly interacting with a criminal in police custody. Resultingly, he tortures him or commits other human rights violations. The theory of differential association in criminology is that "*a person pursues criminal behaviour to the extent that be identifies himself with real or imaginary persons from whose perspective his criminal behaviour seems acceptable*[1]". Torture in police custody is accepted to some extent by many members in police service so much so that they have no difficulty to adopt such behavioural strategies. Then, what about corruption, corrupt practices, corruption-money fixing, nexus criminality etc. The same explanation is acceptable and applicable there too. The individual evaluates his behaviour from the perspective of other individuals working with him. The perspective is favourable to his views and he then behaves in a criminal way.

Criminal Role-Models

A crime-prone policeman/officer has before him many illegitimate success models. Such models who have achieved success by illegitimate means are visible to the new entrants in service. A new subinspector once told me that one X in police service was his role model and he was a terror. The new subinspector wanted to terrorize the people when he performed his functions. He could not do so without violating human rights of others and committing crimes. Success goals in police life for him was to terrorize and rule. Hence, I find that one of the causes leading to police crimes is the availability and visibility of crime-prone or criminal success models in police service. Desiring alone does not and can not ensure that the individual can behave like his role model. There must be the support from the police community and subculture prevailing therein.

The Lokayuktha in a South Indian State issued an order to the director general of police to initiate action against a policeman who was involved in Shylock or loan-shark racket. He gave Rs. 25,000—to a businessman and demanded Rs. 25,000—as interest after 2 years. The businessman refused to pay so much amount as interest. Then he misused the power of his uniform and got the amount back forcefully. On inquiry, it was proved that he was successfully managing a Shylock racket and according to him, he has many role models who became very rich by their loan-shark rackets. No doubt, the Shylock was considered a respectable and an affluent man by his colleagues/associates in service.

Frustration—Equals—Aggression

Policemen react to frustrations frequently by violence—say many people. Of course, they can afford to become violent as there is no one to question them. This was the situation more in the past than at present. People's tolerance of police aggression helped only to develop aggression among the policemen. As democracy came into existence, the people mobilized their energy for reacting to police aggression by initiating newer course of behaviour. New laws were enacted to control police behaviour further and victimological compensation is awarded to the victims of abuse of power/misuse of authority.

Police were told and taught to be mild to frustrations and to control their violence or violent approaches. They are made more accountable. Human rights laws are taught to them. The press and people watch their behaviour. The police are criticized for their violent acts. Departmental and judicial actions are initiated against those who express uncalled for violence.

Frustrations of police are diverted to their selves as well. In a south Indian State, policemen (officers too) were found to commit suicide and on inquiry, it could be learnt that they resorted to suicide as they could not withstand their frustrations within and outside the police department. Strangely enough, many States do not have police counselling services to help the policemen who experience tensions/mental frustrations. How many policemen/officers take to drinks or drugs? They do so to release their tensions and frustrations? Once a few policemen were found drunk during their working hours. At another day, a very senior police officer came to inspect the parade in drunkenness. Once it was alleged that the policemen drank alcohol seized by them during a raid and the number of such instances may be plenty. There is an allegation that police officers do not take serious actions against drunkenness by policemen. Although the service (conduct) rules say that drunkenness while on duty is a misconduct, a substantial number of cases are ignored, indifferently treated or lightly punished. If the drunk creates nuisance, then it may increase the probability of departmental actions. Why do the policemen show a lenient attitude or tolerate such misconducts?

Frustrations of policemen to their sexual needs may find expression in their showing aggression. The media bring news about police misbehaviour in sexual areas. Peeping, exhibitionism, heterosexual aggression, indecent talks, homosexuality etc. may be related to sexual frustrations. A casual study showed that many a policeman suffered sexual starvation as they could not go home and lead a normal family life. Masturbation could be noticed among policemen as an easily available method of releasing their sexual frustrations. 92 per cent of the policemen interviewed by me admitted that they resorted to masturbation as a release mechanism to their sexual frustrations. More than 90 per cent admitted that they had sex dreams. Many had nocturnal emissions. During off-duty hours/days, some of them were found to go out for heterosexual patting to busy bazars, public transport omnibuses etc. In some cases, complaints were received for indecency in sex-behaviour. Homosexuality was noticed in few cases and on an analysis, I could understand that enforced bathlorhood for those who were married and sexual starvation for several months together were certainly the reasons for sexual indecency among the policemen. Brothels would be noticed near police camps and they could invite sexually starving policemen to make a visit to the prostitutes. In the case of higher-ups, such sexual starvation might not be seen as they used to stay with their family and children. Nevertheless, they could be seen to involve in sex-enjoyment as there again could be variety seekers who had no moral guilt to involve in extramarital sex-contacts.

Defence Against Guilt

Some policemen experience guilt when they involve in committing forbidden acts. They have anxiety, fear and apprehensions of danger for them. In some, a mental change takes place in due course. Consequently, they give up their frustration—equals—aggression attitudes and approaches. In those who do not do so, one sees the development of some defences against the guilt they have. They find out a way of managing the guilt generated by a conflict between what they do and what they feel about their doings. Some may take to drinks, others may to drugs. Some may eat a lot or may involve in some pleasure giving activities. Some may blame others or the whole environment; others may rationalize their illegal activities. Thus they seek a sort of psychological protection against their activities. Those who do not have any guilt feelings for what they do are called "psychopaths". They need clinical therapy. Often, they do not go for clinical consultations.

Group Crimes and Police Subculture

There is a view that some of the crimes policemen/officers commit are typically a group phenomena. In police, there exists the *esprit de corps* (an internal cohesion) even in the commission of certain categories of crimes. Crimes are committed in police subculture and one sees them as a cooperation action, shared tradition etc. The entire group is aware of what is going on in the subculture, but it tolerates, encourages and promotes. For, the crimes thus committed by group cohesiveness ensures free and easy life, money and pleasure etc. As a result, there is the joint commitment of the members who constitute the group. It is otherwise called the *consensus crimes* in police.

Some policemen who are not inclined to become a member in the group cohesiveness are driven to the culture. Certainly, they are not attracted as they have conscientious objections to such activities in the subculture. Their sensitivity to the subculture is not honoured and precisely therefore they have no option but to become members in the group if they want to continue in the subculture. In due course, they realize the fact that the subculture is rewarding and then they willingly become a member in the subculture. Later, they may resist any order transferring them to another unit as the pleasure or being in the group is certainly "a pleasure" for them. They become a part of the subculture. The members in the group have common values, common attitudes and common rules for behaviour. They support commission of various kinds of police crimes.

Criminologists who have studied syndicate crimes could attest the view that the organized crimes became successful only if they could establish some relationship or partnership with enforcement agencies. In police, one may find criminal nexuses established between police and organized criminals. The police support syndicate crimes and the group cohesiveness will be in favour of organized crimes. Every new individual born into the group has in some way to come in terms with their norms which may be arbitrarily imposed upon him.

Attack on Policemen and Police Crimes

Policemen are attacked everywhere and the attack is on the increase. During 1994—' 98, the number of police personnel killed or injured on duty is:—

***Police Personnel Killed or Injured during 1994—98**

Year	*No. of Police Killed*	*Personnel Injured*
1994	585	3630
1995	516	3430
1996	626	3151
1997	597	3832
1998	634	3760

* *Source:* Crime in India: 1998, Government of India.

The higher is the rank, the lesser is the causality. During 1998, Gazetted officers—5, Constables—429, Head constables—107, Assistant subinspectors—34, Subinspectors—48, and Inspectors—11 were killed. Those who got injured were constables—2528, head constables—459, Assistant subinspectors—171, subinspectors—330, and inspectors--133. Gazetted officers were the rest and they constituted 2.1 per cent.

National Crime Records Bureau, Government of India writes: "the very nature of policeman's job generates animosity thereby endangering their own life in the course of discharge of their official duties." No doubt, when policeman attacks people, the people and the press make an issue out of it. On the other hand, when people attack the policeman, they keep silence or ignore the same. This attitude and approach taken by the politicians and the press/people make police crimes highly visible and crimes against police quite invisible. I asked some journalists to speak out the double standard in their approach. They told me that "crimes by police is nothing new, Crimes against the police is something new in India" and they said further that the press did not give publicity on crimes against police and the reason was that crimes by police was more heinous than crimes against police. It is a controversial issue and it does not come within the scope of the subject under discussion.

Police Crimes after Independence in India

The police are to enforce the law—fairly and justly. Yet, they make decisions, sometimes, to violate the laws. The allegation against the police is that they take the law into their hands and at times, they themselves become the laws. In such instances, the police become law makers and law enforcers. It is no easy task to govern people thus as the people have freedom, rights and dignity. People say: "the policeman who has a sense of duty, a sense of justice, a sense of dignity does not make laws and enforce them. He obeys the laws and enforces them".

4823 people can not be wrong in their assessment. In a study conducted in January, 1982, the views and opinions of people on police performance were analysed[2]. The study revealed the reluctance of police to aid the citizen in distress, undue delay in the disposal of petitions and complaints, lethargy, inaction, unwillingness to register cases, half hearted investigation, perfunctory inspection, indepth interrogation, partiality, susceptibility to corruption, informal arrests and other human rights violations etc. People do not consider them as criminal and there are many reasons for it. Murder, kidnapping, rape, arson, robbery etc. are treated by people as crimes committed by people and not by police. They see informal arrests by police, but do not treat them as abduction. They see third degree methods but do not look at them as voluntarily causing hurt/

grievous hurt etc. Moreover, some people consider that such police acts are necessary and essential for the management/maintenance of law and order or for preventing crimes in society. Commission of crimes for prevention of crime or for management of law and order—this earlier public approach is no more accepted now. Crimes must be called by their "proper names" and that is the public's attitude to police crimes and criminality today. Earlier, in the above study, it was noted that 48.02 per cent of the people were favouring the use of third degree methods by police in absolutely necessary cases. Today, people do not say so, rather approach the Human Rights Commissions for getting victimological compensation. People consider third degree methods as crimes and so do they with respect to many other commissions and omissions by police. Is police crime a crime?—that question is to be answered. Yes, the police crime is a crime and must be treated as such. But the policeman who violates the law does not regard him as one who violates the law. Till recently, police crimes were treated under *hidden criminality*, but today, they are not. Corruption and corrupt practices in police were disfavoured by the people in the 1982 study mentioned above. They thought that the policemen in the lower ranks were most highly corrupt. But today, people do not think so. Mafia, enforcement crimes etc. are seen among the high, higher and highest echelons in police hierarchy. The police crimes come to police attention, but the police do not take actions. More serious offences do not necessarily lead to arrest by police. Why? The law violators are law enforcers there and sometimes, they enforce law through law violations. The allegation is that the police treat many police crimes as trivial acts and thereby they give a cover to their own illegalities. For example, a traffic violation by a police officer is not rightly treated as a violation by his colleagues. If the violation is by a very senior police officer, the violation may become the law for the time being. Once a deputy inspector general of police violated the law on "one way traffic" and the policeman saw his car going to the wrong direction violating the "one way traffic rule". Immediately, the policeman became wild to all other vehicle drivers who obeyed the traffic rules and said "the rule is different until the D.I.G. leaves the spot".

People blame the police for many things including the registration of false cases to the concocting of evidence in genuine cases— the study observes. The people find the policemen favouring the politicians of the ruling front and certainly, the impartiality of the police is questioned. A substantial portion of the citizens see the succeptibility of the policemen to many other extraneous sources as well. There are laws, rules and orders to control the police, but the police violate them. It means the law can not control the behaviour of people including policemen. The policemen are always in a more advantageous position to commit crimes than the ordinary people in society. Recently, an inspector of police and a few constables were convicted by a court for forcing a suspect to eat human excreta and to drink human urine. Allegations are there that the policemen forcefully compel the suspects to drink urine if they are interrogated in depth by employing torture and other inhuman methods. There is a belief among some policemen that fresh urine mixed with green chilly has good medicinal effect on the tortured. Whatever that be, the policemen themselves admit that they involve in administering miscarriage of justice from the beginning of crime investigation and it may be seen during all the stages of crime investigation[3].

Police Views about their Own Crimes

In a study conducted after collecting the views of 254 police officers who were directly concerned with the investigation of criminal offences, it has been revealed that the police officers committed many types of offences during the investigation of crimes[4]. The police resort to unwritten and illegal procedures or strategies which are certainly of a questionable nature. When F.I.Rs are registered, the police add somethings from their pocket to draw up legally admissible F.I.Rs. There exists the practice of verifying the information prior to recording of the F.I.R. Later, they dress up the case and many cases fail in the court just because they are dressed up. They dress up a case or manipulate the F.I.R. for making it stronger or weaker or to satisfy vested interests etc. Allegations are there to prove that police investigators accept corruption money from the accused/his party, from the victim/his party or both. The above mentioned study reveals that many police officers admit the fact of accepting corruption money from many sources during the investigation of criminal cases. The study further shows that the police adopt many objectionable methods which include threatening witnesses, forcing them or making people as witnesses against their wishes. Police officers are candid to admit that there exist informal arrests, illegal detention of the arrestees even more than 15 days, extorting confessions, torturing suspects, using filthy language and epithets etc. The study brings to light a glaring fact that a sub-system which is bound to investigate a crime in an honest and fair way does not claim that the individuals working in the subsystem do everything as per law and procedure established by law. They resort to several tactics, methods and strategies which are legally unjustifiable. No doubt, a series of illegal acts done in the name of administering justice or in the pretext of administering justice cannot ensure real justice to society.

The abòve study exposes the methods of collecting material evidence against suspects in criminal cases. According to the study, 79.27 per cent of police officers admit that they make the suspects to collect some relevant evidence. 35.37 per cent say that they ask the suspects to recover an evidence already hidden by police themselves. 12.80 per cent state that they cook up evidence and record them as having been collected by the suspects. In such cases, the quality of justice administered is of a meaningless nature. The tutored witnesses, false witnesses, touts of police are produced before the courts of law. According to police officers, many witnesses give different versions to them and to the court. Resultingly, many criminal cases end in acquittals.

In police criminology, the questions that need answers are: "Why do the police do so? Are they not crimes? If they are not crimes, then, what are they? Police officers advance a lot of justifications for their acts. Antiquated laws are not applicable to the changed socio-economic and politico-legal milieu and therefore violation of certain procedures becomes a necessary evil in administration of criminal justice. The retributive spirit with which the people want to deal with criminals pressure the police to adopt objectionable strategies. The non-co-operation of the public, witnesses and prosecutors make the police subsystem to have recourse to many objectionable strategies. Lack of professional ethics in police officers is cited as another reason for some to commit offences while enforcing the laws. Inadequate police training and ignorance of scientific methods, lack of commitment to do the job in an honest way may be other factors for police violations of law. To add further they think that police functionaries are not properly supervised. There is no prick of conscience for some police functionaries even when they flout the rights of the informants, witnesses and suspects. Inculcation of moral values is lacking among some police officers.

Police officers, owing to their lack of information and thanks to ignorance, give least priority to the collection of material evidence in crimes. It leads to perfunctory investigation and concoction of evidence, manipulation of records and production of false/tutored witnesses before the courts of law. There is no accountability for many illegal things police do. Partiality and prejudices work against administration of justice. The political pressure and succeptibility to corrupt practices pay the way for miscarriage of justice. In spite of them, the police officers do not feel that they commit crimes. Instead, they think that they do administer fair justice to the people! According to them, informal arrests, illegal detentions, unauthorized methods of dealing with suspects are justified as they are intended for punishing the accused. For some of them, the end always justifies the means. Use of third degree methods during interrogation turns law into an instrument of torture, but many police officers are not prepared to reconcile with the truth. The study shows that police investigators add to, dilute or destroy evidence and that too, for them, is for administration of justice or interpreted justice. The ideal objectives of law and law enforcement are defeated by such acts of unscrupulous police officers. Some of them do so as they do not want to jeopardize their own interests for the interest of justice administration. All these are crimes in every sense and they are made worse by the culpable indifference and negligence of the higher ups in the hierarchy and they, to some extent and in many cases, can remedy the situation. The climate of illegality can be explained by raising many grounds, but such justifications and rationalizations may mitigate the subjective responsibility of individual police officers in certain cases, but can never justify the miscarriage of justice committed by the powerful against the weak.

Courts and Police Crimes

Where administration of justice is involved, the services of law courts must be profoundly consistent. The courts can not and should not tolerate torture, discrimination, bias, violation of human rights laws etc. for, they are crimes and it is this deep sense of justice which has given rise to a court system for controlling, guiding and directing the police in their activities.

291 acquittal verdicts were scrutinized to learn the judicial grounds of acquittal[5] and every judicial ground is directly or indirectly related to a police crime which is serious or otherwise. For example, cases were acquitted by courts on the grounds or (1) omissions in the F.I.R., (2) preparation of the F.I.R. in the wrong way, (3) false recording of facts in the F.I.R. etc. F.I.R. is an important document and in such an important document, any omission is a serious matter leading to miscarriage of justice. If an act leads to miscarriage of justice, then it is a crime committed purposefully or otherwise. What is the meaning of making *mistakes* in F.I.Rs? Mistakes in the F.I.Rs mean indifferent ways of questioning the informant or purposeful manipulation in the recording of the same. The ritualistic way of recording F.I.Rs may not serve any purpose other than defeating administration of justice. It is a misuse of power and abuse of authority.

Reasonable delay to inspect a scene of crime is understandable; but undue delay is not. The courts acquit criminal cases just because of inordinate delay to inspect the scene of crime. They smell rat in such instances. Hasty and insufficient inspection is found to be another cause of acquittals. Why do they conduct such perfunctory investigation if they are not ill-motivated? In history, one takes note of the fact that criminal cases were treated as private cases. Seeing that such a system could not ensure full justice to the criminal, the society entrusted the task of inspection of the scene of crime and its full investigation to trained police investigators. The society thought that the poor victims of crime ought to get justice and thus hopefully and courageously entrusted the work of investigating crimes to police and provided sufficient fund, personnel and resources for the same. But, the police functionaries did not become scientific in their approaches. Unscientific ways of inspection, defective handling and packing of evidence resulting in contamination of evidence, preparation of defective scene mahazars, destruction of evidence owing to the mishandling of it by unauthorized personnel etc., the study reveals, became grounds of acquittals in criminals cases. Acquittals are going up alarmingly high and they show that the system paves way for miscarriage of justice. Miscarriage of justice is a crime. During the British rule, the people remained silent and did not raise their voice against the miscarriage of justice by enforcement agencies. The multitude of the weak and defenceless human beings, the crimedoers and the victims suffered the ill-effects of miscarriage of justice. Even after India became independent, the people did not react to police crimes as they were ignorant of the ways of reacting to miscarriage of justice. Even after 50 years of freedom in India, the situation does not change much to the better. The people can not be silent about the injustices they suffer today and certainly, they are not prepared to compromise or compound with injustices. They rush to the press, politicians, media and courts when they want to react against enforcement crimes particularly when they are committed by police functionaries. Earlier, an incidence of compelling a member of the Dalit community to eat human excreta was discussed. The court which convicted the police officers for their acts allowed a certain victimological compensation to the one who could not but eat human excreta in police custody. It is seen in the media that the people are collecting money for filing a case against the convicted police officers for claiming reasonable and adequate victimological compensation.

Defective scence mahazars, contamination of evidence, destruction of evidence, unscientific ways of inspection etc. indicate negligence in the duties entrusted to the police and grave violation of the trust which the people have on them. In every acquittal, justice is killed. Either a guilty escapes or an innocent suffers and in every case of acquittal, one observes miscarriage of justice.

The courts of law observe: (1) physical evidence seized but not exhibited in court, (2) material evidence collected, but not sent for forensic examination as grounds of acquittals. Why? What happens in between the seizure of the evidence and its production before the court? Why do the police refuse to send material evidence for forensic examination? There is scope for suspicion and the suspicion centers around manipulations and concoctions. They are, if they take place, nothing but crimes. If crimes mean violations of laws, then manipulations and concoctions are violations of law and to that extent crimes in every sense. When a patient dies because of the negligence, indifference, callousness of a medical practitioner, then the next of kin of the deceased can claim compensation. Likewise, when a criminal case is damaged by the investigating machinery owing to its lack of interest, overenthusiasm or special interest etc., then the victims have a right to get compensation and that is what the world community is for in these days. People treat them as crimes. They want to enact new laws and punish the guilty. Actions once considered as authorized and practised by police are gradually becoming socially unacceptable and illegal today. Police crimes have become a new and special area for criminologists today. Any police action which disregards the fundamental rights of citizens and human rights of the police is treated as a crime.

Police Crimes and Witnesses

Key witnesses turn hostile to prosecution, statement of witnesses contradict one another, unbelievable version of witnesses etc. become major causes of acquittals of criminal cases. Why? What is the responsibility of police in producing such hostile, contradicting and unbelievable witnesses before the courts? They cause waste of time, energy, money and man-power. The prosecution becomes an exercise in futility. The police can not establish the needed "rapport" with their witnesses. Criminal cases are acquitted in large numbers and in such a situation, the issue has to be evaluated from the view of the accused in crimes. He is subjected to many types of agonies and at the end, he is acquitted. It means nothing for the law-enforcement agencies, nevertheless means a lot for the accused. Doubtlessly it concerns his dignity and the act of the law enforcement agency disregarding the rights of the accused is not justified under any human law. Any legal system which makes such practices legitimate or authorized can not be treated as a fair (legal) system as the practices go contrary to the fundamental principles of absolute respect for human dignity and of the protection of human life under law. In this way, the system contributes to lessening respect for human beings and opens the doors to many ways for abuse of power/misuse of authority by the law enforcement agencies. Certainly such acts are destructive to the trust in relations between the people and the legal system. Practices which authorize and promote miscarriage of justice by way of acquittals are radically opposed not only to the good of the citizens but also to the common good of the society. Any practice permitting or authorizing tutored, hostile, unbelievable, untrustworthy, false witnesses before the courts of law is a crime and precisely, therefore, such a practice is looked down upon. Production of touts, witnesses who give contradictory versions or witnesses who are hostile to prosecution are police crimes which no law must or can legitimize.

The courts of law observe (1) use of unauthorized methods/means employed by police, (2) confessions proved to be not voluntary, (3) foisting of cases on the accused, (4) illegal arrests by police, (5) innocent persons chargesheeted, (6) charge made on civil matters, (7) false framing of charges as the judicial causes of acquittals. There are laws which make such practices illegal and the police/prosecution are bound to obey them. In the case of an intrisically unjust practice, such as resorting to illegal arrests, chargesheeting of the innocent persons etc., it is never licit to permit it. It is a fact that such illegal practices have been in existence from the British past and they have been supported by the powerful subsystems functioning in the justice system. People, as a result, have been suffering the bitterness of such permissive police practices. Today, there are growing signs of a rethinking in this matter and therefore people are not prepared to extend their cooperation with unjust and illegal practices. They become hostile to prosecution and make complaints against the police functionaries. They name such practices as police crimes. Police crimes—i.e., abuse of power/misuse of authority during law enforcement or crime investigation—raise difficult problems of conscience for the common man and he expresses it by showing non-cooperation. They do not want to take part in morally and legally evil actions.

Police produce many documents during the trial. The courts find that the documents do not tally with facts in issue. The courts reject the recovery of physical evidence. Physical evidence produced is not accepted during the trial. Police fail to corroborate witnesses' version by production of physical evidence. They produce insufficient evidence. Moreover, physical evidence produced contradict the versions of witnesses. The courts of law acquit criminal cases in such situations and till now, the law and authorities do not treat such practices as illegal and criminal. If they are not acceptable, then they are just rejected and thus the chapter is closed. Why don't they treat them as crimes? Why don't they proceed against the crime-doers? Why don't they initiate criminal actions against them? Till today, such questions are not asked as the questions are found to be unnecessary and out of question in the present legal system. The refusal to treat them as crimes and the reluctance to initiate actions against the crime doers are serious crimes. They commit acts which are intrinsically incompatible with human dignity and with the dignity of the legal system. The authentic meaning and purpose of the legal system are defeated by such inactions and refusals. Those who do so must be punished, for the law and the legal system entrust the duties to the responsible concern of the enforcement authorities, not to make arbitrary use/misuse of them, but to maintain them with a legal sense and care. Production of irrelevant documents, inadmissible pieces of physical evidence, false evidence and insufficient evidence etc. before the courts of law must be treated as culpable as they are nothing but crimes committed by law enforcement/ crime investigation agencies. In some cases, the courts of law acquit the accused granting benefit of doubt and in other cases the courts pronounce verdicts of acquittal with honour. Acquittal with honour means that the accused is innocent and there is no justification in subjecting him to the ordeals connected with arrest, detention, remand and other pretrial procedures. Every crime investigator has a legal and moral obligation to be at the service of administering justice.

The courts find (1) circumstantial evidence not believed (2) circumstantial evidence not adequate, (3) circumstantial evidence suspicious. Consequently, the police and prosecution are not able to bring out truth in the trial. If truth can not be brought out after a trial, then the whole exercise of investigation becomes meaningless and trouble causing. Administration of justice is sacred and inviolable. Authority and power must not be abused in the name of administering justice or in the pretext of administering justice. Truth not brought out through a trial is a serious offence and precisely therefore it is absolutely unacceptable. To be truly a people at the service of administering justice, the police must propose this truth constantly and honestly in their work.

In a study conducted after eliciting the views and opinions of the members of legal profession (judicial officers, prosecutors, defence counsels and so on), it is revealed that the police investigation is inadequate[6]. Why?

Inadequate and perfunctory investigation of crimes means miscarriage of justice and violation of laws and procedures established by law. They further mean that the crime investigators do not see their role in administering justice in its deeper sense—in an atmosphere of incorruptibility. Policeman's support and promotion of fair justice must be accomplished through justness which finds expression in conducting investigation in the most adequate way. This is a particularly pressing need at the present time when the people look at police actions as crimes committed under the colour of their power and authority.

The Accused and Police Crimes

An accused in a crime may be the best person to speak about many crimes committed against him by the enforcement and investigation agencies. In a study conducted after collecting the experiences which acquitted persons had in police cases[7], it is revealed that:—

1. The police maintain hostile, suspicious, aggressive attitude to suspects in crimes.
2. The police frighten, threaten, physically torture, mentally torture, physically and mentally torture, illegally detain suspects in crimes.
3. The police unduly influence people to become witnesses, enlist persons interested in prosecution, make false witnesses, resort to threat and coercion to witnesses or make witnesses against their interest.

The findings in the above study expose the nature, extent and intensity of illegalities during investigation of crimes. If illegalities are called by their proper names, then they are crimes under law. No man-made laws in criminal jurisprudence will accept such atrocities committed during crime investigation. Respect to law and procedure established by law requires the exercise of conscientious application of them during investigation of crimes. Torturing suspects or creating false witnesses etc. can never be considered a form of administration of justice, even when the motive and intentions are apparently or solely to ensure criminal justice to the accused. Rather, such strategies and illegal acts run completely counter to man's aspirations and desires to ensure human rights justice and criminal justice through the police. The achievements are counterproductive. Society can not leave the crime unpunished. Police crimes certainly cry to humanity for justice and that is how several laws punishing the law enforcement agencies and ordering victimological compensation to the sufferers of injustice are enacted. No criminal loses his personal dignity just because he commits an offence and every policeman himself must guarantee this to all in society. It is precisely here that the real worth of police service to man and humanity is exhibited and proved.

The above study conducted after gathering the live-experience of the accused from police investigators shows further that the police do cook up witnesses, material, documentary and circumstantial evidence. The police investigators who 'pad up' evidence may advance many "moral claims" to justify their otherwise illegal and immoral acts in so doing. There are professional police witnesses who make a living from the testimony they give in courts. Some witnesses are having unhealthy relations with the accused while others are having healthy relations with the victims. There are situations in which witnesses are hired by the victims/his party and the police entertain all such methods and strategies to administer justice in society! They fail to understand that from injustice, only injustice will come out. The various methods and strategies which would seem to be at the service of administering justice to people or criminals and which are frequently used with that intention, can only open the door to new threats against administration of justice. Experience proves that many illegal and criminal strategies the police resort to have a high rate of failure in the long run. And that is what one sees now. The courts disbelieve the police and the Indian Evidence Act—1872 has many provisions to that effect. The above mentioned research study shows that the material evidence produced by police before the courts are not always genuine ones. What about the records produced by the police investigators? They too are of the same nature. If the study reveals the truth, then the police commit crimes which ordinary people may not. They commit such crimes as a part of the justice system and cause the system to act upon them. A police culture of crime thus fights against many other types of crimes in society. Then comes the question: "Who is the real criminal?"—the police or the people?

Police crimes are not crimes of recent origin. They have been in existence for centuries, but no one looked at police crimes as "crimes under the laws". The accused people in criminal cases say that they influence investigating officers to get acquittals and they succeed in their attempts. The police investigators become susceptible to influences! The accused offer remuneration, exert pressure and do many other things to make the police to become vulnerable to their desires. Political intervention, intervention by superior police officers, social higher ups, those influential with police and so on are just a few methods adopted by the people. Some of the accused misused the investigating/other police officers to influence the prosecution lawyers for winning their cases. In such cases, the detection, investigation, chargesheeting, trial etc. become just rituals intended to fool the people, courts of law and the legal system. The law enforcement and crime investigation agencies want to have a judicial burial of criminal cases. If a criminal case is decided by a court of law, then it becomes the final decision on the matter unless appealed against. The police crimes too thus get a judicial burial and that is the reason why some police officers say "Let the case have a natural death" and by natural death, they mean a judicial burial. A judge can take a decision only on the basis of what is presented before him. The police and prosecutor can present a case in many ways before the courts of law. One may notice violations of law and morality even in the presentation of criminal cases before the courts of law. Who is bothered about the large scale acquittals in criminals cases? Even academicians are not and the accused will never be. Police officers are not generally and the people are not always. Thus crimes by people, crimes by the defence, police crimes, prosecutors' crimes, crimes by witnesses, pre-trial crimes, crimes committed during the procedure etc. are mixed together in many ways so that a *decent* burial for the crimes committed by the accused and by others comes from a judicially pronounced judgement from a court of law. Acquittals by trial or after the trial of criminal cases and that too by proper engineering for an anticipated acquittal is a crime which must be dealt with in police criminology.

People and Police Crimes

People have always resisted silently or loudly police crimes. Down the centuries, history shows that people had a sense of anquish and of severe discomfort when they thought about going to police stations or interacting with police officials. No doubt, such an attitude had not come from vacuum as they were brought on by intense sufferings which people had in the past. The atmosphere in police custody, as a rule, can threaten the already fragile equilibrium of an individual's mind with the result that on the one hand, the man under police custody, in his isolation and helplessness, finds no assistance from police functionaries and on the other hand, those close to him are made incapable of offering any assistance to him by the police themselves. Transparency is lacking and this is aggravated by a police cultural climate which fails to perceive human values in interactions with people.

In a study[8] conducted by collecting the felt impressions and views of the people, it is revealed that:—

1. The people are aware that the criminal cases end in acquittals in large numbers and one of the prime reasons for the deplorable situation is defective police interrogation.
2. The people maintain the view that the police investigation in general is inadequate and needs improvement. Defective recording of facts, manipulation of genuine facts in records, failure to collect relevant evidence, unsatisfactory approach to witnesses, unauthorized ways of handling suspects, acceptance of undue influence/ illegal gratification etc. are identified as the causes of inadequate investigation.
3. They take note of the indifferent ways of inspection of the scene of crime, lack of supervision, ignoring of inspection, unnecessary harassment to witnesses, unworthy method of questioning and use of unauthorized means of communication etc. as reasons for large scale acquittals.

Are they crimes to do so? People see such police doings, but generally they do not view them as crimes. According to many people, crimes are those committed by the people and not by the police. Whenever a policeman commits a crime while he is in police uniform, people have a tendency to treat it as a part of his duty. People do not and can not think of a police without police "muscles", police "looks", police "languages" and police "behaviours" and more often than not, the police muscles, talks, looks and languages may be unacceptable to the dominant culture, yet the people tolerate them. They do not think about "crimes" when police commit them. The public respond to police misbehaviour in an informal way and in an unorganized manner since the policeman's misbehaviour is not usually treated as falling into a clear category of crimes. There is no official labelling of police misbehaviour as criminal and therefore the public too do not look at it from a criminological angle. For example, a policeman, suppose, speaks indecent language. The public hear it and then forget it. On the contrary, if a person other than a policeman in uniform does the same thing, people may file a F.I.R. and treat it to be a crime. The policeman is thus segregated from others whenever he speaks filthy language or utters epithets. As the people generally ignore such use of vulgar language by a policeman in Indian culture, he may continue to commit the something thereafter. The assumption here is that police crimes bring some advantages to policemen and the returns thus they get make them to continue to commit crimes. For any sort of crimes to be prevented or controlled, there must be some official dealing of them. In the case of police crimes, there is no official dealing with them unless strong protests and complaints are registered. There must be some official reactions for every police crime. Whenever a witness is harassed, whenever a suspect is tortured or whenever concoction of evidence is resorted to, there must be official reactions to such acts. They will put such acts under clear category of crimes.

The above mentioned study brings to light the public awareness of the use of coercive methods, use of abusive language, detention of the arrestees in an illegal way, resorting to informal arrests, cruel and aggressive treatments etc. But the public swallow them often and there is no official action always against such illegalities seen in police subculture. The public take note of the fact that the police become susceptible to political interference and they see the susceptibility in all ranks in police hierarchy. The people observe acceptance of corruption money, favours, gifts, patrol for police vehicles etc. and they see the effect of such pushers and pullers in police works. Certainly, they are crimes of the first order, nevertheless, they are not labelled so. Neither the politicians nor the police officials do treat political interference a crime in police work. If they treat so and if they treat police susceptibility to political interference a crime, then it will be possible to avoid the potentially negative effects of political interference and police susceptibility. Today, everybody distrusts the police and the above study reveals that the police suppress facts, suggest falsehood, pad up evidence, overexaggerate or underestimate facts etc. to prosecutors and courts. What do they gain by such illegalities? What action is initiated against them for such illegalities? Police crimes are so repetitive and so clearly dangerous to the society that really very serious actions are required to control and prevent them. Adherence of such a policy will considerably reduce the extent and intensity of public criticisms against the police.

Victims and Police Crimes

Victims of crime, victims of abuse of power or misuse of authority—all are victims in the study of police victimology. Like police criminology, there is a branch called police victimology which focuses its attention to the victims of abuse of power/misuse of authority by police. I have discussed the subject in detail in my recent book titled *Police, Victim and Victim Justice*. In many cases a suspect in a crime may become both an accused and a victim. Refusal to cooperate with the police, irritating behaviour of the suspects etc. may provoke a police officer to become wild. A police officer once threatened to employ third degree methods on an arrestee in police custody. He said it repeatedly and that night the detinue committed suicide. In some instances of custodial deaths, the victims may be the aggressor. Ego-clashes, heated arguments between the police and the suspects, lack of respect shown to police uniform/

authority etc. may result in the commission of crimes by police on the victims.

For every police action, there will be a victim or victims on the other side. Are the victims necessarily the victims of abuse or power/misuse of police authority? This is an issue that is often discussed in police criminology/victimology. Do the police misuse their power/abuse their authority just because the victims belong to a different religion, caste or subcaste other than the same to which the police officer is a member? Allegations are heard from the members of the scheduled castes/tribes that they are ill-treated or treated without dignity just because they belong to a lower caste/community. Policemen/officers themselves make complaints against their superiors alleging that officers belonging to the higher castes treat them without dignity and esteem. True or false the allegations, the fact remains that such accusations are made by the police functionaries themselves.

Police is a male dominated service in India. Precisely therefore, the females feel disturbed to go to police for service. Just recently, a deaf and dumb girl was molested in a police van kept in a court compound. Another woman raped by policemen committed suicide. Prostitutes are ill treated in police custody and the allegations are numerous and all of them are not baseless or groundless.

Police in India do not have a juvenile wing and usually, the policemen dealing with adult criminality deal with juvenile delinquency as well. Allegations are plenty to show that the police do not honour the provisions of the Juvenile Justice care and Protection of children Act—2000 when they deal with juveniles.

Harry Elmer Barnes speaks about trial by battle or ordeal[9]. The trial involved physical or mental torture. According to Barnes, the torture follows the following pattern. (1) The victim is, as a rule, housed in a cell or dungeon which was cold, verminous, damp and small. (2) He is given very little food. (3) A stage of frustration is followed. He is to face mental torture. He is shown instruments of torture (4) then comes the stage of markless injury—i.e., torture that leave no visible physical signs of injury. (5) Afterwards comes the stage of *marked injury*. The body is stretched on a ladder. Sometimes thumbscrews or other methods of penetrating the flesh may be employed. Afterwards, salt water is applied. (6) At the final stage, i.e., the *fatal end*, the victim is killed by means of physical torture. He says further that a few victims can go through all these stages as most of them confessed their guilt before the torture became very cruel, inhuman and severe. The trial by ordeal is not now seen practised as it used to be in the past. Today, the trial by ordeal is practised in such a way that the victim is subjected to torture without causing visible physical injury. The United Nations are fully aware of the victimization of suspects in custody and therefore a number of human rights laws has been adopted by them. The reports of the National Human Rights Commission give live examples of victimization and torture of suspects in police custody. Evidence in hand shows that the establishment of Human Rights Commissions and Human Rights Courts in India (after 1993 when the Protection of Human Rights Act was enacted) did not eliminate physical or mental torture in custody.

Victimization by police, police torture, police brutality, abuse of power/misuse of authority by police etc. are not new phenomena in India. But they have become more obvious and conspicuous because of the larger number of people involved in these days. The press brings them out and the legislators make use of them for attacking the ruling government. After India became independent, the political parties and various organizations sponsored by political parties raise their protests through demonstrations. The policemen want to control the demonstrations or suppress them. They act as the coercive weapon of the government in power. In such situations, it is difficult to distinguish police behaviour from that of the demonstrators. Police stone at the people and the people too stone at the police. The stone throwing continues to an extent that the police use excessive force to suppress the demonstration. Stark says that in such situations, the police are the major offenders. Why do the police become major offenders in such situations? Commissions of Inquiry appointed after a police operation on mobs, sometimes, point out that the police are major offenders. Here, doubtlessly, the police feel a threat to their power, authority, persons and security. They, then, respond to such threats and they use excessive force to suppress the mob violence. The policeman in such crowd behaviour of the police behaves like a member in the mob. The police justify their actions and do not feel guilty for what they do in such mob control operations. Usually they say that they are provoked to anger. Policemen are professionals and they have good training to deal with mob. They must have control over their emotions. If they do not show such controls, it means that they lack sufficient expertise in the area of mob control. O.W. Wilson says: "The officer . . . . . must remember that there is no law against making a policeman angry and that he can not charge a man making him angry". Stark adds that most policemen "reject the legal, administrative and moral limits imposed on their use of force. They condone and even advocate using violence well beyond that permitted by these limits[12]". The law permits the police to use force when they see violence directed against them, to others and to both. But, no law permits the police to use excessive force or more force than what is required to handle a situation. Some policemen think that they are empowered to use fore against anyone in their custody even when the detinue is found to be helpless, fragile and defenceless. They extend the permission granted by law to areas which do not require the use of force. But some do so as they think that the use of violence is necessary to protect the status of their profession and to teach the people that they are empowered to employ force on anybody at their desires and fancies. Such people misuse their power and abuse their authority to coerce respect for them. This is a police crime and the victims of such disrespectful acts deserve victim compensation. Somehow or other policemen have developed wrong notions and perverted perceptions about public behaviour. Westley says: "The police believe that certain groups of persons will respond only to fear and rough treatment[13]".

Police victimology is not a developed branch in police criminology. How do the police make people victims of their abuse of power/misuse of authority? I asked this question to some lawyers and they said many ways the police could make people victims of their abuse of power/misuse of authority. Some of them are:—

1. Use of "throways" by police. It means that the police carry some implements or tools which they plant on suspects. Later, they take them into custody as suspects making plans to house-breaking or burglary.
2. The police plant some evidence in a place of search and later seize it from there in a formal search.
3. The police take people in custody and make them as carriers of drugs or contraband articles.
4. The police take a person in custody and make him an accused in a case for which the list of suspects is not closed. The police produce their touts as witnesses to attest the story that he too is involved in the case.
5. In order to show that the life of the policeman is threatened, they plant on the suspects some knives or similar weapons.

Policeman has an ego and he wants to maintain it. Any question/ challenge to his real or imagined authority is not tolerated. Police victimology deals with the acts, atrocities and abuses of police power with an intention to victimize the people. Chevigny writes that the policemen consider the courts "as a mere adjunct to their purpose. Distortion of the facts becomes the most pervasive and the most insignificant of abuses. The police ethic justifies any action which is intended to maintain order or to convict any wrong doer, (i.e., anyone actually or potentially guilty of crime)".

Enforcement and Police Crimes

Police Enforcement Crimes and Injustice is a title authored by me and I have discussed in detail various types of crimes police commit during the course of their duties. Again, *Indian Police and Nexus Crime* is another title authored by me and there I have dealt with many types of crimes the police commit owing to the unholy nexuses they establish among them, politicians, businessmen and so on. Enforcement Crimes and Nexus Crimes become the part and parcel of contemporary police criminology. Criminologists who study the current trends in police crimes can not ignore them. For, such crimes are serious problems today. The President of India, in his telecast to the Nation on the Eve of the Independence Day 2000, spoke about the damaging effects of nexus crimes in India. There is no way enforcement crimes may be proceeded against. If a police officer does not register a case as per the law under which he ought to have registered the case, there is no law under which proceedings may be initiated against the police officer who purposefully damages the case. This is enforcement crime. Likewise, if a police officer omits a particular witness, then nothing can be done against him. If a police officer registers a case after having conducted a preliminary inspection of the scene of crime, nothing can be done against him. Likewise, the laws can be violated with immunity during the course of crime investigation and the justice system is helpless to proceed against the law violators. The weakness of the system may be profitably and advantageously exploited for the commission of nexus crimes. Suppose, a police officer becomes lenient in his action against a particular crime-doer as a result of some nexus understanding. Some studies show that the probability of arrests increases when the person to be arrested belongs to the political party in opposition to the ruling government. If discrimination is shown on the basis of political affiliations, then nothing much can be done against such discriminations. A nexus police officer can not maintain an image of full enforcement. The enforcement may be partial or even to the extent of lawless law enforcement.

Police Crimes not Included in the Statistics

Official statistics do not include police crimes. For, police crimes are usually not treated as crimes. If at all a policeman is accused of an offence, it is not treated separately. Only a few types of crimes like death in police custody, rape in police stations etc. are given in official statistics. The figures relating to corruption/bribe are extremely poor and show only the iceberg of police crimes.

Why do police commit crimes? A general theory of criminality can not successfully explain police criminality. Moreover, criminologists have not made any serious attempts to find out the etiology of police crimes. The traditional definitions of crime are related to the crimes committed by people and not policemen in uniform. Therefore, the traditional explanations of crime and criminals may not be strictly applicable to police crimes. For, the police criminals are people in police uniform with power and authority and they abuse/misuse the authority conferred on them. They are in an advantageous position and they do not have many to be afraid of. The chapter that follows contains a theory of police crimes and the last chapter is on enforcement criminology.

References

1. See, Daniel Glaser, *Criminality Theories and Behavioural Images from Delinquency, Crime and Social Processes*, D. R. Cressey & David A. Ward (ed.), Harper & Row, New York, 1969.
2. Alphons L. Earayil and James Vadackumchery, *Police and the Society*, Kairali, Trivandrum, 1985.
3. James Vadackumchery, *Indian Police and Miscarriage of Justice*, APH, Delhi, 1997.
4. James Vadackumchery, *Indian Police and Miscarriage of Justice, op. cit.*
5. James Vadackumchery, *The Police, The Court and Injustice*, APH, Delhi, 1997.
6. James Vadackumchery, *The Police, The Court and Injustice, op. cit.*
7. James Vadackumchery, *The police, The Accused and Criminal Injustice*, APH, Delhi, 1997.
8. James Vadackumchery, *The Police, The People and Criminal Justice*, APH, Delhi, 1997.
9. Harry Elmer Barnes, *The Story of Punishment: A Record of Man's Inhumanity to Man*, Patterson Smith, Montclair, N. J. 1972.

10. Stark, *Police Riots* from *Theory of Collective Behaviour*, The Free Press, New York, 1963.
11. O.W. Wilson, *Police Administration*, McGraw Hill, New York, 1963.
12. Stark, *op. cit.*
13. William A. Westley, *Violence and the Police*, American Journal of Sociology, 49 (July) 1963.
14. Paul Chevigny, *Police Power: Police Abuses in New York City*, Random House, New York, 1969.

CHAPTER—11

Police Criminology: A Theory that Explains the Etiology of Police Crimes

Law enforcement or policing needs able-bodied men. People and the police think so. The physique of the policeman/officer determines the way he behaves—say some people in society. As per the laws, the police have to identify criminals, detect crimes and prevent criminal activities. Skolnick speaks about the "working personality" of a policeman. They have strong physique and Skolnick[1] says that they become sensitive to signs of danger. Policemen are attacked and there exist threat to their lives. They become suspicious of the people, their gestures, manners, body language, activities etc. They are inclined to think that all these lead only to crime, violence and attack on policemen. The suspicion which the police have about people make them to commit certain types of crimes which for the people are nothing but human rights violations. Informal arrests and use of epithets on public etc. may be examples in point.

Like Skolnick's "*working personality*" of the policemen, Niederhoffer[2] tells about the "*authoritarian personality*" of the cops. He thinks that the policemen's love of power and toughness makes them to look at the public with a cynical attitude. The policemen often come in contact with criminals, antisocial elements in society and dishonest men. Their frequent contacts with such people make them, sometimes, to behave the way they behave. Policemen see others as criminals and they, at times, behave like criminals. According to McNamara[3], there is an increase in the authoritarianism in police as they work more in police service. He found police with two years of service having more authoritarianism than those who had less than two years of experience. Their increased authoritarianism is likely to lead them to crimes and criminality.

Police enjoy a lot of discretion in taking decisions particularly when they arrest people. Some researchers hold the view that they take into account the immediate and pressuring situations when they arrest people even when arrests are not warranted. Bittner[4] finds that the policemen arrest a person when they see that the individual to be arrested is a potential risk to law and order than on the basis of the actual risk he causes. Instances are plenty to show that the police arrest people on the basis of political pressures and do not arrest people again on the basis of political pressures. Sometimes, the police arrest people if the individuals question the authority of police to effect arrests. Personality clashes between the policeman and the individual to be arrested may be another reason for the arrests. Informal arrests are notoriously commented by the people. Whenever the policeman arrests people without justifiable cause, the action is said to be misuse of authority/ abuse of power.

A police officer in uniform may think that he has a lot of authority and he wants the people to respect his authority. He expects the people to obey him and respect his authority without questioning. If someone questions his authority he may react to it in an aggressive way. Westley[5] finds enough evidence to show a police subculture which justifies the use of violence to coerce respect. Respect is something that must come from the abdomen—from the heart of one's hearts and is not something that may be coerced. Behind police crimes, one observes police reactions to coerce respect for his authority. No doubt, the police, as a law enforcement agency, enjoy occupational status. But, the people's respect for the occupational status must not come from coercion, violence or pressure. No civilized law will accept the attitude of a policeman who says that a person who talks disrespectfully to a police officer must be treated with brutality. Respect generates respect and a trained policeman will exhibit respect to people who talks back in a disrespectful manner.

Coercing respect to the occupational status of policemen or to the authority/uniform of the cops has not yielded in creating an enviable image of the police service. It has helped only to develop public hostility to police. Researches show that the more public hostility the police receive, the more isolated they become. The policemen become "loners" in the community and the people call them violent, indecent and atrocious.

Departmental Tolerance to Police Crimes

Some researchers say that the police department is well aware of what is going on in the police service. Police personnel knows various types of crimes and one's duty is to detect criminals. But, many policemen do not do so; rather they tolerate the crimes committed by their fellow colleagues. Westley[6] says that each policeman makes attempts to protect his colleague in uniform if he can do so. He writes: " . . . . . . .policemen cannot and do not employ sanctions against their colleagues for using violence, and individual men who personally condemn the use of violence and avoid it whenever possible refuse openly to condemn acts of violence by other men on the force".

A station house officer knows how corrupt are the policemen in his police station and so do the policemen about their officer in the station. Many people in the police headquarters know many things about the director general of police just like the director general of police knows many things about his subordinates. They know many things taking place inside the service and certainly they include crooked practices and criminal activities. But everything is a secret and as Sloddard[7], Savitz[8] and Reiss[9] say, there exist a *code of secrecy* in police service. It is this Code of Secrecy which encourages criminality in police subculture. Policemen know how do they manipulate criminal cases and how do they concoct evidence in each case. But they maintain a Code of Secrecy and more often than not, they tolerate such enforcement crimes. The conspiracy of silence is said to be causally connected to police crimes/criminality.

When police behaviour and police crimes are discussed in India, people compare Indian police to British police. Often, they argue that the British policemen are not crime-prone. They blame the Indian police saying that the police in India are crime prone and people unfriendly. One may be inclined to think that the evaluation is not altogether baseless. For, Indian police has a socio-cultural background to become people unfriendly. They were in the British rule and the British wanted a repressive and oppressive police in India for retaining their regime. During the British period, the Indian society, particularly during the independence struggle, offered the police the means and climate to become repressive. The British glorified the police violence as a way to remain in India. After independence, the police in India continued to be aggressive and people unfriendly. India is not a country having a homogeneous society. As a result, the people in India do not hold consistent values. Owing to communalism, casteism, religious bigotry, political ideologies, regionalism, language, linguistic differences, sectarian attitudes, culture, beliefs etc., many riots errupt often so much so that the police in India are exposed to more violence than what is seen in Great Britain. This makes the police to operate differently in India. Whatever that be, some of the police operations become criminal in nature and content. Researches show that the police arrest the poor and the less influential people and they do not exercise just discretionary power when they arrest them. Sometimes the arrestees are manhandled and are proceeded against. Verbal and physical harassment may be seen. Joseph Lohman[10] once said: "The police function (is) to support and enforce the interests of the dominant political, social and economic interests of the town, and only incidently to enforce the law". Though this was said about the police in American democracy, the observations are true in India as well. This is the reason why police criminology becomes important and the police crimes are studied by criminologists.

Nature of Police Job and Criminality

There are dirty and thankless jobs in any society. Collecting human waste by hand may be a dirty job. Likewise, there are certain functions which policemen do not like to do. Orderly duty may be one among them. They may have to guard the corpse, may have to deal with drunkards having foul smells and vomits, may have to obey the orders of the wives and children of senior level police officers etc. Social scientists may call them "dirty jobs", some of which are unavoidable in police work. Nevertheless, orderly duties, guarding of the residence of senior officers, obeying the "madams" etc. may be quite unpleasant and some of the policemen do such duties as they have no option, but to yield. Certainly, they react to such undesirable situations and negative energy is generated. The energy generated can not be destroyed, rather can only be converted. It has been demonstrated that some policemen transfer their aggression towards their '*dirty*' jobs to others. In some instances, they commit crimes just to reestablish their homeostasis in such situations, Policemen have to do the '*dirty*' job, but are forced to keep silence about the unpleasant nature of the work from the public. This makes them to involve in the commission of crimes.

Once a lady constable said: "When prostitutes are caught from the brothels, they are locked up. The police officers insist lady constables to remain in the lockups with the prostitutes. Many hate to do so". She said further that such police works make them to hate them and others in society. Their self hatred and hatred towards others convert them to behave people unfriendly. Once a police officer behaved indecently to a woman constable and she had to tolerate his sexual indecency. She said that she would be harassed if she raised her voice against such '*superior's* misbehaviours and many things were possible in the rigid disciplinary structure that existed in police department. No doubt, such misbehaviours, if they exist, are crimes under law.

Superiors enjoying powers abuse their authority unless they have an upright conscience and values. Dharma in India upholds this. Kautilya while approving the use of strong-arm tactics during investigation said: "Guilt against a suspected person shall be established by the production of such evidences as the instruments made use of by the accused, his accomplices or abettors, the stolen article and any middlemen involved in selling or purchasing the stolen articles. . . . . For, owing to one's accidental presence on the scene. . . . . . or to one's accidental resemblance to the real thief. . . . . . who under fear of torture admitted himself to be the thief. . . . . . one, though innocent is often seized as thief. Hence the production of conclusive evidences shall be insisted upon". The arbitariness in taking decisions was an anathema to the concept of Dharma, but what is seen today in organized policing is the violation of this principle of Dharma which is now treated as crimes under police criminology.

A Theory on the Causation of Crimes

Criminologists have studied crimes committed by people other than the enforcement agencies and they have proposed many theories which might explain crime and criminal behaviour. The quest for locating the causes of crime has travelled a long way from satan's instigation and innate deprivity to victimology and victim's role in the causation of crimes. The pleasure-pain thesis of the hedonistic calculus of the classical school does not explain why a policeman commits crimes during the enforcement of laws. What type of pleasure does a policeman derive when he manipulates police records to see that an accused is punished? The theory is of a questionable nature and is not applicable to police crimes. Positivists with Cesare Lombroso (1835—1909) as the father of modern criminology stressed the role of biological factors in criminal behaviour—but did not say anything about police crimes and torture of people by police during crime investigation or enforcement of law. The apelike ancestors of his theory of atavism is rejected in toto to explain crime and criminal behaviour.

Darwin's theory of evolution influenced Lombroso to formulate his theory on crime. According to him usually large ears or occasionally very small or standing out from the head as in the chimpanzees, pouches in the check like those of lower animals etc. were seen in the criminals. His theory does not merit discussion in police criminology as he himself discarded his biological determinism[12] later in 1911. Nevertheless, a revised version of Lombrosian explanation may be given to interpret police crimes. Policemen in India are nicknamed as tiger, leopard, lizard etc. and they show the animal like behaviour of them. In other words, their behaviour resembles sometimes, the behaviour of wild animals. It is not behavioural atavism, rather may be the defects in the formation of human personality and value inculcation.

The chromosomal linkages with crime is a variant of biological positivism. The XYY males were found to be subnormal in intelligence and hyperaggressive. Torture in police station, inhuman and degrading treatment in police custody etc. may be seen all over the world and I have not come across any study on chromosomal abnormality and police crimes. As the studies so far conducted do not establish a causal relationship between chromosomal abnormality and crimes in the general public, I do not think that the same has any causal relationship with police crimes as well.

Sigmund Freud and his psychoanalytic theories speak about the influence of biological drives and criminal behaviour. Certainly, all human beings are innately aggressive and their animal instincts are controlled by their superego norms. The superego formation in the right direction may result in the shaping of an unright conscience in children and that may prevent commission of crimes, nevertheless Fraud believes that it may not change the fundamental human nature. Freud's views try to establish that people do not choose to commit crimes. They are rather driven to it as a result of an inadequate formation of superego or an overeffect of the 'id' complexes. A combination of physical (animal) drives and relatively weak learned inhibitions makes a man to commit crimes. As far as police crimes are concerned, this explanation may hold good to some extent particularly in the case of torture in police custody. However, this can not explain the causes of nexus criminality, corruption, manipulation of records, concoction of evidence etc. where one can not see a combination of physical drives and weak learned inhibitions.

Sociological positivism of Emile Durkheim (1858—1917) to begin with and later of Shaw (1929) and Shaw and Mckay (1942) looked at crime from the point of view of social disorganization or lack of community control. To some length, the approach may explain police crimes. Crimes that take place within the police community may be owing to the disorganization and deterioration in the department. The anomie theory of Robert K. Merton (1938) and the differential association theory of Edwin H. Sutherland (1939) give some explanations to some types of police crimes.

If anomie theory is applied to police crimes, it is possible to say that the policemen/officers who want to achieve success in life financially, professionally and otherwise do not and can not achieve their goals owing to several barriers that stop the achievement of the goal through legitimate means. Such people experience frustrations and strains. They then do not bother about the means adopted to achieve the goal. Hence, they are strongly motivated to have recourse to criminal or illegitimate means. They commit many types of crimes from informal arrests to nexus crimes. Certainly, the anomie theory brings out the facilitating environment to become criminals in uniform and further elaborates its impact in motivating policemen/officers to commit crimes.

In an environment that promotes crime and criminality, it is possible to see many people involving in the commission of many crimes. Edwin H. Sutherland explains the process of becoming criminals through his differential association theory. According to him, people engage in the commission of crimes because of their predominant (intimate) contacts with criminal behaviour patterns. The theory has limited application in police crimes. Nevertheless, there are many crimes which are invented by police and their association has noting much to do with the commission of such crimes. Henry Goddard's theory of low intelligence and criminal behaviour too has very little to do with police crimes. All positivists—biological, psychological and sociological—do not give a causal explanation of police crimes. Policemen/officers observe the laws and they violate the law and precisely therefore an explanation given by the positivists will be of little use to understand all kinds of police crimes. Policemen consciously/unconsciously believe that they observe the laws and they are not law violators. Since many of their law violations (corruption, torture, nexus crimes etc.) are generally tolerated and no action is initiated against most of them, many in society usually do not label them as criminals. This attitude of the public makes them to feel that they can afford to involve in the commission of some crimes. As such, they behave as if they enforce the law even when they violate them. Edwin Lemert speaks about citizen's reaction to crime and criminal behaviour. Some people violate law even before they are labelled as criminals. Likewise, the policemen violate laws and the people do not react to their violations. For instance, people in India once admitted that the police were legally permitted to employ torture on people. Lemert's view of *primary deviation*—i.e., commission of crimes before labelling the crime-doers as criminals-may be applied to police personnel when they commit crimes before the people identify them as criminals. But, when the people identify policemen/officers as criminals, the new public knowledge will alter the police perception of their acts as criminal. When this happens, the policemen/officers may take precautions for not identifying them as crime-doers, still they may commit crimes. This is called "secondary deviation". Today, there is a wide recognition of secondary deviations in police service and this necessarily requires the need for studying police crimes scientifically. Police criminology has a greater scope now than what it had in the past. Public definition of police crimes and police criminals becomes objects worthy of study in police criminology. Howard Becker's audience reaction to crime is of primary importance to study police crimes. The awareness of human rights laws, nexus criminality, enforcement crimes etc. makes the audience reaction to police crimes very powerful. Becker says: "The deviant is one to whom that label has successfully been applied; deviant behaviour is that people so label". People today label many police behaviour as criminal and police criminology deals with them. People who did not see police torture as crimes in the past do see it as crime today. People who used to offer money to police today think that they are giving corruption money and the police commit corruption (crime). People who did not react to illegal detention earlier do shout at police saying that illegal detention is a crime. People who did not show any reaction to police when crimes were acquitted in the past go for claiming compensation when the criminal cases are acquitted. Private complaints against the police are on the increase in the recent past.

Causes of Police Crimes

Why do the policemen commit various sorts of crimes? People, police and administration bring a number of "crackpot" theories to explain them. The commissions of inquiry appointed to probe into police excesses/ crimes etc. do not make any indepth analysis of the problem. Retired or serving judges study the cases from angles other than criminological and bring out a report making some recommendations which are sometimes of an indifferent nature. Lack of supervision, disrespect to law, neglect of duties, overenthusiasm in execution, defects in disciplinary controls etc. may be brought as the explanation of police crimes. They come in print and in the media and the pet theories of crime/police crimes advanced by some of the learned commissions are of no utility for anything They are sometimes used for initiating administrative actions against some functionaries or are kept in the archives for the researchers to study. The commissions of inquiry put forward many personal opinions which are nothing but an etiological explanations in some specific cases.

Police crimes, some historians say, are inherited from the British past and certainly, many of the crimes committed by police are seen for several decades. What makes the police to repeat their crimes? The resources of psychology, biology, sociology, criminology and their allied fields were not utilized to study police crimes in detail. For, the people think that people alone commit crimes and the policemen are to investigate, control and prevent crimes. They do not study policemen as people committing crimes. If policemen accepted corruption money, people justified it on the ground that they did not get sufficient salary to live. If a suspect was tortured, people said that they deserved harsh treatment. If the police manipulated records, they were justified on the ground that they needed such manipulations to see that the accused were punished. People and police officers often say that third degree is necessary to eliminate or clear up crimes. What is "necessary" is something they alone know and certainly, the view is subjective, arbitrary and capricious when the same is evaluated from criminological perspectives. Barnes and Teeters write: "Innumerable instruments are used to beat a suspect into submission; rubber hoses, clubs, electric shocks, fists, blackjacks, and kicks in various parts of the body, notably the groin. Not infrequently men must be hospitalized because of the torture to which they were subjected[13]". How could they be justified as necessary from criminological perspectives for eliminating crimes? How can they be explained in the light of the theories brought out by criminologists so far? The theories of poverty, greed, blighted neighbourhood, geographical factors, topography, climate etc. cannot explain the causes of police torture/inhuman treatments.

Push-Pull-Ego Factor Theory of Crimes

Walter Reckless and Simon Dinitz proposed self-concept and containment theory. They said that self-concept is the key factor in explaining crimes. According to them, a "favourable self-concept directs an individual toward law-abiding behaviour and an unfavourable self-concept directs him or her toward delinquent behaviour". Their theory is criticized by criminologists under many counts. Good self-concept and bad self-concepts are concepts that lack clarity and the critics asked: "Why do boys with bad self-concepts refrain from committing crimes?" Conversely enough, "Why do boys with good self-concept involve in the commission of crimes?"

I wanted to study five officers of the Indian police service. I found—

1. One of them had no prick of conscience to misuse his official vehicles for his personal needs.
2. Another one disowned his subordinates whenever they were in trouble.

3. Another one claimed false T.A and D.A. even when he did not travel.
4. Another one encouraged the use of torture by his subordinates
5. The last one manipulated records and concocted evidence. All of them were working in police department and they committed crimes in different ways. Why? The middle level police functionaries were studied and I could notice many types of crimes committed by them. They were involved in the use of filthy language to nexus crimes. What about the policemen? They too were committing crimes of various descriptions. And all of them were law enforcement officers. Reckless and Deniz might say that there might be some kind of self—factor that caused some to accept corruption money, to employ torture, to misuse official vehicles, to manipulate records, to effect informal arrest, to detain suspects illegally, to engage in nexus criminality etc. Different people commit different types of crimes and there is only one question. What is the nature of crime each one commits?

Reckless and Denitz asked: "What is the difference between those who are and those who are not affected? What sorts of individuals are they who succumb and what sorts are they who remain immune?" I think that these questions are irrelevant as everyone succumbs to some sort of crimes. In police, once I did an experiment. I asked 32 police trainees a few questions and they were as under:—

(Please read the questions before answering them)

1. Do you accept corruption money?
2. Suppose you are offered Rs. 50—as corruption money, will you accept it?
3. What will be your attitude if you are offered . . . . .
   —Rs. 500/—?
   —Rs. 5000/—?
   —Rs. 50000/—?
   —Rs. 500000/—?
   —Rs. 5000000/—?
   —Rs. 50000000/—?
4. What is your resistence level to corruption money?
5. If you are not yielding to corruption money, will you yield to:—

(a) Women?
(b) Promises?
(c) Promotions?
(d) Positions of higher status?
(e) Liquor?
(f) Anything else?

6. If you do not yield to any of the above, then will you yield to:—
   (a) Threats?
   (b) Harassments and Victimization?
   (c) Demoralization?
   (d) Anything else?

7. Are you an angel to resist all these temptations and tribulations? If you feel that you can not answer the questions honestly, please return it without writing anything on it.

I received 18 answer sheets stating that they would yield to the temptations and the rest without writing anything. I asked them to tell me the reasons why they did not answer the questions. The obvious reply was that they would yield to temptations and tribulations and they were not angels. As human beings, they can not but commit crimes. Thus, they stated that they were condemned to commit crimes. If that is true, then the syllogism will be:—

All men are criminals
Policeman is a man
Therefore the policeman is a criminal.

If everyone commits crimes, then, what is the meaning in locating or identifying a self factor (in each one) which differently responds to the confrontation of nonconforming and illegal alternates and choices? Reckless and Dinitz classified boys as "good boys and bad boys" and they did it on the basis of the "good or bad" self concept each one had about himself/herself. I have not seen a single person (in my life) who has a "*bad self-concept*" in his entire life. I also have not seen a single person who has a "good self concept" every time in his life. Every one has a mixed self-concept. When people pray, they do not claim to possess a "good self-concept". They are sincere and open and most of the people reveal their real identity when they are before the Almighty. Reckless and Dinitz say that "a good self-concept" is the product of favourable socialization at home and that a "bad self-concept" is the product of unfavourable socialization at home.

Donald's study on self-concept shows that the socialization at home and schools determines the type of self-concept—i.e., good or bad. Kinch finds prosocial, antisocial and asocial types among the delinquents when they were studied from the point of view in self-perception. It is seen that the prosocials had a stable family background and adjustment in schools; the antisocials had a family background with weak discipline; and the asocial had a family background which showed parental rejection. Broken homes, illegitimate births, poor peer-group relationship etc. too were found in the case of asocials. Whatever that be, how far does the self-perception by the types of delinquents affect their involvement in the commission of crimes?

There is no perfect family anywhere. There is no perfect socialization anywhere. There is no perfect human beings. As a result, I am of the view that it is just impossible to have a perfect self-concept or self-perception in anyone. Children born and brought up in the same family and by the same parents become criminals and non-criminals. Why? The various factors, forces and agencies that operate on an individual while he is socialized can not be assessed objectively as many of them are invisible or unknown to the assessors.

I have interviewed many offenders/convicted persons and I could find that a good many of them possessed "good self-concept". I have interviewed many people whom I knew well that they were involving in the commission of crimes. I could learn that many of them had "good self concept." I have also interviewed many policeman/officers and I could take note of the fact that many of them did have "good self-concept". Although they assessed them to possess "good self-concept", I would say that all of them had only "mixed" self concept. They felt *good*—and —*bad* at the same time. I could not see a perfect man possessing only "good self-concept". When I compared the self-concept of police functionaries to the same of the offenders/convicts, I observed no significant difference between the two categories. Police committed crimes which they did not accept as crimes whereas the offenders/convicts admitted that they committed crimes. A policeman who tortured a man justified his act whereas an offender who caused grievous injury to another did not question: "What does good or bad self concept do with the commission of crimes?" Any person having a good or a bad self concept may commit crimes and I observe no positive relationship (cause-effect relationship) between self-concept and commission of crimes.

The policemen/officers who committed the offences claimed that they did many acts (use of epithets, torture, informal arrests, illegal detention etc.) for social welfare. They made attempts to rationalize their criminal deeds whereas the offenders/convicts did not do so. Those who accepted corruption money had their rationalizations/justifications. Some policemen deflected blame from themselves to the people who offered corruption-money. They said that the corruption-money they accepted did not usually hurt anyone. The people who offered corruption-money could well afford it. The nexus criminals forced them to become nexus partners. When they tortured the suspects or committed human rights violations, the policemen/officers claimed that their victims really deserved such treatment and injury. The aggressors here assumed the role of administrators of justice to the victims. They blamed the law, courts, judges, police hierarchy, political system etc. for the crimes they committed. They argued that some of their acts were due to the compulsions they had from the higher ups in police department or from the politicians or from the government in power. Those positions were taken by the constables upwards and most of them claimed that they had good self-esteem. The offenders/convicts did not take such a mental position. Most of them did not deny their responsibility for what they did.

Police Crimes and Neutralization

Sykes and Matza speak about the process of neutralization. In other words, the previously internalized norms, morals and values are put aside and the voice of conscience is silenced during the process of neutralization. I could notice the process of neutralization in police crimes. The process of neutralization certainly protected many policemen/officers from self-blame and blame of others after their act. Some policemen/officers were found to create defences before they committed any offences. Sometimes, the policemen/officers knew for certain that their behaviour was illegal. Such people, I have observed, accepted neutralization without raising any objections.

When police crimes are studied, a criminologist may be tempted to study:—

1. the self-concept of the policemen.
2. the images and perceptions they have about themselves.
3. the values the policemen possess.
4. norm retention or norm erosion.
5. process of neutralization etc.

All of them may be the self factors and they may have the power, strength and potency in causing police crimes or in preventing police crimes.

When police crimes are studied, a criminologist may be interested to study again:—

1. the culture/subculture of police.
2. the criminal/non-criminal subculture of police.
3. the means and methods the police adopt to achieve their end in the existing situations/society.
4. the rules, customs, laws under which the policemen work etc.

The police commit crimes concurrently with their activities for prevention or control of crimes. Police are not meant to eradicate crimes from society.

A Theory in Police Criminology

A theory in police criminology has never been a concern for criminologists till date. Police as crime-doers was not studied principally because the organization was created and is maintained for fighting against crime and criminals. The physiological, emotional, cultural and social factors that influence the police to commit crimes, somehow or other, did not capture the attention of criminologists. Of course, court verdicts, commissions of inquiry, news papers and media etc. time and again bring out various types of crimes which the police commit, but they are not seriously taken into account by researchers and academicians to formulate a theory in police criminology. They are more concerned with "criminology for police" than "police criminology".

Police observe the behaviour of people and the policemen assume that the people are completely different from the police personnel. They expect the people to be consistently law abiding whereas they do not say so with respect to their brethren in service. For example, the policeman does not tolerate the use of epithets by the common man, nevertheless, he tolerates the same behaviour when committed by a member of the police service. Likewise, he does not accept torture by a human being against another while he has no difficulty to accept—even to appreciate—torture by a policeman against a fellow citizen. They protect or overprotect policemen in such instances. When a policeman commits human rights violations, people and the media criticize him. They use the social and cultural values to judge the behaviour of the policeman and say that the police behaviour does not conform to social expectations. Sometimes, the police violate the laws in force and the people criticize them as violators of law. People then keep away from police even when they are well aware that they cannot easily avoid the police or ignore them. Police do play significant role in society.

Policeman, just like any other human beings, has all the basic drives like hunger, sex etc. They are motivating forces. Many filthy expressions have sex-contents. When a policeman speaks vulgar language, it contains filthy words and the people view it as degrading to human dignity. Likewise, whenever a man on the street utters vulgar language, it is also a degrading behaviour. The social environment of the policeman is very active and is populated with people who critically observe police behaviour—who do criticize the police particularly when their behaviour does not conform to the people's expectations, social values and legal norms.

The criticisms of the people and the exact meaning of what the people speak about the police are not meaningfully accepted by the young recruits to police department. The unusually active youngsters behave the way they want although it is not always true with respect to some in the department. As age and experience play their role in police behaviour, they become mature in their dealings. I notice that the older a policeman/officer becomes, the more he is human rights friendly. The instinctual drives in him are not expressed nakedly by him. The older policeman/officer exerts restraints, self-control and self-effacement.

The kind of person a newly recruited policeman/officer is to become is determined by many factors operating in the department. Everyday observation of the newly enlisted policeman/officer will make him to accept social demands during law enforcement. The instinctual drives will be modified in due course by the kind of interactions that take place between the older members and the newly recruited policemen/officers. The police subculture exerts influences and thus there takes place behavioural modifications. Thus they behave in accordance to the expectations and attitudes that are found to be "normal" in that subculture. Young policemen/officers who are not corrupt in the beginning may become corrupt in due course thanks to the influence exerted by the police subculture. One may notice that a subinspector/assistant superintendent of police who is not corrupt in the beginning becomes very corrupt when be becomes a deputy superintendent/inspector general of police as the case may be. In a democratic country, the politicians may interfere in police work. They may create a subculture which accepts policemen/officers who are their men. In such a situation, some policemen/officers who cannot go along with the subcultural currents may withdraw themselves and show behaviours which are characterized by a passive and withdrawn detachments. They find satisfaction within themselves rather than in the activities of the department which is politicized. In such people, their childhood experience and value formation are of great significance/importance. Police criminology gives a lot of stress to the early childhood development of personality, value inculcation and conscience formation.

The Tarde's theory of imitation and Sutherland's differential association theory may help, to a limited extent, to understand police crimes. Repeated exposure to police crimes such as illegal detention, manipulation of records, registration of false cases, concoction of evidence, padding up, nexus criminality, corruption etc. may encourage a new recruit to have recourse to such activities. There is a school of thought which advocates the view that the best way of preventing police crimes is to make police stations "crime-proof" (by exercising police functions as per law and procedure established by law). A newly enlisted policeman once said that he used to get Rs. 50—every day from the station writer who always told him that he could make use of the amount for patrol to come to the police station. The new constable knew very well that he was given Rs. 50 as his share from the corruption money they received every day. He knew further that his elders in the department wanted to silence him by offering the share in corruption money. In such a subculture, the new constable started to think why he should not enjoy the same privilege when he becomes an "Elder" in the department. After about 6 months, he became a part of the subculture and felt annoyed if he was not offered his share in the corruption money every evening. As days and months elapsed, he placed more demands and pleaded for an enhanced amount as his share from the corruption money. There came a situation that he became restless if he did not get his share in the corruption money. In his discussion with his colleagues/superiors, he used the words "your share", "my share" and constantly kept an eye on the amount of corruption money transacted in the police station subculture.

Expectations of the Society for Particular Ranks in Police

The difference between a constable and a director general of police in committing crimes may be only the difference that is seen among the policemen of different ranks. A constable commits crimes which he can and a director general commits crimes which he can. Basically, they are human beings. They have their own attitudes, expectations and feelings about them and their functions. People in society use adjectives that qualify the behaviour of each rank in police service. I asked 487 people to describe the work of the constables, head constables, assistant subinspectors, inspectors, officers of the Indian police service including the director general of police. The adjectives used by them to qualify the policemen/officers were then studied to know the difference between a constable and a director general of police. It has been noticed that the people used the same adjectives for all in police service. For example, with respect to the adjective "susceptible" to political interference, they said that the constable could be influenced by the politicians in the local area whereas the director general could be by a politician of a higher level and status. The same was true in the area of corruption, nexus crimes, enforcement crimes, human rights violations etc. The rank might not make much difference. In employing torture on suspects, the constables, headconstables, subinspectors and so on were blamed. They used adjectives like "serious, trustworthy, conscientious, nasty, undependable, honest, corrupt, earnest, sensitive etc." to all in police department and the rank did not make much difference. People attached more responsibility to higher ranks. At the same time, they said that the higher one went in the rank, the more invisibility was noticed in his criminal behaviour.

Police Needs and Police Crimes

Maslow classified human needs under four headings—(1) Physiological needs, (2) Safety needs, (3) Love and esteem needs, (4) Self-actualization needs. The policemen/officers have their physiological needs satisfied by the regular income they get from their job. People say that "no policeman has ever died out of poverty although some have died of prosperity". Whatever that be, I may subscribe to the view that policemen do not commit crimes for satisfying their physiological needs. What about the safety needs? The policemen do have and they do feel some degree of security that they will be protected from many dangers. Love and attention may be lacking in police as I find a sort of morbid fear—phobia—anxiety—apprehension of danger, punishment etc. in many, probably more among the lower levels than the same among the higher levels. The anxiety—i.e., what will happen if I do not succeed in my work—makes some to have recourse to undesirable tactics and objectionable strategies. The esteem needs work very strongly in some. They want the esteem of others as well as the need to feel useful and necessary to others. They want to be important in society and among police officers/men. How can they achieve their esteem needs? Some do so by committing crimes of various descriptions including nexus criminality, enforcement crimes, corruption etc. They want luxurious houses, gadgets, life-style and pleasures. They can not get them in the normal and legitimate way. They commit crimes and become richer and more important in life.

Self-actualization needs make some policemen/officers to resort to any fair or foul means to achieve the goals through short cuts. During investigation of crimes, some torture the suspects to obtain a confession, some concoct evidence and some produce touts or tutored witnesses and thus become important. In many police functionaries, I notice that the self-actualization needs become paramouht and may be a very important source of motivation for them. I asked 61 policemen/officers in a casual way to tell me the most powerful factor that forced them to behave in a cruel and hostile manner. Most of them answered me that they would tolerate anything except a challenge to their authority and power. I asked 171 people in society—that too in a casual way—the most powerful factor which forced the police to behave in a hostile manner to the people. Most of them subscribed to the above view.

The police work in a highly disciplined set-up and the authority of superiors is respected. They expect the people to respect police authority without raising any question. In a democratic set up, it is not possible as the people question many of police activities. This irritates some policemen/officers who may resort to aggressiveness when their authority is questioned. Policemen/officers brought up in a rigid (disciplinary) atmosphere can not express positive feelings toward others when their authority/power is questioned. They become hostile to people and often are found to be less socialized and cooperative with people. Policemen/officers, often, complain that the people are not cooperative. But, they never ask the question to themselves—i.e., "how cooperative are they to the people?" What I see among policemen/officers is that those who work under restrictive, autocratic and authoritarian superiors are likely to be very conforming and obedient to their superiors, but are not seen to be sociable and law-abiding when they are away from their rigid superiors. Extreme strictness to subordinates in a democratic set up produces a sizable minority of policemen/officers who are chronic rebels in the department. They commit many crimes which they may not if they work under a more permissive and democratic atmosphere.

Disciplining the Policemen/Officers and Police Criminality

According to "*police interpretation of behaviour*", the cure for any delinquency is enforcement of stricter discipline and infliction of punishment. What I have observed is that an extreme strictness, disciplinary methods and infliction of punishment does not always guarantee prevention of police crimes. Punishment may be needed to control police crimes, but the fact remains that in spite of rigid discipline and strict enforcement of punishments, police crimes continue to exist in police subculture. Why? A punitive superior creates aggressiveness, hostility and vengeance among the subordinates. They express such behaviours, often, when they get opportunities. Punitives attitudes on the part of superiors aggravate police crimes rather than discourage them and as said above, they suggest, furthermore, that the punished subordinates may learn to display to others the same attitude of hostility and aggression that are expressed toward them by their superiors. Perhaps, gentleness is more rewarding than punitiveness. Extreme punitiveness causes an "avoidance behaviour" among subordinates and not refraining from the commission of crimes.

Learning and Police Crimes

Edwin H. Sutherland speaks about the process of learning in criminology. I am not discussing here the differenctial association theory proposed by Sutherland. I am interested in the impact of classical (Pavlovian) conditioning and instrumental (operant) conditioning in criminology. Ivan Pavlove and some psychologists say that conditioning has a tremendous influence on the psychology of learning. A telephone call, for instance, comes from a politician of the ruling party to a police station. A telephone call to a police station (a stimulus) invokes a certain response. The response is found to be favourable to the party which calls the police station. The telephone call from the politician may be called an "unconditioned stimulus" (in Pavlovian psychology, it was the *acid* which was the unconditioned stimulus) which is represented as *US*. The favourable response to the politician's call from the police station may be called an "unconditioned response" (In Pavlovian psychology, it was the salivation). Every time, a favourable response is given, the officer in the police station is blessed with political patronage. He thus makes corruption money, involves in nexus criminality, commission of enforcement crimes etc. Everytime, an unfavourable response is given, he is scolded, transferred to distant places, harassed and victimized by departmental superiors and political hierarchy. Whenever a telephone call comes, the policemen think that it is a call from politicians/other influential persons for getting a decision favourable to them. Hence, they avoid attending telephone calls or purposefully tell that the concerned officer is not present in the station. I do not know how far the Pavlovian (classical) conditioning can be applied to such behaviours in police stations, nevertheless, I notice that patterns of police behaviour (this includes criminal behaviour by police) that involve strong emotions (severe anxiety, fear, hatred, disgust etc.) may be the result of classical conditioning.

A telephone call—favourable response from the police station—advantages for the police personnel and this is seen in many areas of police work so much so that it is just not possible to take away political interference in police work. A situation has come into existence that a policeman/officer can commit any type of crimes if and only if he has the political patronage. Miller found that learning had more of a lasting impact if it was accompanied by an action. For example, if the word "*tap*" was accompanied by a tapping action, then the learning had a lasting quality. During the induction training period, each word of command in the parade ground is accompanied by an action. For example, "attention" is a word of command. When the command is given, it is followed by a physical action. If the physical action is not followed, then the trainee is given a punishment. "First obey and then question"—this principle is adhered to. The impact of this sort of conditioning is that the trainees develop a response mechanism which strictly obeys the word of command without questioning. For they know well that any questioning is likely or certainly to follow punishment. Resultingly, a fear of authority is seen among police functionaries. After the training, when they are in the operational field, the same fear of authority continues to operate strongly in many of them. When a telephone call from the higher authority is received, many police functionaries obey it. They are afraid of disobeying it. The telephone call may not be always to do the right thing in a legal way. Necessarily, police crimes come into being. Authority is not restricted only to departmental superiors. It is also vested with politicians and political set up in a democracy. Hence, people rush to politicians to get a favourable decision which may not be always fair and legal.

What about the operant or instrumental conditioning in police work?—in police committing crimes? In this sort of conditioning, a policemen/officer is positively motivated in order to respond appropriately. In other words, there is a reward which satisfies a policeman/officer whenever he does an act. Corruption-money for doing illegal acts may be an example. The money is given as soon as the work is done or even before the illegality is committed. In nexus crimes, this can be seen. There is a relationship between the police response and reward.

A police officer used to do everything as per law and procedure established by law even when he had severe pressure from many sources to do illegalities. Every time, he did not listen to the orders from the higher ups to commit illegalities, he was punished in some way or other. After a few such bitter experiences, he changed his style of working. He listened to instructions from powerful sources without examining the merits and thus he started to receive rewards. He said that he committed many crimes and he did so by learning things. Through trial and error, he learnt how to make a luxurious living. Some policemen/officers who were honest and upright in the beginning of their career became corrupt and involved in nexus criminality as they served long in the department. It was through learning and experience that they became so.

Human Motives, Motivation and Police Crimes

A policeman has power and authority. He can use them and misuse them depending upon his criminal motivations or environmental events or in many cases upon both. William Bonger spoke about criminal motivations and stimulating situations through which the criminal motivations are executed. There are policemen who resist strong temptations amidst strong environmental pressures and they do not commit crimes. They are not many. When corruption money (environmental stimulus) is offered, many yield to the temptation and accept it. Even when someone does not offer any corruption money, some policemen/officers create situations to make corruption money. Why? The criminal motivation may be responsible for such a behaviour. Psychologists say that motivation is an energizing power which drives a person to a destination. He wants to satisfy his drive. Some policemen/officers tell me that they are very hot-tempered. They do not have control over their aggressive drives. Such people, I think, are inclined to perceive their environment as causing anger in them and they become hot-tempered without any reason. Some policemen/officers become angry to a certain category of people. A low caste officer may express anger to a person born in a high caste family. I think that it is because of the wrong perceptions which he has towards people in high caste communities. No doubt, perception is a process that directs motivations.

Motivation and police crimes may be an area which is unexplored or insufficiently explored by criminologists. Psychologists put the motives in a continuum that ranges from the most rudimentary—biological and primitive—to the most complex (socialized and abstract). They talk about the primary motives (sustenance motives, avoidance motives and species—maintaining motives etc) and speak of homeostasis, elimination, sex, sleep, hunger, thirst etc. I am particularly interested in studying police behaviour form the point of view of (1) fear and anger, (2) aggression, (3) pleasure, (4) pain avoidance etc.

Fear and anger are two drives which are very strong in human beings. External stimuli or the thoughts of them arouse them. Subsequently, they are expressed in a man's behaviour. With the perception of the drive-arousing stimuli, the arousal begins. When a person is taken into custody by police or when he thinks about the police, many physiological changes are seen in him. Increase in heart beat, respiration rate in fear etc. are found. When the police threaten the suspects, they may exhibit such physiological symptoms. When the policc interrogator sees such physiological symptoms, naturally they work as external stimuli which may motivate him to resort to methods and strategies which may further aggravate his anger. My observations and studies on police behaviour make me to conclude that the emotion of anger in police finds expression when they are motivated by the emotion of fear in people. The police become angry to the weak and helpless who express fear to police. To the strong and fearless, the police are found to be meak and mild.

Fear in suspects may be related to pain avoidance—another primitive drive in people. I find that the people in Indian culture are generally afraid of police and they want to avoid the pain of going to police stations. Their perception of police interaction with them as a painful experience makes them to express fear when they see them. Certainly, it is a learned perception and has a history of development in Indian police. The police are fully aware of people's perception of police action and they know for certain that the people want to avoid their painful experience with them. This idea in police or police thought about people's fear of them works as a stimulus to cause anger in them. This motivates some to commit crimes in police service. Policemen have to encounter many painful situations particularly during law and order management or in searching for criminals etc. Sometimes, they resort to aggression to defend them from attacks. Aggressiveness, psychologists say, may be a drive that is related to the need to defend the organism from attacks. Whenever a policeman catches a hardened criminal, a terrorist, a naxalist, he may express aggressiveness. In such situations, he becomes aggressive not for committing any crimes, but to defend himself from the attacks. He takes advantage of his capacity to become aggressive. Pleasure is a drive and sometimes they commit crimes for obtaining pleasure. Drinking while on duty, uttering filthy expressions and epithets etc. may be examples in point.

Secondarv are those drives that are modified by learning. The primary motives can be modified by learning and the police training is essentially meant for it. The police have to interact with many others and precisely therefore they cannot express their primary motives in a naked way or as they want them to be expressed. They have to behave in a social context. As such, the social motives become important in police interactions.

Social Motives and Police Criminality

Human beings need qualities that make them human in their behaviour and the policeman is not an exception. A policeman must learn them through his association with other fellow human beings. Certainly, a policeman has his "ego-needs" and he is concerned with them. Social motives are, say Maslow, necessary for self-esteem, recognition and approval. The social motive is necessary to have the feeling of the "need to be needed" in human beings. Studies show that the policemen who do not have adequate development of the social motives in them commit various types of crimes while they are on the job. For example, they want self-actualization. They want to prove that they are good investigators of crimes. This motive becomes a dominant force in their behaviour. They may work hard ignoring food, rest, physical danger etc. for their self-actualization. In doing so, they may commit atrocities or concoct evidence to prove the crime and they do so if they are not adequately socialized with human values. A subinspector shouted at a woman at the top of his voice. After ten years of service, the same officer did not do so in spite of the fact that he faced a similar situation. It means that he could subordinate his primary motives to secondary motives. How? The learning that has taken place in his official life affected his behaviour.

Achievement motivation (David C. Mc Clelland) is a secondary motive characterized by ambition, desire to go up and the like. A police officer may not sleep when he wants to achieve his ambition—may be detecting a sensational crime story and its criminal. He may prepare plans and strategies to detect the crime and in his overenthusiasm to achieve quick results, he may involve in the commission of human rights violations.

Emotions and Emotional Behaviours in Police Crimes

Man is a rational animal—say the philosophers; nevertheless, only a small part of man's behaviour results from rationality—say the psychologists. Whatever may be the views of philosophers and psychologists on the behaviour of man and his rationality, I may say that man lives in a society which gives a lot of importance for reasoning and rationality in human behaviour. Precisely therefore, a policeman has to be rational in his behaviour. If he is not rational in behaviour, then he becomes "emotional". Researches prove that emotions lead to criminality—emotions inhibit criminality. Fear, rage and joy are emotions. Likewise, grief, despair, apathy and depression are also emotions. Anxiety is an emotion which has many special qualities. Policemen, just like some people in society, may drink alcoho for reducing anxiety connected with their work. There is a view that anxiety lies at the basis of a great deal of police crimes. Anxiety is aroused by concern about the future and some policemen/ officers become corrupt and nexus criminals owing to their anxiety of their future. Some policemen/officers show extreme anxiety just before their retirement on superannuation. They say that they could not make their "life financially safe as they were not corrupt in their lives." They express a lot of anxiety and say that they do not know "what lies ahead" of them in the future. The anxiety is found to be a painful emotion and in order to reduce the pain, some people become corrupt or involve in illegal activities. If anyone interferes with another's secondary motives, it is likely that he experiences anxiety. Whenever man experiences frustrations in life, he is likely to respond to it with anxiety or with aggressiveness or other defence mechanisms.. Anxiety, I see, is a painful emotion and whenever one is exposed to a painful situation causing anxiety, he is more likely to eliminate his feeling of anxiety than to eliminate the situation that is the cause or source of anxiety. Crimes may be committed during the process of eliminating the feelings of anxiety.

Policemen/officers become always a target of attack by the press and people for many things they do—even legally and fairly. The constant attacks make the police to feel anxiety every time and I have specially noticed such anxiety symptoms more among the high and higher level of police functionaries. They, therefore look up, down and around before they act. I have further noticed that the middle level functionaries in police express lesser anxiety than what higher level officers show. Lower level police functionaries, as a rule, are found to exhibit less anxiety as they are sure that the middle and the higher levels are more accountable and responsible to what they do. Psychologists subscribe to the view that anxiety is stressful and painful and is found to be the characteristics of "weak" persons or persons possessing a week 'ego-structure'.

Anxiety in police functionaries, my studies show, is always a check to their behaviour/misbehaviour. Hence some anxiety (not too much) is always good and helpful to control police behaviour/misbehaviour.

Control of Emotional Behaviour in Police

As years get elapsed, many policemen/officers become "mature" and the maturity in them certainly controls their behaviour. As one is exposed to many situations in life, he learns many things and understands that he must control his emotions. This happens in police service as well. In due course, every person becomes or ought to become more socialized/ more civilized. Necessarily, this curbs down and controls his hostile or negative impulses. As a person advances in his age (service), he acquires/ ought to acquire a stability of emotions. Whenever I see young and newly enlisted policeman/officer behaves without controlling his negative or hostile emotions, I used to think that he will change soon and I notice such changes in police. If counselling is given to them at the appropriate time, the change can be speeded up. The psychological boundaries between young policemen/officers and their environment can be easily penetrated by an expert counsellor and their behaviour can be easily corrected. Superior officers who have acquired a maturity in their emotions do so and their timely advice result in the change of temper, noice level and body language of young policemen/officers.

Push—Pull—Ego Factor Theory in Criminology

In my book titled *Indian Police and Nexus Crime*, I have discussed in some detail my theory—i.e., Push—Pull—Ego Factor Theory—in criminology. The Push Factors are those forces which are found operative in every individual and we have discussed about some of them earlier in this chapter. Emotions, instincts, drives, the subconscious, the unconscious etc. may work as *Push* Factors in an individual.

Any *Push Factor* in a normal individual has a *Pull Factor*—i.e., a force that drags the individual through a particular path to a destination. The *Pull Factors* are seen in the environment which surrounds a human being. There can not be a push factor if there is no corresponding pull factor. It means that there is a pull factor in the environment which will satisfy the hunger. The pull factor has the capacity to drag a man to a destination. A man can reach the destination in a legitimate way or in an illegitimate way. If he reaches his destination in an illegitimate way or acquires the object in an illegitimate way, he commits a crime. How? This will be discussed later at length in this chapter.

Pull Factors in Criminology

Every individual lives in a society. He is limited in time and space. He develops in an environment which is conducive for his development. There are many factors which exert force on an individual. Policemen/officers work amidst people and respond to many situations/environments consisting of significant people and severe pressures. The kind of individuals the policemen are today is to a great degree a product of the interaction they have experienced with other people. Experts in child psychology attest to the view that the basic attitudes, feelings and values as adults are decisively decided by the childhood relations with parents, siblings, home environment etc. Does it mean that police crimes or the police attitudes to crimes have something to do with the early personality development/value formation of each policeman/officer?

There existed a contraversy which occupied the attention of the psychologists for many years. Finally, many psychologists came to a consensus that the heredity and environment together decided the personality of an individual. The "hereditarians" and the "environmentalists" have their controversies even today. According to the "hereditarians", a person develops his criminal personality primarily owing to differences in inherited potential and the "environmentalists" would argue that the criminal personality result primarily from differences in environment. Let them have their controversies.

My researches in the area of criminology in general and police criminology in particular give me ample evidence to show that there is a third factor that comes into being as a result of the interaction between the hereditary potentials and the environments. This third factor is called "*Ego*". If we call hereditary potentials "*Push Factors*" and environmental forces "*Pull Factors*", then the new product which comes into being in each person is what I wish to call "*Ego*". It is from this, the "*Push—Pull—Ego*" Factor theory is developed. Hence the theory is

Hereditary Potentials interacts with Environmental Forces resulting in Ego and the Ego is a new product which behaves legally or illegally as the case may be. Every individual has his/her own Ego and it is this ego which makes him a distinct individual. This is called "Ego-identity". The twins are not identical in their behaviour although they may be identical twins. One may commit crimes while the other may not commit similar crimes. Children born of the same parents and brought up in the same environments may not commit the same kind of crimes. There is individual differences and it is because of the differences in "Ego" factor in each person that individual differences are seen.

The Ego, The Push-Pull Factors

In the development of criminological thoughts, little or no research has been conducted to study the role of "Ego" (the product of Push-Pull Factors) in the commission of crimes. The philosophical psychology mentions about Ego as a deciding factor in human behaviour, particularly when a person makes a choice. Nevertheless, they too do not say that the Ego is the product of push-pull factors. As they are not criminologists dealing with crimes and the etiology of crimes, they do not talk anything much about the part played by "Ego" in the commission of crimes.

Criminologists, especially those who are interested in the sociology of crimes discuss a lot about pull factors in the causation of crime. One of the earliest explanations involving environment (The *Pull-Factors*) was proposed by Xenophone, Plato, Aristotle, Horace, Thomas More and they dealt with the economic conditions and crimes. Karl Marx spoke about economic determinism and brought poverty as an etiological determinant in crimes. None of them was a criminologist and precisely therefore they could not give any explanation to various types of nexus crimes, corruption-Mafia, enforcement crimes, economic offences, smuggling, investment frauds etc. seen in the present day society. Police crimes were unheard then and their approach was of no use to understand more about crimes of today. Nevertheless, they brought out the impact, relevance and effect the *Pull Factors* (environment) in the causation of crimes.

All poor people are not criminals and all affluent people are not non-criminals. Frank Tannenbaum and William Bonger raised objections to the Economic Determinism of Karl Marx when they advanced the theory of *facilitating environment.* According to them the society ought to provide facilitating envoronment for the people to commit crimes. I do not and cannot agree with them. As I said earlier, every push factor in a person has a pull factor which alone can satisfy a push factor and therefore every individual goes after or search for the facilitating environments even when the society does not provide such facilitating environments as they are. William Adrian Bonger (1876—1940) believed that the economic system in the society provides a "climate of motivation" for crime and criminal behaviour. If at all the economic system provides such a climate of motivation for criminal behaviour, it does not mean that all people who live in such a system must become criminals. It means that there is something that works in every individual and that something makes him to commit the crimes. It is not the *Push Factors*, but is the *Ego* which is the product of the push-pull factors in a person that makes a person to commit crimes. What has the economic system to do when a person is informally arrested or illegally detained?—or when a false case is registered against him? Crimes are committed by scholars, businessmen, politicians, law enforcement officers, poor men, inventors, scientists, social workers, terrorists, naxalites, priests, pujarees, police officers and certainly the economic system or poverty can not be a cause in all such crimes always. There are several environmental factors (*Pull Factors*) and the economic system is just one among them.

Emile Durkheim (1858—1917) said that crime was both normal and functional. He introduced his version of 'anomie' which meant lawlessness, (i.e., the pull factors in society could create lawlessness). He too did not say anything about the "Ego" factor in individuals who committed crimes. The concept of anomie was extensively developed by Robert Merton. He was against the biological theories and psychiatric approaches (especially the psychoanalytic theory of Sigmund Freud). Robert Merton emphatically advocated the view that the *social structures* made some people to commit crimes. Social structures—i.e., the *Pull Factors*—,I think, may pull the individuals (having the *Push Factors*) to goals which, as Merton says, are the aspirations of all within a society. But even in any social structure, there will be men who are not pulled much by the social structures and they may not then commit crimes.

The "class-oriented theories" proposed by Hermann Mannheim gave a different interpretation for the commission of crimes. According to him the lower class people committed crimes because they could not reach the middle class goals by the approved means of the society. If that explanation is accepted, then there is no difficulty to explain the behaviour of constables or the lower class functionaries in police. But researches show that all classes in police—in any society—commit crimes of the same, similar or different nature. This is because of the Ego of the individual and it is the product of the pull-push factors—i.e., the psychological and sociological factors, Frederic M. Thrasher showed the importance of subculture in crime and criminal behaviour. According to him, the social disorganization made the gang to develop and the slum life was primarily responsible for the gangs to commit crimes in Chicago. Certainly he gave a lot of emphasis to the pull factors in a disorganized society and underestimated the importance of individuals and their pull factors. If crimes are seen in police service, then they must be due to the disorganization in the department? Certainly, the disorganization may be a factor, but not the only factor. The push factors are important and different people commit different types of crimes. I think that they do so because each one has Ego which is individualistic. As two individuals are different in many ways, the two "Egos" of two individuals too are different in a variety of ways. It is this difference which makes them to commit different types of crimes.

Criminologists consider Thrasher's approach as the forerunner to the present subculture theories of crimes. Albert K. Cohen developed subculture theories. If his approach is adopted in police criminology, then one may say that the lower class functionaries in police is constantly measured by the middle class measuring rods. In other words, the lower class personnel in police accept the goals of the middle class in police and naturally they can not meet those goals by means approved by the society. Hence, they become corrupt or involve in corrupt activities to become richer and reach the middle class level. The lower class police personnel function within the institution run by the middle class officers who again function within the institution run by top level police functionaries. Each class evaluates and judges the lower class with its measuring rods (standards) and therefore one class sees the activities of the other class as criminal or non-criminal. I admit the importance of subculture (*Pull Factor*) in the causation of crime, nevertheless, I can not overlook the influence of the push factors in an individual living in a subculture and the role of his "Ego" in the commission of crimes. How to decide the lower, middle and higher class in police? Can it be decided merely on the rank each one holds in police hierarchy? I know a director general of police who could not become a bus conductor in a public transport undertaking. He later got into the Indian police service. Likewise, I know a deputy inspector general of police who could not get the job of a subinspector, but became a deputy inspector general as he got into the Indian police service. Hence, it is wrong to classify police personnel on the basis of the rank one holds in police hierarchy. Every person who occupies a rank in the police hierarchy has his own ego formed from the push and pull factors. The Ego develops and develops in a person as he grows older and older.

The positivists of Lombrosian period and later times believed that crime was the result of forces beyond the control of the perpetrator. But, they were not talking about the pull factors in the environment. However, they found different elements of determinism. The classical school of criminology brought the concept of free will and for them crime was the product of the free will exercised by the crime-doers. David Matza took a middle position between the classical and positivist views and adopted an approach called "soft determinism". He said that the delinquents drift into delinquency. According to him, a delinquent drifts between conventional and criminal behaviour "responding in turn to the demands of each, flirting now with one, now with the other, but postponing commitment and evading decisions". Why do they do so? The explanation may be given by the pull-push-ego factor approach. The "Ego" which is the product of push and pull factors takes a decision and thus commits crimes.

The differential opportunity structures theory proposed by Richard Cloward and Lloyd Ohlin give emphasis to the pull factors in the subculture. According to them, if a juvenile has little or no access to illegal or criminal means, then he would not adopt criminal means to achieve his goals. In other words, pull factors are necessary for a person to become criminal. The Push-Pull-Ego factor theory advocates that even in such cases, a person who has a criminal Ego will create many means to commit crimes if he decides so. This is what is seen in enforcement criminality. Even in vigilance department, one sees people committing crimes even where there exists little or no access to illegal or criminal means. To think that there is a society where there exists little or no access to illegal or criminal means is not possible as there exists no such society in the world. Ecologists emphasised the role of pull factors in the causation of crime and made an attempt to explain crime as a function of social change that occurs along with environmental change. For them, delinquency producing factors are inherent in the community. There may not be any dispute over their findings, but at the same time, everyone who lives in such a community does not become a criminal. Why? The answer is given by the Push-Pull-Ego Factor theory.

Home environment and crime—this is an area which has been studied by many, "Broken home is the cause of delinquency"—said some sociologists interested in the study of criminology. Later, it was said that home environment along with other factors was a causative factor. Healy and Bronner, Glueck, Rosen, Abrahamsen and a number of others have done special researches to study home and environment and their impact upon delinquency and crime. In the history and development of criminological thoughts, extensive researches were conducted to study the importance of religion, age, mass-media, school and many such factors in the causation of crimes. I am not interested to discuss them in this book. I want to say that so much work has been done on the effect and importance of pull factors in the etiology of crime and especially of delinquency. According to some, the pull factors alone are responsible or guilty in crime. As early as in 1885, it was said in France that "the social environment . . . . . . is the bouillon for culturing criminal". And, just recently a director general of police in his private talk on police crimes said: "Every society has the criminals they deserve. The policeman is the product of the society and if he is a criminal, it means that the society is found to be one where he can grow." The sociologists give an undue importance to the pull factors or shift the emphasis from the characteristics of the individual offender to the characteristics of the society and social milieu in which he lives. Policeman lives in a cultural and social milieu and he commits crimes which may be unknown to the society, people and the milieu. The Supreme Court of India and various High Courts in India have time and again given directives to police offices and sometimes punished them for crimes which they ought not have committed. A few of such instances may illustrate it further to show that the policeman commits crimes which the society does not approve of.

In D.K. Basu Vs. State of West Bengal[15], the Supreme Court of India issued certain directives to police officers showing their obligations after arrest. The Supreme Court took notice of custodial violence and certainly, it was a crime of the first order. The directives contained preventive strategies and precautions against misuse/abuse of authority. The court observed that any form of torture or cruel, inhuman, or degrading treatment would fall within the inhibitions of Article 21 of the Constitution of India whether it took place during investigation, interrogation or otherwise.

In Joginder Kumar Vs. State of Uttar Pradesh[16] and others the Supreme Court found that the police detained people in their illegal custody. It would mean that the people in authority could violate the law and the violation of law is what is called crime in society. The Supreme Court took note of the observations of the National Police commission that nearly 60 of the arrests were either unnecessary or unjustified action accounted for 43.2 of the expenditure of the prisons.

The Supreme Court of India has punished many police officers for their crimes committed during the enforcement of law. In Jaspal Singh Vs. State of Uttar Pradesh[17], the Supreme Court found that a detinue was beaten, manhandled and tortured by the CBI in the precincts of the Court. The Supreme Court said that the incident was indeed symptomatic of the degeneration in the respect for law, human dignity and human rights by police. Accordingly, the Court punished the officials of the CBI. In Afzal Vs. State of Haryana[18], the Supreme Court convicted three police officers for imprisonment. The Secretary, Hailakandi Bar Association Vs. State of Assam[19], the Supreme Court found that the police filed a false and fabricated report to mislead the court and to obstruct the court from reaching the correct conclusion by submitting such a false report. The Court punished the police for the same. In Delhi Judicial Service Association Vs. State of Gujarat[20], the Supreme Court punished police officers for forcing a Chief Judicial Magistrate to consume liquor and for assaulting him. The Chief Judicial Magistrate was tied with a rope and sent to the local hospital for medical examination. Thus, any number of cases showing abuse of power/ misuse of authority could be cited to show the crimes committed by police functionaries under the colour of their uniform and the criminologists today study such behaviours from academic angles.

Richard Cloward and Lloyd Ohlin held the view that a juvenile would not commit crimes or adopt criminal means to solve his problems if he had little or no access to illegal or criminal means in a given social structure. I think that there is a point in what they speak and their view can be applied to police crimes. The police officers commit crimes because they get opportunities to do so in the given social structure in which they live. There is an approval of some forms of crime in the police subcultures. The subculture therefore becomes a pull factor and the police officer who has such a pull factor commits crimes. As a product of the Pull and Push Factors, I take note of the force of the *ego* of the individual.

The Ego in Police Criminology

Sigmund Freud has discussed in detail the concepts of Ego and Superego in human behaviour. The *Ego* about which I wish to talk is not the Freudian Ego, but is the *Ego* which is the deciding principle in crime and criminal behaviour. It is a product of the Pull-Push Factors. How is the Ego formed?

Formation of Ego and Criminal Behaviour

Sigmund Freud (1856—1939) said that human personality consisted of three elements—the ego, superego and id'. According to him the Ego was a reality principle which constantly attempted to achieve an acceptable balance between the 'id' and 'superego'. The 'id' for him was the reservoir of urges, desires, drives and animal instincts. The 'superego' was the 'dos' and don'ts' and it constituted the society's moral principle. His theory doubtlessly was good for psychoanalysis and therapy. Nevertheless, one doubts very much the relevance of the theory in explaining criminal behaviour and particularly the police crimes. Of course, he said that an inadequate formation of the 'superego' or the overeffect of the 'id energy' might cause criminal behaviour.

I find it extremely difficult to understand his view. What is "adequate superego?—inadequate superego?" How does it influence people to commit crimes? Can superego repel a person from committing crimes? If so, how? Again, what is meant by an overeffect of 'id energy'? If the 'id' energy is very strong, then according to Freud, a person ought to commit crimes. As Sigmund Freud was not very much concerned with crime and criminal behaviour—or rather more concerned with personality disorders and their treatment, let us not bring him to explain crime and criminality. The *Push-Pull-Ego* Factor theory takes into account all factors which operate within and outside an individual and explains the causes of crimes in an understandable way.

The interaction between the push and pull factors takes place in a way which may be outside the control of the self. The consequence is the formation of the Ego which is the human conscience. The individual may or may not be fully aware of the push-pull factors and in all situations he is not. Hence the formation of his conscience is not within his power and control. The people around him can control some of the environmental factors, but not all. Hence, the formation of human conscience is not within the power or control of the environment as well. The pull factors are many.

Cause of crime or causes of criminal behaviour—the history of criminology is a history of finding out the causes of crime. Though many theories have come into existence, none of them could explain the causation of crime in precise or specific terms. Why do people commit crimes? In Push-Pull-Ego Factor theory, there are the Push Factors—and—Pull Factors. The Ego is the product of Push-Pull Factors. Water is formed by Hydrogen and Oxygen. Just like that, the Ego is formed by the Push-Pull Factors in an individual. The Water is neither Hydrogen nor Oxygen and just like that the Ego is neither the Push Factors nor the Pull Factors. The Ego is a new product which is unique in every individual and it behaves in every situation. Water can be classified into many kinds like pure water, partly pure and impure and like that a human ego can be pure, partly pure and impure. Pure water can be made impure and impure water can be made pure. Likewise, an impure ego can be made pure and a pure ego can be made impure. It is the ego which behaves. Depending upon the purity of ego, a man commits/does not commit crimes. The Push factors can be biological, psychological, constitutional, endocrinological or anything of that kind. The Pull factors can be sociological, cultural, socio-cultural, ecological, political or anything of that kind. A human person develops his Ego and forms a new product as a result of the interaction between the Push and Pull factors.

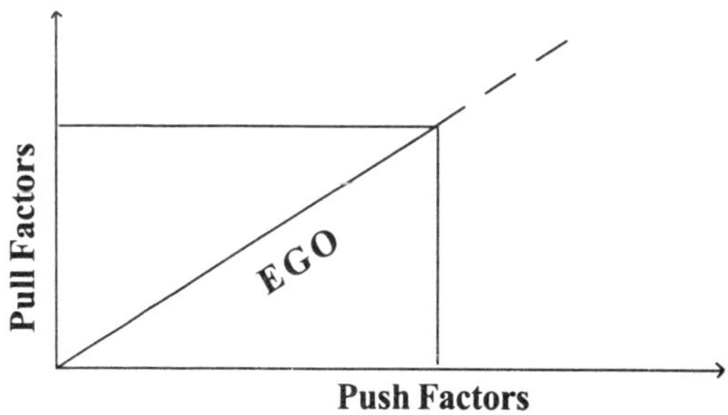

The Ego develops as a person grows older and older. As an individual grows older and older, he is exposed to more and more pull factors. The Push Factors are constant in an individual and the Pull Factors are not. Resultingly, as the Pull Factors are more, the Ego gets developed.

Ego and Human Conscience

Human conscience is described in various ways in various disciplines and I wish to call it the inner voice in a man. This voice activates him or makes him to behave in a particular way—rather than in another way. Once a police officer came to me and said that he has done something according to his conscience and therefore he has no conscience prick. He experienced mental satisfaction. He claimed himself to be a conscientious man. O.K., so far so good.

Human conscience is something which can not be physically seen, but is something that is experienced. In order to explain human satisfaction when he does something, we need a concept and I call it a conscience which one manifests through his "Ego". Ego expressions thus mean to me the expressions of the human conscience.

Earlier I said that H_2O=water and likewise the Push and Pull Factors make the human Ego. I also said that the water may be pure, partly pure or impure. But how? H_2O is always pure water, but in Ego, the Pull Factors can be pure, partly pure or impure. In ideal conditions, the Pull Factors are pure and in such a condition, the human conscience will be pure and accordingly the ego—expressions. But, such an ideal condition never exists so much so that there can be no pure conscience for anybody. Hence the human conscience may be drawn as:—

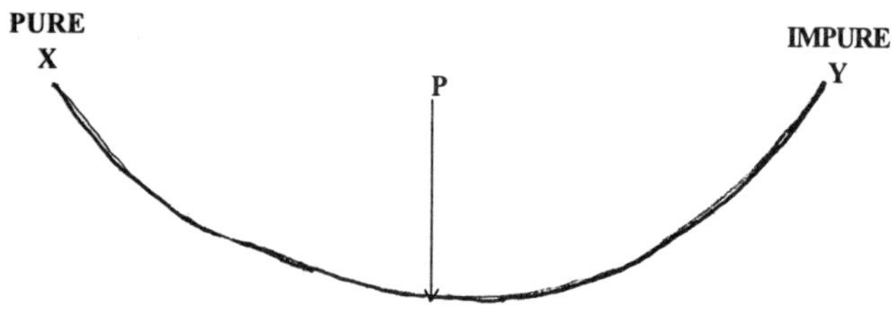

BOARDER LINE HUMAN CONSCIENCE

In the above curve of human conscience, the pure conscience is at X and the impure conscience is at Y. P is the boarderline. In PY, a person starts to experience conscience prick at P, the threashold to impure conscience. If a man behaves from the XP area of his conscience, he feels metal peace and no conscience prick.

In criminology, we study criminal behaviour. In police criminology, we study police behaviour which is criminal. How is criminal behaviour caused? After answering this question, let us go to police crimes.

Think about an infant/child. The infant/child bites the nipple of its mother when he/she experiences frustrations to suck the milk. No doubt, it is an aggressive act and a child is not supposed to do so. The mother is the provider of milk for the infant and to such a provider, the infant must not behave the way he/she does—i.e., biting the nipple. Yet he/she does so. It means that the Push Factors in him/her are so strong that he/she does things the way he/she is compelled or forced to do.

What happens afterwards? After biting the nipple, the child has no feeling of guilt—no conscience prick. Why? His conscience is not formed. His Ego is not at work. The socializing agents takes the responsibility of forming the superego concepts in his conscience/ego. He is taught many things and more especially the do's and don'ts. Sigmund Freud speaks about superego and the formation of superego in human infants. The responsibility for the formation of superego is given to the socializing agents—namely, the mother, parents, teachers, community ... I have no difficulty to agree with the argument that the socializing agents do play a decisive role in the formation of the superego concepts in a developing infant/child. But, that is not enough. According to me, the socializing agents form only one part of the Pull Factors which act on the developing infant/child.

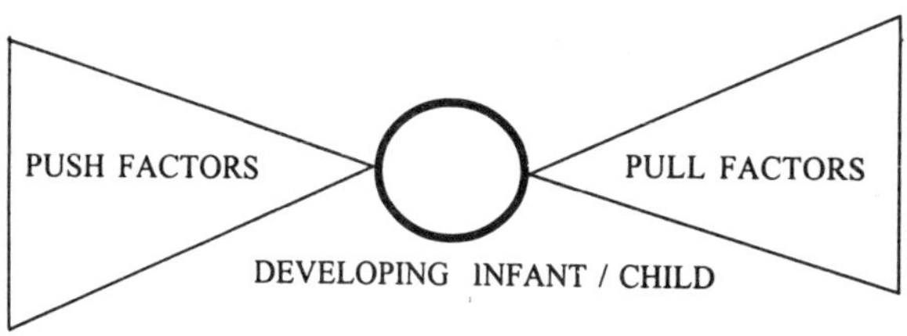

Earlier, I have brought out that the sociological, cultural, sociocultural, economic, family etc. environments form a part of the Pull Factors. The Pull Factors also consist of many other forces and they are:—

The socializing agents inculcate values, norms and do's/don'ts etc. to human conscience. Life experience adds further. Life is not a straight line. It has curves and the lessons one learns through his life experience adds to the conscience. Thus the values inculcated by the socializing agents may be modified by life experience. To it, the values inculcated by reading books or absorbed through the media may be added. They too modify the conscience. The pressures exerted by the environment make changes in human conscience. These Pull Factors interact with Push Factors which are inherited—psychological, biological, constitutional etc. The interaction which starts at birth continues till death and as the pull factors and push factors interact more and more, there will be changes in the human conscience. The *Ego* thus changes from birth to death. According to the

PULL FACTORS
Socialising Agents
Life Experience
Self Reading
Environmental Pressures

changes in the Ego, the conscience (inner voice) feels satisfaction/pleasure etc. If a man behaves contrary to the voice of his conscience, he experiences guilt for what he has done. This is what I call to be Push-Pull-Ego Factor theory in criminology and the theory is applicable to all sorts of crimes committed by human beings.

Examination of Conscience and the Egogramme

I have asked many of my students to draw their egogramme—i.e., their conscience and I have noted that none could do so. The reason has been that they did not/could not know how the interaction between the Push-Pull Factors worked in them. The daughter of a prostitute does not become a prostitute, but the son of a priest may become a thief. How? It is because of the conscience that one commits crime and the other does not. The Ego is the cause of crime and a person possessing an upright conscience can not commit crimes. This theory was subjected to an experimental study which was as follows.

Methodology

Police officers/men from various ranks were administered a research tool and they were requested to respond honestly to the statements given therein. The study took four years for its completion. The responses were then analysed for studying the formation of their conscience (Ego) at the time when the research tool was administered.

It was presumed that all policemen/officers committed police crimes of some kind or another. It was further presumed that a person had guilt feelings if he possessed an upright conscience when he committed the crime. Guilt feeling meant that he felt that he did something which he ought not have done.

The respondents to the tool were given five options to indicate their intensity of the guilt feelings and another five options to show the frequency of occurrence of their guilt feelings.

The research tool was as under. Every item started with "when" as follows:—

"When I tortured a suspect . . . . . .", and the respondent could mark any one of the options shown under the "Intensity" and under the "frequency of occurrence" of the feeling of guilt in him.

Research Tool to know the Intensity and Frequency of Occurrence of Guilt Feelings in the Following Situations

You may mark ✔ under any of the options given under the caption "*Intensity*" and under "*Frequency*"

	GUILT FEELINGS									
	INTENSITY					FREQUENCY				
Situations	Severe	Prefound	Moderate	Mild	Nothing	Very often	Often	Some times	At times	Never

1. When I uttered filthy words/epithets ...
2. When I accepted bribe/illegal gratification ...
3. When I tortured a suspect ...
4. When I harassed a witness ...
5. When I humiliated a person ...
6. When I informally arrested ...
7. When I illegally detained ...
8. When I tutored witnesses ...
9. When I concocted evidence ...
10. When I violated human rights ...

11. When I manipulated records ...
12. When I registered false cases ...
13. When I showed disrespect to witnesses ...
14. When I became partial ...
15. When I became susceptible to influence ...
16. When I threatened suspects ...
17. When I coerced witnesses ...
18. When I did not listen to petitioners ...
19. When I became a partner to nexus crimes ...
20. When I received kickbacks ...
21. When I got payoff ...
22. When I employed excessive force on a law and order situation ...
23. When I employed foul means during investigation ...
24. When I uttered vulgar language during patrolling ...
25. When I was not gender decent ...
26. When I was indecent to women in custody ...
27. When I received favours from people ...
28. When I was given share in corruption money ...
29. When I forced people to have recourse to corruption money splitting ...
30. When I resorted to mooching/scrounging ...
31. When I resorted to chiseling ..
32. When I abused my power ...
33. When I misused my authority ...
34. When I victimized people ...
35. When I unnecessarily used my muscle power ..
36. When I offered false testimony in courts ...
37. When I expressed pseudo-authority ...
38. When I misused government vehicles ...
39. When I misappropriated public money .
40. When I misappropriated government materials ...
41. When I wrote the confidential report of subordinates dishonestly ...
42. When I behaved in a prejudiced manner ...
43. When I disowned my subordinates ...
44. When I initiated false disciplinary inquiries ...
45. When I punished the subordinates unjustly ...
46. When I showed blind eyes to organized criminal activities ...
47. When I performed duties in an indifferent way ...
48. When I made false accusations against colleagues/associates ...

49. When I saw political interference to torpedo justice ...
50. When I was pressured to do injustice ...
51. When I saw injustice among my subordinates/associates ...
52. When I neglected my duties ...
53. When I wrote special reports dishonestly ...
54. When I produced touts in courts ...
55. When I influenced unduly the prosecutor ...
56. When I exerted undue influence on the defence counsel ...
57. When I prepared a false mahazar ...
58. When I influenced the defence witnesses ...
59. When I delayed decisions ...
60. When I did something in a perfunctory way ...
61. When I made the prosecution witnesses hostile ...
62. When I made a cognizable case into a non-cognizable one ...
63. When I made a non-cognizable to cognizable one ...
64. When I refused to register a F.I.R ...
65. When I misbehaved with the poor and downtrodden ...
66. When I ill-treated people on the basis of their caste/community ...
67. When I showed disrespect to the old ...
68. When I did not produce the detinue before the court in time ...
69. When I tortured the innocent ...
70. When I managed to get fuel for police vehicles from the public ...
71. When I had entertainment without purchasing tickets ...
72. When I hired taxi without paying the fare ...
73. When I travelled in bus without purchasing tickets ...
74. When I misbehaved with children ...
75. When I behaved under intoxication during duty hours ...
76. When I misappropriated seized property ...
77. When I misbehaved with people during a search ...
78. When I did not show due respect to article during a search ...
79. When I located any article which was already hidden at the place ...
80. When I suppressed facts ...
81. When I suggested falsehood ...
82. When I exaggerated the facts ...
83. When I underestimated people ...
84. When I absented myself from duty ...
85. When I misdirected the accused in crimes ...
86. When I saw that the innocent was punished ...
87. When I misused official position to run private business ...

88. When I participated in false encounters ...
89. When I encouraged the commission of crime ...
90. When I did not do anything to prevent the commission of crime ...
91. When I prompted/promoted crime and criminality ...
92. When I showed misconduct ...
93. When I made false promises ...
94. When I was responsible for lawless law enforcement ...
95. When I caused miscarriage of justice ...
96. When I behaved in an unbecoming way ...
97. When I caused a bad image for the department ...
98. When I created interpersonal rivalry ...
99. When I behaved with hostility and vengeance ...
100. When I behaved well according to my conscience ...

The study revealed that:—

1. One and the same person did not have the same intensity for different situations. Against some, he had *severe* feeling of guilt and against others he had only *mild* feeling of guilt.
2. The frequency of occurrence of the guilt feeling depended upon the nature of intensity of the feeling of guilt. If the intensity was mild, the frequency was "at times" and if the intensity was *severe*, then the frequency was '*very often*'.
3. Every one experienced guilt when he committed a wrong act as per his conscience. His conscience was the decider of right and wrong. Depending upon the formation of conscience, the intensity of guilt was strong and the frequency was frequent.

After getting the research tool filled up by the respondent, I analysed it meticulously. Some of them were taken on a random basis and I took those responses with "severe/pound feeling of guilt" and "very often/ often frequency". I could locate the supervisory officers of some of them. I also could meet some of their subordinates. I held elaborate discussions about the behaviour of the respondents with their superiors/subordinates. For example, one has given profound feeling of guilt "when he tortured a suspect and if he has given that the frequency of occurrence was "very often/often", then the expected assessment from the superiors/ subordinates would be that he never employed torture on the suspects. The conclusions were:

1. The more severe/profound a policeman/officer had the guilt feelings, the less he involved in the commission of crimes.

2. The more frequent one had the occurrence of guilt feelings in him, the less times he involved in the commission of crimes.
3. What I could notice was that the more upright was the formation of one's conscience, the chances of his committing crimes were less.

As the second part of the research was time consuming and laboursome, I did not continue my research work with more supervisors/ subordinates. Moreover I was fully convinced about the validity of my theory even without more researches in that direction. I thought that it would be a waste of time to do so. My conclusions are:

1. The Ego (Conscience) which is the product of Push-Pull Factors is the cause of crimes.
2. Formation of an upright conscience is an effective way to control/prevent crimes.
3. Police crimes are the result of defective ego (conscience) formation.

Push-Pull-Ego Factor theory of crime causation may lead us to many more conclusions, namely:—

1. Punishment has limited value and impact to prevent crimes. It can at the most control the commission of crimes for a temporary period.
2. Correction of the crime-doer/reformation of the criminal may take place only if a change in his conscience (Ego) takes place. A change in one's 'conscience' means a change in his behaviour.

Push-Pull-Ego Factor theory is applicable not only with police crimes, but with all sorts of crimes. Nevertheless, this discussion is limited to police crimes and control of police crimes.

Push-Pull-Ego Factor Theory and Control of Police Crimes

How to prevent/control police crimes? At the outset, we may admit that no crime will be fully prevented for ever. A crime can only be controlled. Police crime can also be never prevented, but can be controlled. Strengthening the human conscience (Ego) is the best method to control any crimes and police crimes are not exceptions to this general rule.

So long as objective tests for understanding human conscience have not been developed by Indian police, it is not possible to know one's values and conscience. The police training institutions, the atmosphere, superiors, subordinates, culture, subculture, training, education work etc. may exert pressure and inculcate new values. Conscience is already formed when a person is recruited to police and certainly it can be modified. Whenever a police officer shows criminal tendencies, the best way to control and correct him is to make an attempt to effect modifications in his Ego—the conscience. For, it is the Ego which takes a decision to behave in a specific way in a given situation. This theory is applicable in all types of crimes and therefore the next chapter deals with enforcement criminology.

References

1. Jerome H. Sholnick, *Justice Without Trial*, John Wiley & Sons, New York, 1966.
2. Arthur Niederhoffer, *Behind the Shield*: *The Police in Urban Society*, Doubleday and Co., Garden City, N.Y., 1967.
3. John Mc Namara *Uncertainities in Police Work*: The Relevance of Police Recruits' Backgrounds and Training, in David J. Bordua, ed., *The Police*: *Six Sociological Essays*, John Wiley & Sons, New York, 1967.
4. E. Bittner, *The Police on Skid-row*: *A Study of Peace Keeping*, American Sociological Review, 32 (October), 1967.
5. William A. Westley, *Violence and the Police*, American Journal of Sociology, 59 (July), 1953.
6. *ibid.*
7. E.R. Stoddard, *The Informal Code of Police Deviancy*: *A Group Approach to Blue-coat Crime*, Criminal Law, Criminology and Police Science, 59 (June) 1968.
8. L. Savitz, *The Dimensions of Police Loyalty*, The American Behavioural Scientist, May-June, July-August, 1970.
9. A.J. Reiss, Police Brutality—Answers to key Questions, Transaction, 5 (July-August) 1968.
10. See Arthus Niederhoffer, *op. cit.*
11. R. Shamasastry, Kautilya's Arthasastra, Mysore Printing and Publishing House, 1967.
12. George Vold B., *Theoretical Criminology*, Oxford University Press, New York, 1958.
13. H.E. Barnes and N.K. Teeters, *New Horizons in Criminology*, Prentice-Hall, New Delhi, 1966.
14. Quoted from Sue Titus Reid, *Crime and Criminology*, The Dryden Press, Hinsdole, 1976.
15. J.T. 1997 (1) SCI=AIR 1997 (SC) 610=1997 (1) SCC 416=1996 (9) Scale 298=1996 (8) Supreme 581=1996 (4) Crimes 233 (SC)=1997 Cr. L. J. 743.

16. Joginder Kumar Vs. State of Uttar Pradesh, A.I.R. 1994 SC 1349=1994 (4) SCC 260=1994 (3) JT 423=1994 Cr. L. J. 1981=1994 (2) Crimes 106=1994 (2) Scale 602=1994 SCC (Cr.) 1172.
17. 1995 SCC (Cr) 832=1995 Supp. (3) SCC 234=1994 (1) Scale 326.
18. 1996 SCC (Cr) 424=AIR 1996 SC 2326=1996 (7) SCC 397=1996 (I) JT 328=1996 (1) Scale 340=1996 (1) Crimes 58 (SC)=1996 Cr. L. J. 1679.
19. 1996 SCC (Cr) 921=1996 Cr. L. J. 2518=AIR 1996 SC 1925=1996 (9) SCC 74=1996 (5) JT 88=1996 (4) Scale 290.
20. (1991) 4 SCC 406=AIR 1991 SC 2176=1991 (2) Scale 501=1991 Cr. L. J. 3086=1991 (3) Crimes 232.

CHAPTER—12

Enforcement Criminology

Any person who is empowered by law can abuse his authority or misuse his power. Law enforcement may mean law violations and contain a series of violations of law by those who are bound to enforce the law. Originally crimes were private matters. The concept of personal justice was in existence then. The Code of Hammurabi from 1900 B.C., the Roman Tablets of laws from 450 B.C., the Mosaic Code, the laws of the early Greece as seen in Iliad and Odyssey, and the laws of Tacitus (Germanic people in 98 A.D) speak about personal justice. As days went on, it became difficult to enforce private justice. Thus came official actions against crimes and criminals. Crimes were treated as acts committed against kings (State) and thus the State became the injured in every crime. The State enforces the law through people appointed for the purpose and if they commit crimes during the enforcement of law, then what must be done? They are given a statute for enforcing its provisions. And they enforce the provisions violating the principles of justice or they do not enforce the law as they are bound to do for the State. In such a situation, what can be done. Are they committing crimes then? For example:—

1. Abkari Act contains a lot of provisions for the Excise Officials to enforce. They do not enforce them. By doing so, they make advantages for them.
2. Central Excise law permits the Excise Officials to employ their discretion. They use it to their advantage.
3. Sale Tax law allows the officials to interpret the law this way or that way. They interpret it to obtain benefits for them.

4. Forest laws, Income Tax laws etc. have similar provisions which the officials can use or abuse them in such a way that they get gains.

No doubt, it is not only unwise but also impossible to remove all types of discretion from the enforcement officials. Laws can not be enacted to comprehend every situation. Discretion must be used with honesty and integrity in approaches. A professional and ethical orientation that is legal must be seen in every enforcement action. The officials perform their duty for the State and if the State commits offences, then there is no effective remedy against such actions. Enforcement criminology deals with the crimes committed by the officials of the State during the enforcement of laws or in the pretext of enforcing the laws. Crimes thus committed by the officials are intentional acts or omissions and they do so without any justifications. Their behaviour is not sanctioned by the State. There is a contractual relationship between the State and its officials and the officials have a legal duty to perform the work entrusted to them in the manner expected from them or in the way they are bound to do. In manipulating, interpreting, executing the law, they have no right to do so to their advantage, benefit or gain. Everything must be done legally to the advantage of the State. Here, they do not do so and that is why enforcement criminology says that they are violating the canons of the State. Acts or omissions which the officials do are voluntary and that proves that the officials have control over their acts.

Why do the officials manipulate the law? Certainly, it is for their advantage (also for the advantage of others and not at all for the State) and the evil intent becomes very obvious. Enforcement criminology makes the evil intent of the doer the essence of his crime. He does not do the same thing in the same way for all and precisely therefore, the act is the result of one's executive volition. Criminal jurisprudence makes the wrongful or criminal intent as the essence of crime. The criminal intent, the principle says, needs not necessarily be to do the very act forbidden by law, but it must, at least, be to do a wrong thing. In the above cases, it may be difficult to say that the acts/omissions done by the officials are forbidden by any law, but it can certainly be stated that their acts/omissions are done with an intent to commit a wrong thing and thereby to make some advantages or benefits for them. Therefore, their acts/omissions are crimes—say criminologists.

Mens Rea in Enforcement Crimes

Mens Rea which means the criminal intent may be specific or general.

If a forest official commits an act that results in an injury to the public, then it is presumed that he has had the required criminal intent unless otherwise proved. After a fair assessment, a Central Customs Officer decides that an amount of 3 lakhs must be levied as the custom-duty for the articles. Later, on the basis of a *nexus* understanding, suppose, he pockets one lakh rupees and levies only one lakh rupees from the passenger, then he misappropriates one lakh rupees. The amount is due to the public and it is an offence committed by the official. He has the necessary *mens rea* and enforcement criminology deals with it accordingly. Here, the official has no specific *mens rea* to commit a crime against a specific individual, but he has the required *mens rea* to commit an offence against the public. The official plots with the passenger to criminally misappropriate the amount due to the public and together they carry out the criminal intent. Hence they have the specific *mens-rea* to commit the offence.

After committing the offence, they do not have any remorse over the crime thus committed. In all cases of enforcement crimes or nexus criminality, one may notice specific *mens rea* and not a general *criminal intent*. The superior officers/supervisors of the customs officer have a liability over the crimes their subordinates commit. If they keep proper vigil and supervision over the acts of their subordinates, certainly they can prevent the crimes their subordinates commit. But, they do not and that alone provides a facilitating environment for their subordinates to commit crimes. They have the general *mens rea* in such instances. Enforcement criminology justifies punishing those committing crimes with a general *criminal intent*.

Enforcement Crimes and Welfare of the State

Enforcement officials abuse their power, misuse their authority and discretion to commit crimes. Any crime threatens the welfare of the State and enforcement crimes injuriously affect the welfare in many ways. But, the State does not take action against the offenders. There is no complaint against anyone. The public do not make complaints. The nexus partners are the beneficiaries. The enforcer of law—i.e., the official of the State/the State—is the offender. He interprets the law to his advantage. He has no defence or justification for what he does. The defences given under the chapter General Exceptions in the Indian Penal Code—1860 or justifications shown in any special and local laws can not be brought to establish the non-liability for the crime committed by the enforcement officials. The question is: "what punishment can be given to an enforcement official if he misuses/abuses his authority and power?" "What is the punishment for nexus crimes or enforcement crimes?" The State or an official of the State is the offender here and how can the punishment be awarded? The State does not provide punishment for many crimes committed by the enforcement officers. Suppose, a sale tax officer/income tax officer makes an untrue assessment of the income and fixes the tax, certainly, he has misused his power/abused his authority. He does so purposefully to put the assessee in trouble or to force the assessee to approach him with offers and offerings. He is doing a harmful act and he has the support of the law to do such harmful acts. What is the remedy for the people in such situations? Enforcement criminology has to deal with such types of criminal behaviour by the enforcement officials.

Statistics on crimes may not include enforcement crimes as many events that would be crimes otherwise are not treated as crimes now. Many *de facto* criminals are not punished even when they commit offences under law. It does not mean that they are not criminal. They are, but are not treated as *de jure* criminals. Likewise, an enforcement criminal may not be a *de jure* offender, but he is certainly a *de facto* criminal.

Enforcement officials are legally bound to enforce laws as per the laws and procedure established by laws. But, they may not and they do so purposefully. They have the legal and nonlegal ways of reacting and they have the option to select one. Their selection may depend upon their values and they may select to act in a nonlegal way. In such situations, enforcement criminologists say that they commit crimes. But they are not labelled as criminals. Some, enforcement officers misuse their official vehicles for personnel purposes. They say that they use the vehicles for official purposes. Whenever they use the official vehicles for personal purposes, they are not labeled 'criminals'. Why? Whenever an enforcement official engages in corruption money splitting/corruption money fixing, he is not given the status of a criminal. Why? On the contrary, he calls a pickpocket "a criminal" and his status has the effect of a life sentence for him. If at all he is acquitted by a court, he enjoys his status as a criminal all throughout his life. The society refuses to erase that label and the same society fails to call enforcement criminals "criminals" in society. Why?

"Red tapism"—everyone knows it to be an evil, a crime. But, the society looks at it in a mild way. Hoarding of files is what is otherwise called 'red tapism'. Purposeful delay caused in taking decisions and the crime is sugarcoated by a word "administrative delay". Every file is an essential commodity and a decision on it too is an essential commodity. Bureaucrats do not understand the gravity of their so named "administrative delay" which causes irrepairable damage to many and the society does not look at the bureaucrats who do so as crime-doers! Why? The society does not label them as bureaucratic criminals! Why? The legislators do not enact laws to punish such delay causing criminals! Why? *Nulla Poena sine lege* (No punishment without law) attitude is seen and the crimes of bureaucratic hoarding of files and purposeful causing of delay in decision making are on the increase. To them their bureaucratic might is their right and they know no other codes.

Government renders monopoly services and the people can not get them from other places. The officials responsible for rendering services to people do not do it with honesty and sincerity and then people go after help. The cases registered against Government decisions are numerous and the records in any High Court in India will prove that maximum number of cases is filed against Government decisions. Does it mean that the bureaucracy is so inefficient that it can not take just decisions? Does it mean that the bureaucracy is so efficient that it takes wrong decisions? Every unjust decision taken by the bureaucracy is a violation of law and to that extent is a crime. The society has not so far assigned the label "criminal" to such bureaucrats and therefore they enjoy a status which is different from the same of the criminals so labelled. Cesare Lombroso said that a criminal was a moral degenerate? Is a bureaucrat who abuses his power/ misuses his authority a moral degenerate? Some officials know well that they are doing a wrong thing when they take illegal decisions; yet they do so. Why? Are they the mental or moral imbecile of the metaphysicians? They repeat their illegal acts and can they be called "recidivists"? Are they hardened criminals? Are they the victims of adverse circumstances? Do they suffer from inferiority complex or oedipus complex? Can they be the victim of unsavory environment or do they suffer from some defects in their heredity? They are criminals—says enforcement criminology, but the society needs time to give that label to them.

Enforcement criminologists may argue that bureaucrats and enforcement officials commit crimes as a matter of choice. They do not do so as a means of livelihood. They are men of status, education and fixed income. They have people who have chosen to commit a wrong thing as they have the power to do so and authority to execute their illegalities. People who commit minor offences are sometimes put behind bars and those who misuse their power/abuse their authority are not. Why? Enforcement criminals are not criminals by accident. They do not commit crimes under the influence of liquor, drugs, sudden provocation or hunger. Their crimes are real crimes—and not '*accidents*' and the illegality is committed after discussions and deliberations. There are plenty of examples to prove the truth. And that is what one may see in preplanned raids to harass or humiliate some individuals and that is what one sees in taking no decisions on vital issues and the list is very long. When Topinard, the French Antropologist coined the term '*criminology*' in 1879, he never thought about enforcement crimes and enforcement criminology. Down the decades, no serious studies were conducted in the area and even today, criminologists have not entered the field to study crimes by enforcement officials and bureaucrats.

Causes of Enforcement Crimes

Why do enforcement officials commit various types of crimes from corruption to nexus criminality? from manipulation of records to hoarding of files?—from indecision to wrong decisions?—from harassment to people to calculated loss of money/status for them?—from humiliations to humourings? Action, inaction and overaction—these may be the three ways a bureaucrat or an enforcement official may be behaving. Inaction and overaction—both are violations of law and principles of administration. What is the remedy for the victims of inaction or overaction of the bureaucrats/enforcement official? Inaction or overaction may not be the characteristics of bureaucrats/enforcement officials. But they exist under the existing circumstances in India or are observed in the present set up. Why? Enforcement criminology like to know which variables produce inaction or overaction—or—enforcement crimes of other descriptions.

History proves that the bureaucrats/enforcement officials have been exercising an absolute and almost tyrannical powers over those who came before them for their monopoly services. The enforcement officials have power and authority, fund and resources, strength and will to exercise their decisions and descriminations. The people were helpless before them. Laws guiding the decision and behaviour of the officials have been vague and the officials took it upon themselves to interpret the spirit of the law if the vagueness did not suit their objectives which were sometimes their whims and fancies. Personal interpretations of the law, rules and regulations paved the way for unjust discriminations which ultimately meant the execution of administrative decisions as they wanted. The people became defenceless. The rules were applied unequally to citizens and the execution of unequal rules necessarily invited corruption and corrupt practices. One could observe corruption from time immemorial. The people had no option but to yield to the administrative decisions which were sometimes unjust and unfair. Some went to courts, but it was a time consuming, laborious and painstaking process. There was uncertainty as well. This dragged many to offer corruption money to the bureaucrats/ enforcement officials. Thus corruption became rampant in society.

In history, one sees that the enforcement officials—wherever they worked—were harsh to the people who came before them. They could be made mild only by oiling them with behavioural patterns which they loved. The presumption has been that they were transacting business for the king or for the government. Hence, they could afford to be harsh and cruel. Their superiors approved their behaviour and they exploited this privilege, many a time, to their advantage. The classicists Bentham and Beccaria spoke about utiliterianism and pleasure theory to explain criminal behaviour. The theory may explain the behaviour of bureaucrats/enforcement officials as their behaviour gives more utility and pleasure for them when they involve in exercising their freedom of choice to their advantage. Any decision taken for the government or in the pretext of ensuring advantage for the government is protected by the presumption that they do everything for the pleasure of the greatest number of people. This is a protection or is a protective cover for their decisions which are otherwise or sometimes unfair or unjust. Their decisions with a calculated move to obtain advantage, utility or pleasure too is protected by the principle of largest pleasure for the largest number of people. Punishments are not awarded for their unjust and unfair decisions. Hence, they take it for granted that they can do anything without being afraid of any punishment for what they do.

Enrico Ferri (1856—1929) did not say anything about enforcement criminality. Nevertheless, he said that crime was produced primarily by the type of society from which the criminal hailed. Some bureaucrats/enforcement officials say that they belong to the society and represent a cross section of the same. They argue further that enforcement crimes can be reduced only if the society changes. Therefore, correct the society before correcting the enforcement functionaries. I interviewed 70 enforcement officials (not police) to know how criminality would creep into their work. I learn that novices to government service do not generally show criminal tendencies. They want to be just, honest, not prejudiced and not partial. They have high ideals! But, in due course, they show symptoms of criminality—inaction/and/ overaction and they become a part of their style of functioning.

An enforcement official told me:

"I have seen many officials accepting corruption money and I wanted to become a government functionary just to make money. I got a government job and it was in enforcement. I wanted corruption money. I knew that I could not get money unless I created some hurdles for others. I watched how others in the department do and I did the same thing in the same way.

Then they approached me with money and I am what I am today because I created hurdles for others.

Many enforcement officials were candid enough to say that their initial contact for involving into enforcement crimes was another enforcement official in the same department. The associates in the department often agree to aid the beginners. In a particular department, the associates collect the corruption money and distribute the same among others who form the group. The associates teach values and philosophy of service. Another official told me:

"Treat all officials in the department fairly because a government employee's worst enemy is another employee in the same department and only by treating other employees decently, can one expect to get along with them. Anyone may cause harm and life becomes miserable".

People from all walks of life—with different socio-economic backgrounds—with different educational achievements—with different political ideologies—enter into government service. In India, caste and birth in a particular religion too are factors deciding entry into government service. 'Multiple factors' theory of crime causation holds the view that many factors are responsible for the commission of crimes. As such, the socio-economic backgrounds, educational achievements, political ideologies, caste, birth, place of birth etc. may work together for causing crimes. In government service too, they may be associated in greater or less degree in the causation of crimes. Nevertheless, they need not always necessarily cause crimes. For, researches show that those conditions are sometimes present when crimes are committed or they are sometimes absent when criminality occurs.

As soon as a person enters into government service, he starts learning many things which he can not learn if he were not in government service. The education is informal and he absorbs a knowledge of the fair and foul ways of performing his job in government service. He learns them from his associates and he learns them before he becomes well versed in his job. He understands that it is possible to abuse/misuse his power and authority for his advantage. The attitude of the subordinates, associates and superiors towards the abuse/misuse of power and authority is an important factor in determining the attitude of the new entrant to government service. If the attitude is favourable to enforcement criminality, then he develops a favourable attitude to enforcement crimes. 'Multiple Factors' exert influence here and thus he becomes an enforcement criminal in due course.

No doubt, power has a controlling effect on government operations and every law enforcement officer enjoys some power and authority. Enforcement service consists of a well organized minority of people who has power to enforce the decisions which are lawful or unlawful. If the enforcement officers decide to enforce their unlawful decisions, then the people become the sufferers. The people are not well organized to fight against the enforcement machinery. Resultingly, they have no option, but to suffer. For, they have little or no power against the enforcement mechanism or if at all they have any power, the mobilization of their power/strength is not easy.

Corruption and Bureaucratic Criminology

Corruption in government service becomes an issue during all elections. Whenever a new government comes into power, commissions of inquiry are appointed to probe into the corrupt practices committed by the previous government in collaboration with the bureaucracy. In some instances, bureaucrats are prosecuted and punished. Recently, a Chief Secretary of a South Indian State was convicted for three years rigorous imprisonment for the alleged corruption. Ministers are chargesheeted and the houses of the bureaucrats are raided. Some raids bring out huge amount of money and savings from unknown sources. Some bureaucrats invest money in other States and maintain bank accounts there and thus they keep their illicit income and savings from the immediate visibility of the people and associates with whom they work in the State. Why do the bureaucrats involve themselves in the commission of crimes and corrupt practices?

The Prime Minister of India in a recent article written by him spoke about corruption in government services and according to some researchers, corruption has been institutionalized by Indian Bureaucracy. William J. Chambliss says: "Organized crime becomes not something that exists outside law and government, but is instead a creation of them, or perhaps more accurately a hidden but nonetheless integral part of the government structure[1]".

There are many laws regulating, controlling and preventing many types of crimes and vices. Prostitution, gambling or gaming, pornography, bootlegging, drug-trafficking, investment schemes, rackets and similar vice syndicates do exist in Indian society. In spite of many laws to prevent such vices, they are seen in many forms and magnitudes. There are special departments specifically created to deal with offenders involved in such racketeering, but the fact remains that they are incapable, helpless, and blind in the enforcement of the laws. Some do encourage such vices or participate in the commission of crimes. Nexus crimes are notorious in the present set up and the syndicate criminals with considerable political power and bureaucratic support engage in conducting brothels, gambling dens, casinos, parlours and bootlegging etc. They, together with some unscrupulous bureaucrats, enjoy the pleasures of the vice without any kind of interference from the law and law enforcement agencies. Why? My book titled "Indian Police and Nexus Crime" throws more light on this issue—especially on the nexus crimes committed by law enforcement machinery. Near the secretariat in a south Indian State, there exists an officers' club where one finds gambling by cards. But, no one initiates any action against the gaming that is going on. Why is this laxity in enforcing laws? The questions are many and answers are few. Criminologists may find out answers to such questions. There are games, blue movies and gambling nights in private clubs—country clubs and one may see bureaucrats everywhere. It means that there is bureaucratic support and encouragement for the promotion of vices in the city. William J. Chambliss writes further: "Typically, this means that law enforcers adopt a tolerance policy toward the vices, selectively enforcing these laws only when it is to their advantage to do so[2]".

Enforcement officials are or ought to be governed by rules and laws, and at the same time, they have a lot of discretionary power vested with them. This is an inevitable necessity. Some, therefore, may abuse their discretion and misuse their authority. Precisely therefore some degree of corruption is not a mere possibility, rather is a virtual necessity—says Chambliss. He adds that the virtual necessity "is built into the very structure of bureaucratic organization". In Indian bureaucracy, a file is examined at various levels from clerks upwards. Everyone exercises his discretion and all of them think that they are right. Some may be doing it for personal benefits and they may get corruption money. In Watiao Vs. State of Manipur[3], an IAS officer was punished by the Supreme Court after enhancing the sentence of imprisonment to him on charges of corruption. In common cause Vs. Union of India, the Supreme Court held the view: "With the change in socio-economic outlook, the public servants are being entrusted with more and more discretionary powers even in the field of disbursement of government wealth in various forms ... If a public servant abuses his office either by an act of omission or commission and the consequence of that is injury to an individual or loss of public property, an action may be initiated against such public servant ... It is high time that public servants were held personally responsible for their malefide acts in the discharge of their functions as public servant". The judgement speaks of enforcement criminology and the Apex court is of firm opinion of fixing the responsibility on the public servants. Instances have been reported that the Supreme Court has awarded compensation to the victims of abuse of power/misuse of authority by government servants. In Paschim Banga *Khet Mazdoor Samity* Vs. State of West Bengal[5], the Supreme Court awarded an amount of Rs. 25,000—as compensation to a person who was denied of medical treatment in government hospitals.

Enforcement criminology holds the view that the people in authority—in government service—can violate the laws they enforce with a certain amount of immunity. For, they are the enforcers of law! Violation of law is what is defined as crime and whenever law violations take place, no matter who violates them, their violations are called enforcement crimes. Accordingly, enforcement crimes come under the scope of enforcement criminology. No government official can or must claim immunity when he flouts the law.

Power Corrupts Power

Power corrupts power; absolute power corrupts absolutely—this may be a cliche, but is pregnant with meaning and truth. The basis of enforcement crimes, perhaps, can be seen in the power one exercises—the power of discretion one enjoys in decision making—the power to misuse/abuse one's authority in favour or against another. Anyone who exercises power assumes a new personality and if the newly assumed personality suffers from personality defects, then he is sure to abuse/misuse his authority and power. As enforcement crimes have not been given a distinct identity by criminologists—are not treated as offences under law—are committed by many government officials, there arises a lot of problems to proceed against the enforcement criminals. For example, an officer hoards a file without taking proper action or another officer destroys an important document during the course of his official transactions, what can the victims do about it? After some time, the crime may be detected, but the offender is not easily identified. A former Vice-Chancellor of a university told me once that some of the orders which he issued on the files were not carried out by the Registrar of the University. After some years, in connection with a vigilance inquiry, the vice-chancellor's orders were traced. It was later learnt that the order of the vice-chancellor was still on the file and has never seen the light of the day. In another case, it was found out that a Chief Secretary of a State took secretly hundreds of files and burnt them. The files, it is said, contained illegal transactions and unlawful activities. Yet in another instance, it was seen that some routine government orders which were issued about 20 or 30 years ago were manipulated by the employees working in the secretariat in a State and were misused for their advantage. By such manipulations in the routine government orders said to have been issued about three or four decades ago, the present employees could establish precedents to get their things done to their favour. If crimes are committed by government officials after a consensus being reached, then no one on earth will be able to even identify the enforcement crimes and criminals. Enforcement criminology teaches that enforcement crimes are as henious as any other crimes and they must be given special identity. The injustice committed by enforcement criminals, in some instance, is beyond human conception, comprehension and imagination. False entries are made, false certificates are issued, false documents are created and thus the crimes are endless and the injustice committed is unimaginably severe. What is the motive's behind the commission of enforcement crimes? No research studies have been conducted on such issues in criminology. Yet, motives can be easily established in many enforcement crimes. According to the Supreme Court of India, "the proof of the existence of a motive is not necessary for a conviction for any offence[6]. In bureaucratic crimes, no one searches for a motive. A secretary to Government yields to the desires of his minister in power. Why? He has the motive to make his position lucrative and advantageous by being a "yes-man" to the minister.

People make complaints that many government officials/clerks are not seen on their seats. Service association/Union leaders and workers sign the attendance register and leave their offices for association/union works. No body controls them or can control them. Some officers/clerks are always on unauthorized leave (French Leave as they say) and they do not do any work. Weeklies, fortnightlies and monthlies are brought to the officers and are read. Thus one may notice that there exists no work culture in many of the government offices. Emile Durkheim and Robert Merton did not think about this sort of office lawlessness when they developed the theory of anomie. Many criminologists found high incidence of crime and delinquency among people in the lower classes. According to some criminologists, the lower class people indulged in committing crimes as they could not attain the goals of the society through legitimate and approved means. The government servants who violate the service rules and norms do commit crimes because they think that they can do anything or afford to do many things without fearing anybody under the sun. The service associations/unions have political patronage and anything they do may be politicized for getting political mileage. Crimes develop in government offices/among government officials as a result of the disorganization within the service. The government officials in India have great security in their job and they get their salary every month, no matter they work hard or not. This sort of assurance they have makes some to become lethargic in their work. While speaking about the development of a subculture of delinquency, Albert Cohen said that the activities in a delinquent subculture would be nonutilitarian, malicious, negativistic, versatile and characterized by short run hedonism and group autonomy. I can not say how far can the observations of Albert Cohen be applied to the delinquent/criminal subculture which exists in government services. Nevertheless, some of the activities they do and decisions they take are malecious. "How a thing can not be done"—this is how some officials look at issues, events and individuals. They become inhuman and anything for them is just a file. They do not or can not find human faces, sentiments and needs behind the files. In-service courses to reorient the attitude of government officials are now organized to effect a behavioural change in them.

Office Environment and Criminality

There is a school of thought which argues that a broken office is the cause of criminality. There exists no one to control the office staff. The chief in the office does not have the moral and administrative control over his subordinates. There was a time the subordinates kept their eyes shut to what they saw at the higher levels of administration. Today, they keep their eyes open to everything they see at the higher/top areas of administration. They make them known to the people through the media and thus an atmosphere is created in government offices that the people do not trust one another. A new entrant to government service develops himself in such an atmosphere. Gabriel Tarde saw "murderers, pickpockets, swindlers and thieves as individuals who had gone through a long period of apprenticeship, just as doctors, lawyers, farmers or skilled workmen. It was that the accident of birth placed them in an atmosphere of crime". Perhaps, the observations are equally true in enforcement/office criminality. Many new entrants to government service violate their service rules, become corrupt in their work, do unlawful things because they are placed in an atmosphere which promotes enforcement/office criminality. Gabriel Tarde believed that it was the imitation which made many people to commit crimes. He said that "men imitate one another in proportion as they are in close contact". I do not think that there is a blind imitation in many things and particularly in criminal behaviour. The behaviour of others may instigate people and a crime-prone individual may be tempted by the instigation. Government officials may become corrupt when they are tempted only if they are corruption-prone. Their Ego plays a role there. Tarde's laws of imitation, I do not think, can fully be applied to bureaucratic criminality. He over-simplifies the causation of crime.

Edwin H. Sutherland's differential association theory has very limited application in the causation of enforcement crimes. According to him, the criminal behaviour is learned. My studies show that a man commits crime even when he has no opportunity to learn the commission of crimes. Adam and Eve as pointed out elsewhere violated the divine law not at all through an interaction with other people in a process of communication. A crime prone person finds and invents means and methods to commit crimes. In enforcement crimes, the chances of communication may be very limited, yet people commit crimes. In organized defiance to authority by government servants, one may take note of the fact that they destroy pubiic property. In one instance, the employees working in the Electricity Board of a State caused mass destruction of transformers and power lines. Likewise, the employees of a State Transport Corporation caused damage to hundreds of buses and in such expression of aggressiveness, Sutherland's differential association has little or no applicability. Sutherland says that a person becomes delinquent because of an excess of definitions favourable to violation of law over definitions unfavourable to the violation of law. In destruction of public property by government employees, there is no law favouring the violations. Enforcement criminology studies the crime and it does not give any importance to learning or differential association. Enforcement criminology questions the postulate of Edwin H. Sutherland that differential association is necessary and sufficient condition explaining crime and delinquency. Enforcement criminality is committed only when an individual becomes a government official. As such the crime has an origin at a later age and the officials who work under the same roof commit various types of crime. If close association with other is the cause of crime, then it is not possible to see a variety of crimes being committed by government officials who work and associate under the same roof. Some crimes committed by the bureaucrats are really invented by them. Sutherland himself admitted the limitations of his theory when he said that criminal associations alone did not explain criminal behaviour. He said further that it was those "associations plus tendencies toward alternate ways of satisfying whatever needs happen to be involved in a particular situation. Consequently, it is improper to view criminal behaviour as a closed system, and participation in criminal behaviour as a closed system, and participation in criminal behaviour is not to be regarded as something that is determined exclusively by association with criminal patterns ... For the reasons that I have outlined and doubtless for additional reasons, differential association of criminal behaviour is invalid". Sutherland was talking on white collar crimes and not at all on enforcement crimes and precisely for that reason his theory is inadequate and invalid to explain enforcement criminality.

The 'Ego', I have explained, of an individual is the product of the Push-Pull Factors and my studies show that the 'Ego' which is the product of those factors causes crimes of all kinds and also the enforcement crimes. It is not and should not be the push or pull factors, nor push versus pull factors, nor push under or over pull factors, but only and always the product of the push-pull factors—i.e., the ego that causes crimes in society. Enforcement crimes are purposive behaviour and the crime is committed with a *mens rea* which I call "*the enforcement mens rea*". Healy and Bronner found out that delinquents suffered from personality defects and disorders. No researches have been conducted to study the personality defects and disorders of government employees and corrupt officials. Nevertheless, my observations on bureaucratic criminals show that most of them lack a feeling of guilt when they involve in the commission of crimes. They show a tendency to disregard values in life. They suffer from adequate superego formation and their Ego exhibits a virtual absence of moral judgements. Egocentricism is seen among them and are often found to be pleasure seeking in life. Officers/clerks born and brought up in certain communities, castes, sub-castes etc. suffer from inferiority complex and their Ego expresses such complexes in their behaviour. Such people had greater chances of being impaired mentally and having more personality disorders than those born and brought up in higher castes/ denominations/communities. Conversely enough, officers/clerks born and brought up in higher castes/communities/denominations have the defects connected with their birth and upbringing. Both commit crimes in their own way and therefore it is not correct to say that the social and environmental factors are responsible for their involvement in the commission of crimes. It is each one's Ego which makes a person to commit a specific type of crimes. Survey of criminological literature shows that various types of crimes have been in existence among the government officials from time immemorial. Man is a rational animal and if rationality is taken away for a moment, he behaves just like an animal. The caste, colour, creed and community do not and cannot take away the animality in man and so long as animality is very much in man, he commits a variety of crimes which are due to the push factors in him. The push factors can be controlled by pull factors and owing to an interaction between the push and pull factors, an Ego is formed which determines the type of crimes he may commit. Wherever there exist 'official crimes' and enforcement criminality, there is the disintegration in office, inefficiency of supervisors, corruption and indifference in official works, political interference and other influences opportunity for involving in the commission of crimes and misconducts. There will be hostility among the members working in the same office. Many crimes committed will be of a clandestine nature and there is little or very little visibility of the same to the outside world. The like-minded people work together. Some will be primarily focused on crimes of gain—i.e., corruption and corrupt practices. They want material gains by illegal or unauthorized means. Delinquent behaviours are accepted means to success for them. They take their associates/superiors as role models to involve in criminality.

In India, the bureaucratic crimes and enforcement criminality have come into being not one day, too soon. I think that they are, to some extent, transmitted from the British past. The bureaucratic culture which is transmitted may be a pull factor in the ego formation of enforcement criminals. Some government employees experience futility in their attempts to find ways and means to success. They compare their fate with others in service and outside. They experience relative deprivation and they involve in corrupt practices to compensate their frustrations. The disparity between aspirations and chances of fulfilment makes them to have recourse to illegal means and methods. Their frustration, disparity feelings and discontentment in life make their Ego to adopt and accept a mode of adjustment or solution to their mental problems.

Push—Pull—Ego Factor Theory and Enforcement Criminology

Enforcement criminology is in its infant stages as criminologists and law do not accept enforcement crimes as crimes having a special identity. My theory—i.e., the Push—Pull—Ego Factor theory—can be applied to explain enforcement crimes. I find that there is a self-factor which I call the Ego that causes people to commit crimes and I want to say that the same ego is the cause of enforcement crimes and bureaucratic criminality.

Every person has the Push Factors in him and Pull Factors outside him. They are there from their birth till their death. A government official too has them. There is the interaction between the Push and Pull factors and certainly, a product has to come into existence. This new product is called the "*Ego*" of the individual and it is unique in every person. Nobody knows fully his "*Ego*" although everyone says that he has an "*Ego*" which is unique to him. No one knows or can know how the pull factors interact with his push factors and precisely therefore no one knows fully and perfectly the product—i.e., the Ego formed out of the interactions. This is the reason why some people who are not corrupt today become corrupt tomorrow or who were corrupt yesterday become honest today. As indicated in the previous chapter, one can effect control over the crimes only if a change in his conscience—in his *Ego*—comes into being.

Enforcement crimes may be a curse in Indian democracy and so long as they persist, there may not be any salvation for the people of this great country. People want a change and for it, researches in enforcement criminology becomes the need of the hour. The findings of the researches must be implemented immediately. A system that was established for ensuring justice to the society must not become a system that promotes and propagates crimes in society.

References

1. William J. Chambliss, *Vice, Corruption, Bureaucracy and Power,* from *Criminology: Power, Crime and Criminal Law,* John F. Galliher and James L. Mc Cartney, The Dorsey Press, Homewood, 1977.
2. William J. Chambliss, *op. cit.*
3. 1995 SCC (Cr) 1130=1996 Cr. L. J. 43=AIR 1996 SC 361=1995 (6) SCC 488=1995 (7) JT 587=1995 SCC (Cr) 1130.
4. 1996 (6) SCC 593=AIR 1997 SC 1886=1996 (10) JT 349=1996 (8) Scale 127=1996 (7) Supreme, 789.
5. (1996) 4 SCC 37=AIR 1996 SC 2426=1996 (6) JT 43=1996 (4) Scale 282=1996 (4) Supreme 260=1996 LIC 2054=1996 (3) SCJ 25.
6. Prem Kumar Vs. State of Bihar, 1995 Cr. L. J. 2634.
7. Albert K. Kohen, Alfred Lindesmith, and Karl Schuessler, *The Sutherland Papers*, University of Indian Press, Bloomington, 1956.

Bibliography

Abrahamsen, D., *The Psychology of Crime,* John Wiley & Sons, New York, 1964.

Arnold David, *Police Power and Colonial Rule: Madras 1859—1947,* Oxford University Press, 1986.

Barnes Harry Elmer and N.K. Teeters, *New Horizons in Criminology,* Prentice Hall, New Delhi, 1966.

Bawa, P.S., *Policing for People,* Rupa & Co., Calcutta, 1989.

Bayley, D.H., *Police and Political Development in India,* Princetion University, 1969.

Bentham, J., *An Introduction to the Principles of Morals and Legislations,* Hafner, New York, 1948.

Chambliss, W. J., *Vice, Corruption, Bureaucracy and Power,* Wisconsin Law Review, 1150—1173, 1971.

Chaturvedi, S.K., *Police and Emerging Challenges,* B.R. Publishing Corporation, Delhi, 1988.

Daudistel H., et.al, *Criminal Justice: Situations and Decisions,* Holt, Rinehart and Winston, London, 1979.

Dwivedi, J. N., *Police Power and Duties,* Allahabad Law Agency, Allahabad, 1950.

Earayil Alphone L & James Vadackumchery, *Police and the Society,* Kairali, Trivandrum, 1985.

Elliott, Mabel A., *Crime and Modern Society,* Harper, New York, 1952.

Eysenck, H. J., *Crime and Personality,* Granade Press, London, 1970.

Ferri, Enrico, *Criminal Sociology,* (trans.) Joseph Killey and John Lisle, Little Brown, Boston, 1917.

Galliher, J. F. and James L. Mc Cartney, *Criminology: Power, Crime and Criminal Law.* The Dorsey Press, Homewood, 1977.

Geis, Gilbert (ed.), *White-Collar Criminal,* Atherton Press, New York, 1968.

Gillin, John L., *Criminology and Penology,* Appleton, New York, 1945.

Glaser, Daniel. *Criminality Theories and Behavioural Images,* American Journal of Sociology, LXI (March), 1956.

Glaser Daniel, *Crime in our Changing Society,* Holt. Rinehart and Winston, London, 1978.

Goddard Henry H., *Feeble Mindedness: Its Causes and Consequences,* Mac Millan Co., New York, 1914.

Gould, Leroy, *Crime and its Impact in an Affluent Society* from Jack D. Douglas, ed., *Crime and Justice in American Society,* Bobbs Merril Co., India 1991.

Iyer Krishna, V.R., *Justice at Crossroads,* Deep & Deep, Delhi, 1992.

Kattakayam, J., and James Vadackumchery, *Crime and Society: Current Issues and Trends,* A.P.H., Delhi, 1999.

Korn, Richard R; and Lloyd W. Mc Corkle, *Criminology and Penology,* Holt, Rinehart and Winston, New York, 1959.

La Fave, Wayne R., Arrest: *The Decision to Take a Suspect into Custody,* Littlc Brown, Boston, 1965.

Lemert, Edwin M., *Social Pathology,* Mc Graw-Hill, New York, 1951.

Mannheim, Hermann (ed.) *Pioneers in Criminology,* Patterson, Smith, Montclair, 1973.

Mehra, A.K., *Police in Changing India,* Usha, Delhi, 1985.

Merton, Robert K., *Social Structure and Anomie,* American Sociological Review, 3 (October), 1938.

Mondale, Walter, *The Accountability of Power,* McKay, New York, 1975.

Neumeyer, M.H., *Juvenile Delinquency and Modern Society,* Van Nostrand, New York, 1955.

Packer, Herbert, L., *Policing the Police,* The New Republic, 4, December, 1965.

Radzinowicz, Leon, *Ideology and Crime,* Columbia University Press, New York, 1966.

Rao, Venugopal, S., *Dynamics of Crime: Special and Socio-economic Aspects of Crime in India,* IIPA, Delhi, 1981.

Reasons, C.E., *The Criminologist: Crime and the Criminal,* Goodyear Publishing Co., California, 1974.

Recfless, W.C., *The Crime Problem,* Vakils, Feffer and Simons, Bombay, 1970.

Reid, Sue, Titus, *Crime and Criminology,* The Dryden Press, Hinsdale, 1976.

Reiss, A.J. (Jr), *Police Brutality: Answers to Key Questions,* Transaction, 5 (July—Aug.), 10—19, 1968.

Remington, E.J., *The Role of Police in a Democratic Society,* Journal of Criminal Law, Criminology and Police Science, Vol. 56, 1965.

Saksena, N.S., *Police Unpopularity: Causes and Remedies,* Indian Police Journal, Oct—Dec., 1974.

Schafer, Stephen, *Theories in Criminology,* Random House, New York, 1969.

Schafer, Stephen, *The Political Criminal: Problem of Morality and Crime,* Free Press, New York, 1974.

Sellin, Thorsten, *Culture Conflict and Crime,* Social Science Research Council, New York, 1938.

Sharma, P.D., *Police and Criminal Justice Administration,* Uppal Publishing House, Delhi, 1985.

Shelon and Eleanor Glueck, *500 Criminal Careers,* Alfred A. Knopf, New York, 1930.

Sutherland, E.H. and D.R. Cressey, *Criminology,* Lippincolt, Philadelphia, 1974.

Tannenbaum, Frank, H., *Crime and the Community,* Ginn, Boston, 1938.

Tappan, Paul W., *Crime, Justice and Correction,* Mc Graw Hill, New York, 1960.

Taylor, Ian *et. al., Critical Criminology,* Routledge and Kegal Paul, London, 1975.

Trilok Nath, *The Indian Police: A Case for a New Image,* Sterling, New Delhi, 1978.

Turk, Austin T., *Criminality and Legal Order,* Rand Mc Nally and Co., Chicago, 1969.

Turner, J.W. Cecil, (ed.), *Kenny's Outlines of Criminal Law,* Cambridge University Press, London, 1962.

Vadackumchery James, *Criminology and Penology,* Kairali, Trivandrum, 1983.

Vadackumchery James, *Police Enforcement Crimes,* and Injustice, Gyan Publishing House, New Delhi, 2001.

Vadackumchery James, *Third Millennium Police: Take off Trends in India,* A.P.H., Delhi, 2000.

Vadackumchery James, *'Why I am not a Policeman?',* Kaveri, New Delhi, 2001.

Vold, George, 13., *Theoretical Criminology,* Oxford University Press, New York, 1958.

Wallerstein, J.S., and Clement, J.W., *Our Law-abiding Law-breakers,* Probation 35 (April), 1947.

Westley, W. A., *Violence and the Police,* American Journal of Sociology, 59 (July): 34—41.

Whisenand, P. M., *Police Supervision: Theory and Practice* (2nd ed.) Prentice Hall, Englewood Cliffs (NJ), 1976.
Wilson, James Q., *Thinking about Crime,* Basic Books, New York, 1975.

INDEX

R

S

T

U

V

W